Law of Tort

John Cooke

Principal Lecturer in Law, Liverpool John Moores University

Pitman

Pitman Publishing
128 Long Acre, London WC2E 9AN

A Division of Longman Group UK Limited

First published in 1992

© Longman Group UK Ltd, 1992

A CIP catalogue record for this book is available
from the British Library

ISBN 0 273 03678 5

Typeset, printed and bound in Great Britain

Contents

Preface

This book is one of a series of six covering the six core subjects required for exemption from legal professional exams. There are a number of excellent textbooks covering tort law already on the market, ranging from the encyclopaedic to revision aids. Why then write another?

The study of law, as well as other subjects, is changing rapidly. The old-fashioned approach was to have students in lecture theatres diligently taking down dictated notes. What they had at the end of the lecture course was a mini-book. This was then learned and regurgitated in an exam. The modern approach is to place more emphasis on transferable skills and delivery methods are more student-centred than lecturer-centred. This change has taken place against a background of rapid expansion in the number of part-time students and open- and distance-learning students.

What many of these students do not have is regular access to teaching staff for assistance. This book seeks to provide an accessible introduction to the major areas of tort which are commonly studied on exempting courses. It is designed to be used in conjunction with a good case book, for students who do not have easy access to a law library. The text should give readers the framework for the topic, which can be backed up by reading of the major cases. Outline coverage of the cases is given in the text and the use of detailed footnotes has been avoided. It is the author's experience that these are rarely used by the majority of undergraduate students.

Application of the principles in the text is illustrated by sample questions and answers at the end of certain chapters. These are not intended to provide model answers to the questions but to give illustrative approaches to different types of problem questions.

I would like to acknowledge the support and patience of my wife Maggie and children, Emma and Matthew. They have had to put up with a number of lost weekends, the constant noise of a word processor and the somewhat distracted and obsessive company of the textbook writer. My thanks also go to Pat 'deadline' Bond at Pitman's for getting the project off the ground and completed. Finally, most of a teacher's best ideas come from his students and colleagues and my thanks go to the common law students and civil law team at Liverpool Polytechnic.

John Cooke
April 1992

Table of cases

Table of statutes

Part I
GENERAL PRINCIPLES OF TORT LAW

1 | General principles

INTRODUCTION

This chapter will attempt to explain some of the basic principles which underlie the law of tort. Introductory chapters in textbooks are notoriously difficult for students to understand as they are written by people with a detailed knowledge of the subject for people who are new to it. The author will inevitably assume knowledge which the reader will probably not have. Readers are therefore asked to read the chapter and pick up what they can but not to agonise at this stage over material which appears impenetrable. As you progress through the book you will be able to usefully refer back to the introductory chapter.

WHAT IS A TORT?

A tort is a civil wrong in the sense that it is committed against an individual (which includes entities such as companies) rather than the state. The gist of tort law is that a person has certain interests which are protected by law. These interests can be protected by a court awarding a sum of money, known as damages, for infringement of a protected interest. Alternatively by the issuing of an injunction, which is a court order to the defendant to do or refrain from doing something. There are increasingly limited circumstances where the victim of a tort may avail himself of self-help.

Other branches of law also defend protected interests and the relationship between these and tort law will be discussed later. (See 'Boundaries of Tort', p. 14.)

ELEMENTS OF A TORT

Tort is a remarkably wide-ranging subject and probably the most difficult of all legal areas to lay down all embracing principles for.

The approach that will be taken at this stage is to lay down a general pattern and then to show some of the main deviations from this pattern.

The basic pattern

The paradigm tort consists of an *act* or *omission* by the defendant which *causes damage* to the plaintiff. The damage must be caused by the fault of the defendant and must be a *kind of harm* recognised as attracting legal liability.

This model can be represented:

act (or omission) + causation + fault + protected interest + damage = liability

An illustration of this model can be provided by the occurrence most frequently leading to liability in tort, a motor accident.

Example

If A drives his car carelessly with the result that it mounts the pavement and hits B, a pedestrian, causing B personal injuries. The act is A driving the vehicle. This act has caused damage to B. The damage was as a result of A's carelessness, i.e. his fault. The injury suffered by B, personal injury, is recognised by law as attracting liability. A will be liable to B in the tort of negligence and B will be able to recover damages.

Variations

We will be looking at these elements of a tort in more detail shortly. Now we will look at some of the common variations on the basic model. The elements of act (or omission) and causation are common to all torts. There are certain torts which do not require fault. These are known as torts of *strict liability*.

Example

An Act of Parliament makes it compulsory for employers to ensure that their employees wear safety helmets. The employer may be liable in a tort called breach of statutory duty if the employee does not wear a helmet and is injured as a result. This is the case even if the employer has done all he could to ensure the helmet was worn. (See also 'Mental Element in Tort', p. 8.)

In some cases the act or omission of the defendant may have caused damage to the plaintiff but the plaintiff may have no action as the interest affected may not be one protected by law. Lawyers refer to this as *damnum sine injuria* or harm without legal wrong.

Example

A opens a fish and chip shop in the same street as B's fish and chip shop. A reduces his prices with the intention of putting B out of business. A has committed no tort as losses caused by lawful business competition are not actionable in tort.

Just in case you thought this was straightforward, there are also cases where conduct is actionable even though no damage has been caused. This is known as *injuria sine damno* and where a tort is actionable without proof of damage it is said to be actionable *per se*.

Example

If A walks across B's land without B's permission then A will commit the tort of trespass to land, even though he causes no damage to the land.

THE INTERESTS PROTECTED

Personal security

People have an interest in their personal security. This is protected in a number of ways. If one person puts another in fear of being hit then there may be an action in the tort of *assault*. If the blow is struck, then the person hit may have an action in the tort of *battery*. A person whose freedom of movement is restricted unlawfully may be able to sue for *false imprisonment*. If personal injury is caused negligently then the plaintiff may have an action in the tort of *negligence*.

The scope given to the personal security interest expands as society becomes more advanced. Until the present century little attention was paid to the psychiatric damage that can be caused to a person. Someone who witnesses a traumatic event can incur serious mental suffering. The advance of psychiatric medicine and changing views on what is tolerable have led the courts to protect certain aspects of mental suffering such as nervous shock caused by witnessing a negligently caused accident. This is an area of law which is still being worked out by the courts in the context of disasters such as the Hillsborough football stadium disaster.

In the area of medical treatment, patients have become less willing to accept the word of doctors without question. The rising tide of litigation in this area has led to the courts having to examine difficult issues such as consent to treatment and the right to life. Here law and morality are inextricably mixed. What, for example, is the legal position if a doctor needs to give a blood transfusion to a patient who will die if he does not receive it but the patient refuses to have the blood transfusion because of his religious beliefs?

Ancillary to a person's interest in his personal security is his interest in his reputation. Where a person's reputation is damaged by untrue speech or writing then he may have an action in the tort of *defamation*.

Interest in property

Property in the broad sense of the word is protected by tort law. A person has an interest in his land which is protected by a number of torts such as *nuisance, Rylands v Fletcher* and *trespass to land*. Interests in personal property are protected by torts such as *trespass to goods* and *conversion*. Where clothing or a car is damaged in a negligently caused accident then a person may have an action for damages in *negligence*.

Economic interests

Tort law will give limited protection to economic interests where the defendant has acted unlawfully and has caused economic loss to the plaintiff. These are known as the economic torts. Such protection is limited because the common law has been cautious in drawing the line between lawful and unlawful business practice. This is a line which is largely left to statute to draw.

A controversial area and one which will be dealt with in the chapter on negligence is the extent of liability for *negligently* caused economic loss. This is an area where tort and contract intersect. (See 'Boundaries of Tort', p. 14.) At present a person can be liable for economic loss which is caused by a negligent statement but in general terms not for economic loss which is caused by a negligent act.

Example

A is driving an excavator and negligently severs an electricity cable which leads to a factory. The factory is forced to close down for a day and production is lost as a result. Any production which had been started at the time of the interruption of the supply and is damaged will be classed as damage to property and can be claimed in a negligence action. Any production which has not been started but cannot be carried out and results in loss of profit will be classed as economic loss and will be irrecoverable. Do you think that this distinction makes sense?

The role of policy

Lawyers are used to dealing in concepts such as duty of care, remoteness of damage and fault etc. When cases are analysed in these terms and there is held to be no liability as there was no duty or the damage was too remote, or the defendant was not at fault, this is referred to as formal conceptualism or black letter law. What is frequently concealed in this terminology is the policy reason behind the decision. Although the lawyer must know the relevant rules of law and these will be the main area of study in this book, a clear picture will not emerge unless the student is aware of the policy issues which have shaped the decision.

Take another look at the example given in the previous section. The court has the choice of allowing the loss to lie on the factory owner by saying that A is not liable, or of shifting the loss to A by holding him liable. The court's decision will be explained by saying, e.g. that A owes no duty to the factory owner in terms of certain kinds of loss or that certain kinds of loss are too remote. But the decision can also be explained in terms of two policy factors. The courts are concerned with opening the floodgates of litigation: i.e. if the electricity cable was connected to fifty factories. Closely connected to this is the role of insurance. Most damages in tort are in practice paid by insurance companies. The court's decision will act as a signal to firms as to who will have to insure against this risk. The decision may also be based on who they think is the best insurer.

Traditionally, English judges did not refer to policy when giving decisions but they are now increasingly prepared to state these reasons. The floodgates argument has been prevalent in the development of the law on both nervous shock and the recovery of economic loss in negligence. When you study these sections bear in mind that one of the factors governing the legal rules imposed is the fear of the courts being swamped by a large number of actions and too heavy a burden being placed on the defendant or his insurers.

The judges are also concerned with maintaining the due administration of justice. This is reflected in the principle that a barrister is immune from liability for his conduct of a case. This rule was introduced because of fear that the action against the barrister would effectively be a retrial of the original case.

Example

A is charged with murder and is defended by barrister B. A is convicted and his appeal to the Court of Appeal fails. If A could sue B for negligence in the way B conducted A's defence and A's negligence action was successful, this would cast doubts on the validity of A's conviction.

The role of insurance

Without insurance the tort system would simply cease to operate. Where a plaintiff is successful in an action the damages will normally be paid by an insurance company.

Insurance may be either first party, where a person insures himself against loss which he may incur, or third party, where a person insures himself against any liability which he may incur to a third party. First party insurance, such as house, personal accident or life insurance is relatively easy to obtain. Most of life's eventualities may be insured against, including bad weather! Where the event which has been insured against occurs there is no litigation, the insurance company simply pays up.

A common example of third party insurance is third party motor insurance. By law a motorist must have this insurance.

Example

A has taken out third party insurance on his car with insurance company C. A's car is involved in a collision with B's car. B successfully sues A for negligent driving. The damages which B is awarded will be paid by C. If B is seriously injured then the damages could amount to over £1 million pounds. Without insurance it is unlikely that B would receive his damages.

Liability insurance is now very prevalent: e.g. most professional people such as doctors, architects, accountants, lawyers and surveyors will be insured for liability which they may incur.

THE MENTAL ELEMENT IN TORT

As we saw previously, it may not be sufficient for the plaintiff to prove that the defendant's act or omission caused him damage in order to succeed in an action. It may also be necessary for the plaintiff to show a particular state of mind on the part of the defendant. Where such a state of mind needs to be proved it is said to be a fault based tort. Where no such state of mind needs to be proved it is said to be a strict liability tort.

The history of fault in tort law is connected to policy and stems from the nineteenth century. At this time the availability of insurance was extremely limited and damages would usually be paid personally by the defendant. In order to protect developing industries the courts evolved a system of tort that usually required proof of fault in order for an action to succeed. The economic argument in favour of fault was supported by the moral and social arguments that fault based liability would deter people from anti-social conduct and it was right that bad people should pay. One consequence of this development was that workers in industry who suffered industrial accidents were largely deprived of compensation.

English law has never succeeded in ridding itself of this nineteenth-century legacy and fault remains as the basis of most tort actions. Understanding of the principle is made more difficult as the spread of insurance has meant that the courts have been able to increase the standard of conduct required in certain situations, while retaining the language of moral wrongdoing. It has been shown that many errors by car drivers which are classed as being negligence (fault) are statistically unavoidable. Where this is the case, the moral and deterrent arguments for fault are certainly reduced if not extinguished. Further problems are caused by the fact that a tort judgment is rarely paid by the defendant himself but by his insurer. What has happened is that fault has often moved away from being a state of mind to being a judicially set standard of conduct which is objectively set for policy reasons.

Example

A was operated on by surgeon B. Something went wrong during the operation and A is now incapable of looking after himself. A sues B for negligence. If the action is successful then A will be awarded £500,000 damages. The question in the case will be whether B was negligent (at fault). At what level should the court set the standard? In order to compensate as many victims of medical accidents as possible, the standard should obviously be set very high. But if this is done the damages which are paid out by the health authority will remove money which could otherwise be used for patient treatment. The standard will therefore be set at a level which is dictated by policy.

There are three states of mind which a student needs to be aware of in tort law. These are *malice, intention* and *negligence.* Where a tort does not require any of these it is said to be a tort of strict liability.

Malice

Malice in tort has two meanings. It may be: (a) the intentional doing of some wrongful act without proper excuse; (b) to act with some collateral or improper motive. It is (b) which is usually referred to.

In the sense of (b) above there is a basic principle that malice is irrelevant in tort law. If a person has a right to do something then his motive in doing it is irrelevant.

Bradford Corporation v Pickles [1895] AC 587

The defendant extracted percolating water in undefined channels with the result that the water supply to the plaintiff's reservoir was reduced. The defendant's motive in doing this was to force the plaintiffs to buy his land at his price. The action failed, as the defendant had a right to extract the water. As he had such a right his motive, even if malicious, was irrelevant.

There are two groups of exceptions to this basic principle;

(a)   Where malice is an essential ingredient of the tort: e.g. in *malicious prosecution* the plaintiff must prove not only that the defendant had no grounds for believing that the plaintiff was probably guilty but also that the defendant was activated by malice. The reason for this requirement is that policy in this area favours law enforcement over individual rights. The result of the requirement is that there are few successful cases of malicious prosecution.

(b)   There are also torts where malice may be relevant to liability. For example, in *nuisance* malice may convert what would have been a reasonable act into an unreasonable one.

Christie v Davey [1893] 1 Ch 316

Plaintiff and defendant lived in adjoining houses. Plaintiff gave music lessons and this annoyed the defendant. In retaliation the defendant banged on the wall and shouted while the lessons were in progress. The plaintiff was held to be entitled to an injunction because of the defendant's malicious behaviour. (See also 'Nuisance', p. 183.)

Also, in defamation cases malice may destroy a defence of fair comment or qualified privilege and may affect the defence of justification where spent convictions are in issue. (See 'Defamation', pp. 235, 238.)

Intention

The meaning of intention varies according to the context in which it is used. Intention is relevant in three groups of torts.

(a)   Torts derived from the writ of trespass. Here intention means where a person desires to produce a result forbidden by law and where he foresees it and carries on regardless of the consequences. The defendant must intend to do the act but need not intend harm: e.g. if a person has a fit and strikes another person this would not amount to trespass to the person. But the test will catch the practical joker who intends to frighten a person but ends up causing them severe nervous shock.

(b)   In cases of fraud and injurious falsehood. In these torts the defendant must make a statement which he knows is untrue.

(c)   In cases of conspiracy. If X and Y combine together and act to cause injury to Z, then Z will have an action provided that he can prove that their primary motive was to cause him damage. If the primary motive of X and Y was to further their own interests, then even if they realised that their act would inevitably damage Z, they will not be liable in conspiracy.

Crofter Hand Woven Harris Tweed Co Ltd v Veitch [1942] AC 435

Yarn for making Harris Tweed was spun by mills on Harris. Crofters who made Harris Tweed began importing cheaper yarn from the mainland. The millworkers' union ordered their members at the docks to refuse to handle the imported yarn after the millworkers' employers had refused a pay rise because of competition from the crofters. The crofters action for conspiracy failed as the union's predominant motive was to advance the interests of its members and not to damage the crofters.

Negligence

Negligence in tort has several meanings. It may refer to the *tort of negligence* or it may refer to *careless behaviour*. It is in the latter sense that the word is used here. In this sense it does not refer to a state of mind. When a court finds that a person has been negligent it is making an ex post assessment of his *conduct*. A person who totally disregards the safety of others but does not injure them is not guilty of negligence, although he may be morally reprehensible. On the other hand, the person who tries his best but falls below the standard set by the court and causes damage, will be liable.

The standard set is an *objective* one. The court will apply the test of what a 'reasonable man' would have done in the defendant's position. One effect of this test is that no account is taken of individual disabilities.

Nettleship v Weston [1971] QB 691

Defendant was a learner driver who was given lessons by the plaintiff. The plaintiff was injured as a result of the defendant's negligent driving. The court held that all drivers, including learner drivers, would be judged by the standards of the average competent driver.

The setting of the standard depends on what the objective of the negligence formula is. If the objective is to compensate the plaintiff for his loss then it is clearly in the plaintiff's interests to set the standard as high as possible. But if the objective is to deter the defendant, then it is counter productive to set a standard which is too high to be attainable. Research has shown that the standard set for drivers is unattainable, even by safe drivers, with the result that the defendant may have been unable to avoid the accident but is still classed as having been negligent.

Strict liability

Whereas fault is a positive idea, strict liability is a negative one. It means liability without fault. In the last century the emphasis was placed by the courts on fault based liability and strict liability was generally frowned on. Some areas of strict liability have survived and Parliament has created others.

No coherent theme links these areas. There are historical relics such as strict liability for trespassing livestock, which harks back to a predominantly agricultural society. The rule in *Rylands* v *Fletcher* represents a largely failed attempt by the judiciary to deal with the problems created by the Industrial Revolution. The rule that an employer is vicariously liable for the negligence of his employee in the course of his employment, in the absence of any fault on the part of the employer, is a pragmatic response to a particular problem.

In the area of industrial safety Parliament has passed legislation which imposes strict as opposed to fault based liability on an employer.

The standard of liability imposed, even within the context of strict liability, varies from tort to tort. There is one example of absolute liability, where no defence is available. This is the Nuclear Installations Act 1965. Most actions, however, permit some defences or exemptions from liability.

What is common to all tort actions is the idea of causation. The plaintiff must always prove that the defendant caused his injury. There are frequently calls for drug manufacturers to be made strictly liable for injury caused by their product. If this were to occur then the plaintiff would no longer have to prove negligence but would still be faced with the difficult task of proving that it was that drug which caused his injury.

OBJECTIVES OF TORT

Tort law has two main objectives, compensation and deterrence. It is generally thought that tort law normally has no punitive function and that this job is performed by the criminal law. There are very limited circumstances though, where *exemplary damages* may be awarded in tort and these do have a punitive function. (See 'Remedies', p. 272.) The fact that the judiciary has kept the award of this type of damages within such narrow parameters, means that they are wary of tort law performing this function.

Deterrence

Individual deterrence

The theory behind individual deterrence is that the possibility of a civil sanction, such as damages, will cause the defendant to alter his behaviour and avoid inflicting damage.

This theory depends on two factors. First, will the sanction actually affect the defendant? We have seen that most awards of damages are paid out by insurance companies. The only financial effect of an award of damages on an insured defendant may be to increase the premium which he has to pay for his insurance. But reputation is also important to some people. A finding of negligence against a doctor or lawyer may adversely affect their career. The second factor is whether the defendant could have avoided the accident. We have seen that it is impossible for a car driver to avoid committing driving errors which the law will label as negligence. If a person cannot avoid an error then he cannot be said to be deterred by a liability rule.

It is now generally accepted that individual deterrence has little part to play in many tort actions. The legal reason that most people drive as safely as they can is the fear of criminal, not civil sanctions. Individual deterrence does have a role where a person's professional reputation is at stake and the reason why most newspapers try to avoid libelling people is the fear of an action for defamation.

General or market deterrence

Academic work on the economic effects of tort liability rules has renewed interest in the role of deterrence in tort law. But this form of deterrence is not individual deterrence but what is known as market deterrence. The idea behind this is that tort law should aim to reduce the costs of accidents. This is achieved by imposing the costs of accidents on those who participate in accident causing activities.

Example

If a car manufacturer were to be charged the accident costs of cars in which seat belts were not installed, then the price of cars without belts would reflect the accident costs. Rather than impose a law which states that cars must be fitted with seat belts, the market, through the cost of cars without seat belts, would enable people to make a choice between the cheaper cars with belts or the more expensive ones without.

Compensation

One of the major aims of tort law is to compensate those who have suffered personal injury. The present system shifts losses from the plaintiff to the defendant when the defendant has been shown to have been at fault. In recent years this system has come under increasing criticism as being an inefficient method of compensating accident victims.

There are three systems which provide for accident victims. These are tort law, public insurance (social security) and private insurance. The largest part in compensation is now played by public insurance. A person who is injured in an accident may become entitled to payments by the state, such as sickness benefit.

Tort damages are distinguished from payments by the state in that the former are payable only on proof that a person caused an injury and was at fault in doing so. The latter are payable on the occurrence of an event and according to need.

The third system is private insurance. This plays a small but growing part in accident compensation. Personal accident insurance or permanent health insurance may be taken out against the possibility of indisposition. This is still relatively expensive in the UK but is being taken up by employers for their key personnel.

A number of criticisms are levelled at the tort system. It is very expensive to administer in comparison with social security. It has been calculated that the cost of operating the tort system accounts for 85% of the sums which are paid to accident victims. For plaintiffs the system is unpredictable, as they do not know whether they will receive any compensation or not. This results in pressure on plaintiffs to settle actions for less than they would receive if they went to trial. The system is also slow and a plaintiff may have to wait years before receiving compensation. The more serious the accident then generally the longer the plaintiff has to wait. Finally, damages are paid in a lump sum. This creates difficulties as inflation may erode the value of the award and no account can be taken of improvement or deterioration in the plaintiff's medical condition.

ALTERNATIVE SYSTEMS OF COMPENSATION

We have already seen that tort damages are only part of the overall picture of compensation for accidents and are a junior partner to state benefits. The position in England and Wales is complex, with a number of possible avenues of compensation open to an injured person. He may be able to obtain tort damages, be covered by private insurance and be entitled to state benefits. Because of the haphazard and uncoordinated way in which the system has evolved the victim may end up being over-compensated. On the other hand, a victim may have no insurance cover, not be able to prove fault against a person and may not have a sufficient contribution record to claim contributory state benefits. This victim will only have the safety net of income support benefit at subsistence level to support them.

One other source of compensation which should be mentioned at this point is the Criminal Injuries Compensation Scheme. Payments may be made for injuries directly attributable to crimes of violence. If the victim goes on to obtain tort damages then any award made under the scheme must be repaid.

In some countries the role of compensating for accidents has been removed from the tort system. In New Zealand a comprehensive no-fault accident compensation scheme was set up in 1972 to replace tort damages in personal accident cases. Where a person suffers injury through accident he makes a claim through the Accident

Compensation Commission. The victim may claim up to 80% of earnings before the accident. Payments are made on a weekly basis and can be adjusted to reflect inflation and the victim's medical condition. The victim does not have to prove fault and a wider range of accidents are therefore covered by the scheme than by tort law. The system of periodical payments avoids problems which are caused by lump sum awards of damages in tort cases. In tort cases it is not generally possible for the court to take into account future inflation or to allow for changes in the victim's medical condition. Under the scheme, a victim may also claim for non-pecuniary loss. This means items such as pain, shock and suffering. Such awards are low compared with those which would be received under a tort system. The advantage of the scheme is that all accident victims receive some compensation and are not put to the trauma, cost and delay of having to sue someone.

In England, the thalidomide tragedy in the 1960s and 1970s aroused interest in the question of compensation. The Pearson Commission (Royal Commission on Civil Liability and Compensation for Personal Injury, Cmnd 7054, 1978) was established and the report proposed a no-fault scheme limited to accidents caused by motor vehicles. Some 188 other proposals were made but it is doubtful whether any reform can be traced directly to these. A no-fault scheme does involve spending money and the implementation of such a scheme depends on the political will to do so. Opponents of such schemes argue that the removal of tort actions will remove an important deterrent to careless conduct.

Despite the political neglect of the Pearson Report, no-fault schemes are now back on the political agenda. Disasters such as Zeebrugge, Piper Alpha and the Hillsborough football stadium disaster have given publicity to the plight of victims. The recent rise in the number of claims for medical negligence has led to calls for these to be removed from the tort system and compensated through a state no-fault scheme. Organisations representing the medical profession which were opposed to such schemes at the time of Pearson are now in favour.

THE BOUNDARIES OF TORT

For reasons of space this section will concentrate on the boundary between tort and contract. This is an area which has caused the courts considerable problems in recent years.

The traditional distinction between tort and contract was that an obligation in contract arose from the agreement or will of the parties, whereas an obligation in tort was imposed by law. It is no longer possible to maintain this distinction. Not all contracts now arise from prior promises made by the parties and the terms of a contract are not always agreed by the parties. Where a person buys goods from a shop it is very artificial to reduce the process to questions of offer and acceptance and, whether they like it or not, sellers have terms of *fitness for the purpose* and *merchantable quality* included in the contract by virtue of the Sale of Goods Act 1979.

There are also problems in analysing certain tort situations into duties imposed by law. Where a person is held liable in damages for a non-contractual statement, the statement was made voluntarily and the recipient relied on the statement. The only point that distinguishes this from a contractual statement is that no consideration was given for the statement by the recipient. Whether the statement was actionable in contract or tort, the key element is reliance on the statement by the recipient.

Does the distinction between contract and tort make sense if one approaches this question from the point of view of *consent*? That a contractual duty can only be imposed where a party consents but a tortious duty may be imposed in the absence of consent. Whether a contractual duty exists or not is determined on the basis of *objective* criteria, not on the *subjective* intention of the parties. This means that although consent plays a part in contract, it is not all important. Conversely in tort, consent may play a role. Where a person is injured during a sporting contest such as football there may be no action in tort, as the injured person may have consented to the risk of injury by taking part in the contest. Tort law also imposes duties on an occupier of land to a visitor to the land. Whether a person is a visitor or not and therefore whether such a duty may be imposed, depends on the consent of the occupier to the presence of that person.

 Can a distinction be drawn on the basis of the objectives of the two actions? Contract is said to protect the *expectation* interest of the plaintiff, whereas tort is said to protect the *reliance* or *status quo* interest.

Example

If A sold B a motor car for £5,000 which was worth £4,000 but A said it was worth £6,000, B's contract damages would in theory be the difference between what the car was worth and what he had been led to believe it was worth, i.e. £2,000. But B's damages in tort would be the amount required to put him in the position he was in before the tort was committed, i.e. £1,000.

The traditional role of tort law has been to protect people against damage to their person and property. This is done by making an award of damages for any loss incurred by the victim. The problem comes, as in the above example, where tort is used to protect *economic* interests. Some people believe that this should be the role of contract and that tort should have no role to play. Contract law aims to make things better and tort to avoid making things worse. But consider the following case.

Ross v Caunters [1980] Ch 297

The defendant solicitor acted negligently in the execution of a will, with the result that the plaintiff was unable to take a bequest under the will. The testator (person making the will) had a contract with the solicitor but the plaintiff did not, because of the contractual doctrines of consideration and privity. The court decided that the defendant was liable in the tort of negligence and the plaintiff was able to recover the value of his lost bequest from the solicitor. But was this a case of the solicitor making the plaintiff worse off or failing to make him better off? Would it not be easier in these circumstances to alter the law of contract so that there is a contract in favour of a third party (in this case the beneficiary)?

Some writers have pointed out that the extent to which contract protects the expectation interest is in practice limited by the rules which restrict the amount of damages which may be claimed. The two most important are the rule that a plaintiff may not recover items of loss which are too remote and the plaintiff must take reasonable steps to mitigate his loss. The effect of these rules is that in many cases a plaintiff will only be able to recover his reliance or status quo loss.

There are situations where a plaintiff may have a choice between contract or tort. If a person receives private medical treatment and is negligently injured he may sue the doctor in negligence or for breach of contract. The substance of the action will not differ, as in negligence the doctor must take reasonable care and in contract there is an implied term that the doctor will take reasonable care. It is unlikely that the doctor will have guaranteed a cure so there is no advantage to the plaintiff in suing in contract to protect his expectation interest. The damages in either case will be the same.

There are a number of technical distinctions between contract and tort. The limitation period, the time in which the plaintiff has to start proceedings, is different and there are different rules on when writs may be served outside the jurisdiction.

THE POSITION OF MINORS

As a general principle anyone may sue in tort. A minor may bring an action through a next friend.

The position of minors as defendants has not been considered very much, probably because they would not normally be able to satisfy a judgment. In principle there is no reason why a person of any age cannot be sued. In practice it may be that the courts set the standard of care according to the age of the child (see 'Breach of Duty'), although in theory the standard of care in negligence is an objective one.

Damage caused before birth has always posed a problem in tort law. It was one of the principal hurdles that the parents of the thalidomide children had to face in their litigation. Legislation has since improved the position.

The Congenital Disabilities (Civil Liability) Act 1976 gives a child a cause of action where it was born disabled as the result of an occurrence which either: affected the ability of either parent to have a normal healthy child; or affected the mother during the pregnancy; or affected the child in the course of its birth; or there was negligence in the selection or handling of an embryo or gametes for the purpose of assisted conception during treatment for infertility. In any of these cases the child must be born with disabilities which it would otherwise not have had.

The child's action is unusual as it is derived from a tortious duty to the parents.

The defendant will be liable to the child if he would have been liable to the parent but for the fact there was no actionable injury to the parent.

The child's mother is not liable under the Act unless the injury can be attributed to her negligent driving of a motor vehicle.

Example

Christine became pregnant and suffered badly from nausea. She consulted her doctor who prescribed a drug to relieve the nausea. Christine gave birth to a daughter who suffered from physical and mental disabilities. Both the doctor and the manufacturer of the drug owed a duty of care to Christine. If the doctor was negligent in prescribing the drug or the drug company in making or marketing it, then all the elements of a negligence action by Christine are present except damage. It is the baby who has suffered the damage and has the action under the Act. The stumbling-block will be causation. It will be necessary to prove that the drug was the cause of the child's disabilities.

Where the disability is a result of a pre-conception event which affected the ability of the parents to have a normal healthy child, the defendant is not responsible if either or both of the parents knew of the risk. If the child's father is the defendant and he knew of the risk but the mother did not, then the father will be answerable to the child.

Further reading

Atiyah, P S, *Accidents, Compensation and the Law* (4th edn by P Cane, 1987)
Fleming, J G, *An Introduction to the Law of Torts* (2nd edn, 1985)
Report of the Royal Commission On Civil Liability and Compensation For Personal Injury (The Pearson Report) Cmnd 7054 (1978) Chs 3 and 4
Williams, G L and Hepple, B A, *Foundations of the Law of Tort* (2nd edn, 1985)

Part II
THE TORT OF NEGLIGENCE

2 | General principles of negligence

ELEMENTS OF THE TORT

To succeed in a negligence action the plaintiff must prove three things: that the defendant owed him a duty of care; that the defendant was in breach of that duty; and that the plaintiff suffered damage caused by the breach of duty, which was not too remote. The defendant may raise certain defences to the action. The most important defences are that the plaintiff consented to run the risk of the injury (*volenti*) or that the defendant was contributorily negligent.

Example

A drove his car over the speed limit and failed to keep a proper look out, as he was talking to the passenger next to him. A's car struck B, a pedestrian, causing personal injuries to B. Analysing this event in terms of the legal categories. A owed a duty of care to B as one road user to another. A was in breach of the duty in speeding and failing to keep a proper lookout (i.e. A was 'negligent'). B has suffered damage as a result of A's negligence.

If B had failed to look before stepping into the road, it would be open to a court to find that B had been contributorily negligent and reduce his damages by the proportion which he was held to be responsible for the accident.

THE INTERESTS PROTECTED

Negligence is the most important modern tort. Other torts are normally identified by the particular interest of the plaintiff which is protected: e.g. defamation protects interests in reputation and nuisance protects a person's use and enjoyment of land.

Negligence on the other hand protects a number of interests and the only unifying factor is the defendant's conduct, which must be labelled as negligent if liability is to arise.

Three interests can be identified as being protected by the tort of negligence. These are: protection against personal injury, damage to property, and economic interests. Economic losses consequential on damage to the person and damage to property may also be recovered.

Examples

A drives his car negligently and collides with B's car. This causes personal injuries to B and damage to his car (property damage). B may recover damages from A for both these losses. But B may lose wages as a result of his injuries and may have to hire a car while his own is being repaired. Both these losses are recoverable as consequential economic loss.

A asks his solicitor, B, to draw up a will leaving A's property to C. B negligently drafts the will with the result that C is unable to take his bequest under the will. C may sue B in negligence for the value of his lost bequest. The interest protected here is C's economic interest and C is said to recover damages for pure economic loss.

Note the difference between consequential and pure economic loss. In the example of the will, C has suffered no personal injuries or property damage and his loss is said to be damage to the pocket or pure economic loss.

Readers are reminded that most defendants in tort actions will be insured and any damages awarded will be paid by an insurance company and not by the defendant himself. When a judge says that he will not impose liability as it would impose too heavy a burden on the defendant, he usually means that it would impose too heavy a burden on the defendant's insurers. In the car example above B's damages would be paid by A's motor insurers and C's damages would be paid by B's liability insurers. In both cases it is compulsory for the defendant to carry insurance against these risks.

A defendant cannot be liable in this tort unless the court judges him to have been negligent (i.e. at fault). This means that the defendant's conduct must have dropped below a standard set by law. Where there is liability insurance the court can set the standard at a fairly high level, as the award of damages will not directly penalise the defendant. But as one of the purposes of the negligence formula is said to be deterrence, the presence of insurance distorts the actual deterrence to the defendant. (See 'General Principles', p. 12.)

PROBLEM AREAS

Negligence has expanded so fast in the twentieth century that at one time it appeared possible that it would make other torts redundant. Its popularity was based on a fairly simple formula of fault backed by insurance. The structure is now creaking due to problems in the insurance market and negligence no longer seems the simple panacea for all legal problems that it once did.

Personal injuries

In statistical terms most negligence actions are brought for personal injuries suffered by the plaintiff. The majority of personal injuries actions are brought in the areas of motor accidents and accidents at work.

An injured person requires compensation for his injuries and the more serious the injury, the greater the need for compensation. It has already been observed that the insurance factor dilutes the personal deterrence objective of negligence. As the other objective of tort law is compensation for the victim, the negligence system can only be supported if it is an efficient and fair method of delivering compensation to the victims. The Pearson Commission established that this was not the case. (See Chapter 1, 'Objectives of Tort', pp. 12–14.)

The inefficiency and apparent unfairness of the tort system at delivering compensation has led to calls for it to be replaced in whole or in part by a no-fault scheme of compensation. No such scheme is perfect and the introduction of such a scheme is a question of political will.

Medical negligence

The number of claims for negligence against medical practitioners has been rising steadily, with a corresponding rise in the insurance premiums which have to be paid by doctors. This has led to claims that England is suffering a medical malpractice crisis similar to the United States. Doctors claim that the the threat of litigation leads to 'defensive medicine': i.e. carrying out procedures in order to avoid being sued, rather than for the benefit of the patient. The rise in the caesarian section rate is often pointed to as an example of defensive medicine.

Victims of medical accidents are not happy with the negligence system. Numerous problems stand in the way of a person who wishes to sue for medical negligence. The action is expensive and legal aid is not easily available; lawyers with the necessary skills in this specialised area are not always easy to find; the system leads to a closing of ranks on the part of the medical profession, which makes it difficult for the patient to find out what went wrong; even if the victim does obtain compensation, this may be many years after the event.

Disenchantment with the system on the part of both doctors and patients has again led to calls for medical negligence to be replaced by a no-fault scheme of compensation. This is now supported by the medical insurers, doctors, professional bodies and victim support agencies.

Economic loss

Complaints about negligence in the area of personal injuries are concentrated on inefficiency and unfairness but at least the law in that area is relatively clear and mature, except in cases of psychiatric damage. The tort of negligence has only recently ventured into the area of economic loss and the law on this subject is unclear and at an early stage of development.

Claims for economic loss in negligence may come about: either where a negligent *statement* has been made which causes financial loss to the recipient; or where the defendant commits a negligent act which has a similar effect. Broadly speaking, claims for a negligent statement may be successful but the courts will not allow actions for negligent acts.

Historically, contract was the proper action where a person suffered economic loss and if a person had no contract they had no action. The reason that negligence (tort) law moved into this area was the perceived injustice created by the doctrine of privity in contract law. This doctrine states that only a party to a contract may sue or be sued on a contract. A party to a contract is a person who provides consideration.

Example

A instructs B, his solicitor, to draft a will leaving A's property to C. When A dies it is discovered that B has drafted the will negligently with the result that C is unable to take his bequest. C's loss is economic loss and in theory C should sue for breach of contract. But C has no contract. The contract is between A and B. The doctrine of privity means that C cannot sue B in contract, which leaves tort law to decide whether C should have a negligence action against B.

It is often useful to consider economic loss cases in diagrammatic form.

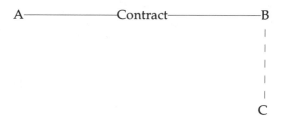

Many of the economic loss cases fall into this triangular pattern. The question for the court is usually whether tort law is prepared to complete the triangle by granting C a negligence action against B.

Omissions

Negligence actions are usually concerned with the situation where A commits a negligent act and causes damage to B. But could A be liable in negligence to B where he omits to do something and B suffers damage?

NB In legal terminology a positive act is known as *misfeasance* and a failure to act as *nonfeasance*.

Liability for failing to take positive steps to safeguard another is traditionally the role of contract. If you want a person to assist you then you have to pay them (provide consideration).

If A sees B drowning then he is under no duty in tort to attempt a rescue. But what if A has some relationship with B? For example, A is B's parent or B is a visitor to A's premises. Would A then be under a duty to attempt a rescue?

LIABILITY IN CONTRACT AND TORT

If the parties have a contractual relationship, can there also be tortious liability? If the answer is yes, then a plaintiff will be able to take advantage of tortious rules, which may be more advantageous. The most important of these will be the rules on limitation. These rules govern the time period within which a plaintiff must bring an action. In contract, time periods generally run from the time a contract is made and in tort from the time damage is suffered.

Unfortunately, as the law stands at present, no clear answer can be given to this question and it is necessary to look at the actual relationship between the parties. There is no doubt that a tortious duty can be owed between parties in a contractual relationship: e.g. doctor–patient and solicitor–client. In the 1970s the courts were enthusiastic about creating such duties. See *Esso v Mardon* [1976] QB 801 (petrol company and tenant); *Batty v Metropolitan Realisations Ltd* [1978] QB 554 (property developer and purchaser); *Midland Bank Trust Co Ltd v Hett, Stubbs and Kemp* [1979] Ch 384 (solicitor and client).

However doubt was cast by a statement of Lord Scarman's in *Tai Hing Cotton Mill v Liu Chong Bank Ltd* [1986] AC 80 at 107.

> Their Lordships do not believe that there is anything to the advantage of the law's development in searching for a liability in tort where the parties are in a contractual relationship. This is particularly so in a commercial relationship. Though it is possible as a matter of legal semantics to conduct an analysis of the rights and duties inherent in some contractual relationships – either as a matter of contract law when the question will be what, if any, terms are to be implied or as a matter of tort law when the task will be to identify a duty arising from the proximity and character of the relationship beween the parties, their Lordships believe it to be correct in principle and necessary for the avoidance of confusion in the law to adhere to the contractual analysis: on principle because it is a relationship in which the parties have, subject to a few exceptions, the right to determine their obligations to each other, and for the avoidance of confusion because different consequences do follow according to whether liability arises in contract or tort, e.g., in the limitation of action.

This statement has received a mixed reaction. Concurrent liability is still accepted but the courts are now reluctant to impose a tortious duty when this would be wider than the contractual duty, particularly in commercial cases.

Reid *v* Rush & Tompkins Group plc [1989] 3 All ER 228

The plaintiff was employed by the defendants and was sent abroad to work. He was injured in a motor accident by a hit and run driver. The plaintiff sued his employers claiming (amongst other things), that they were in breach of duty in tort to take all reasonable steps to protect his economic welfare, arising out of personal injury, while he was acting in the course of his employment. The breach of duty was alleged to be in failing to take out appropriate insurance cover for him or advising him to take it out himself. Relying on Lord Scarman's dicta, the Court of Appeal held that as there was no term in the contract providing for this, the plaintiff was precluded from suing for economic loss in tort.

But in contrast to this, the House of Lords assumed in 1987, that an architect could be liable in tort for economic loss suffered by his client (*Ketteman* v *Hansel Properties* [1987] AC 189).

The following case is a contract action but contains an interesting link between contract and tort.

Johnstone *v* Bloomsbury Health Authority [1991] 2 All ER 293

The plaintiff was employed by the defendant health authority as a junior doctor. The essence of his claim was that by his contract he was obliged to work 88 hours per week and that this was in breach of the employer's duty to take reasonable care for his safety and well being. The Court of Appeal heard cross appeals on the question of striking out the claim.

It was held (Leggatt LJ dissenting) that although the defendants were entitled to to require the plaintiff to work up to 88 hours per week under his contract of employment, they had to exercise that discretion in such a way as not to injure the plaintiff. The health authority therefore had to exercise their power in such a way as not to injure the plaintiff's health. They could not require the plaintiff to work so much overtime in a week that his health might reasonably foreseeably be damaged.

Two of the judges also stated that an implied contractual term in a contract of employment, such as the implied duty to to take reasonable care for the health of employees, is subject to any express terms in the contract. It was only because the defendants had a discretion to get the plaintiff to work 88 hours, rather than an absolute obligation, that the Vice-Chancellor was able to consider the interaction of the express and implied terms. Stuart-Smith LJ dissented on this point. To him it was a question of the interaction of the two terms, the express and implied one. The contract gave the authority the power to require the plaintiff to work up to 88 hours per week but only if this could be done in such a way as not to breach the implied term of reasonable care for the employee's health.

If the approach of the majority were adopted on the point of express terms overriding implied terms, this would reduce the whole of the law of negligence on employer's liability to a question of contract. It is unlikely that the judiciary would take such an approach.

Further reading

Fleming, J (1984) 4 Oxford J Legal Stud 235
Markesinis, B S (1987) 103 LQR 354
Stapleton, J (1985) 5 Oxford J Legal Stud 248

defective product, if the friend had suffered damage. By creating a tortious duty to the plaintiff the House of Lords began the removal of the privity fallacy from English law. (Although it now appears to be staging a comeback!)

(b)   A new category of duty was created: that of manufacturers of dangerous products to their ultimate consumers. This is known as the narrow rule. (See 'Defective products', p. 128.)

(c)   Lord Atkin stated his famous neighbour test as a general test for determining whether a duty of care existed. This is known as the wide rule.

> You must take reasonable care to avoid acts or omissions which you can reasonably foresee would be likely to injure your neighbour. Who then in law is my neighbour? The answer seems to be . . . persons who are so closely and directly affected by my act that I ought reasonably to have them in contemplation as being so affected when I am directing my mind to the acts or omissions which are called in question.

Controversy exists as to how influential the neighbour test has been in the development of duty of care principles. But the test has been much cited and gave the law a starting point for the question of whether a duty of care existed, based on reasonable foreseeability of damage to the plaintiff.

What has always been clear is that this test alone was not sufficient to explain cases where the court found that no duty existed. There were numerous cases after *Donoghue* where the damage to the plaintiff was clearly foreseeable but the court refused to find a duty. One example was that of the builder who negligently constructed a house. The courts until the 1970s refused to find that the builder was liable in negligence to the house owner for the cost of repair. There were also cases of nervous shock where foreseeable shock did not give rise to a duty. Some other factor was clearly required to explain these cases.

The expansion of negligence liability

The neighbour test was originally confined to cases where physical damage was caused to the plaintiff by the defendant's negligence. But in *Hedley Byrne & Co Ltd* v *Heller & Partners Ltd* [1964] AC 465 the House of Lords allowed, in principle, a duty of care not to cause economic loss. They rejected the neighbour test as giving rise to potentially too wide a liability and instead stated that there had to be a special relationship between the parties.

A more elaborate test was put forward by the House of Lords in the 1970s in an attempt to rationalise developments since *Donoghue* and provide a framework within which judges could develop the law. *Anns* v *Merton London Borough* [1978] AC 728 at 751-2 per Lord Wilberforce

> the position has now been reached that in order to establish that a duty of care arises in particular situation, it is not necessary to bring the facts of that situation within those previous situations in which a duty of care has been held to exist. Rather the question to be approached in two stages. First, one has to ask whether, as between the ed wrongdoer and the person who has suffered damage there is a sufficient nship of proximity or neighbourhood such that, in the reasonable contemplation

of the former, carelessness on his part may be likely to cause damage to the latter, in which case a prima facie duty of care arises. Secondly, if the first question is answered affirmatively, it is necessary to consider whether there are any considerations which ought to negative, or to reduce or limit the scope of the duty or the class of persons to whom it is owed or the damages to which a breach of it may give rise

This broad statement of principle legitimised expansion which had already taken place in the duty of care and led to further expansion.

It can be seen that a two stage test was established. The first stage was to establish that the parties satisfied the requirements of the neighbour test. If this was done then a duty would exist unless the court found that policy dictated that there should be no duty. (See below, 'Policy', for examples, p. 33.)

The two stage test altered the way in which the neighbour test was used. Previously the courts had used it to justify new areas of liability if there were policy reasons for doing so. Now, it would apply unless there were policy reasons for excluding it. In other words policy was now to operate as a long stop.

Lord Wilberforce's dicta was followed by a brief but dramatic expansion in negligence liability as the courts applied the two stage test. The high water mark of this expansion was reached in *Junior Books Ltd* v *Veitchi Co Ltd* [1983] 1 AC 520, where the House of Lords apparently extended liability for economic loss to encompass traditional contract liability. (See below, 'Economic loss', p. 56.)

Retraction of negligence

The expansion of liability which took place in the 1970s and early 1980s caused some alarm to the appellate courts, who set about trying to check it and pull it back. The alarm was set off by a number of factors including the difficulties in obtaining adequate insurance to cover the new types of liability and the incursion of tort into traditionally contractual areas.

When changes are made to the law by the judiciary, they are usually not explicit about the socio-economic factors which make these changes necessary but they do need conceptual tools in order to make these changes. Highly influential in judicial reasoning during the period of retraction has been a statement by Brennan J in the Australian case of *Sutherland Shire Council* v *Heyman* (1985) 60 ALR 1:

Of course, if foreseeability of injury to another were the exhaustive criterion of a prima facie duty to act to prevent the occurrence of that injury, it would be essential to introduce some kind of restrictive qualification – perhaps a qualification of the kind stated in the second stage of the general proposition in *Anns*. I am unable to accept that approach. It is preferable, in my view, that the law should develop novel categories of negligence incrementally and by analogy with established categories, rather than by a massive extension of a prima facie duty of care restrained only by indefinable 'considerations which ought to negative, or to reduce or limit the scope of the duty or the class of persons to whom it is owed'. The proper role of the 'second stage', . . . embraces no more than those 'further elements' [in addition to the neighbour principle] which are appropriate to the particular category of negligence and which confine the duty of care within narrower limits than those which would be defined by an unqualified application of the neighbour principle.

The approach taken by Brennan J was to reject a broad general principles approach as taken by Lord Wilberforce and instead adopt an incremental approach. This would develop by looking at the particular category that the case fell into and developing specific rules within that category. So a nervous shock case, for example, would attract different rules from a straightforward physical damage one, as the former creates different problems and is not susceptible to an approach based on reasonable foreseeability alone.

This approach has been adopted a number of times by the House of Lords. For example, Lord Keith in *Yuen Kun- yeu* v *A-G of Hong Kong* [1987] 2 All ER 705:

> Their Lordships venture to think that the two-stage test formulated by Lord Wilberforce for determining the existence of a duty of care in negligence has been elevated to a degree of importance greater than it merits, and greater perhaps than its author intended. Further, the expression of the first stage of the test carries with it a risk of misinterpretation . . . there are two possible views of what Lord Wilberforce meant. The first view . . . is that he meant to test the sufficiency of proximity simply by the reasonable contemplation of likely harm. The second view . . . is that Lord Wilberforce meant the expression proximity or neighbourhood to be a composite one, importing the whole concept of necessary relationship between plaintiff and defendant . . . In their Lordship's opinion the second view is the correct one . . . foreseeability does not of itself, and automatically, lead to a duty of care. . . . The truth is that the trilogy of cases refered to by Lord Wilberforce (*Donoghue* v *Stevenson* (1932); *Hedley Byrne* v *Heller* (1963); *Home Office* v *Dorset Yacht* (1970)) each demonstrate particular sets of circumstances, differing in character, which were adjudged to have the effect of bringing into being a relationship apt to give rise to a duty of care. Foreseeability of harm is a necessary ingredient of such a relationship, but it is not the only one. . . . The speech of Lord Atkin stressed not only the requirement of foreseeability of harm but also that of a close and direct relationship of proximity. . . . The second stage of Lord Wilberforce's test is one which will rarely have to be applied. It can arise only in a limited category of cases where, notwithstanding that a case of negligence is made out on the proximity basis, public policy requires that there should be no liability . . . their Lordships consider that for the future it should be recognised that the two-stage test in *Anns* is not to be regarded as in all circumstances a suitable guide to the existence of a duty of care.

Further consideration was given to this question by Lord Bridge in *Caparo Industries plc* v *Dickman* [1990] 1 All ER 568 when he reviewed the necessary ingredients of a duty of care:

> What emerges is that, in addition to the foreseeability of damage, necessary ingredients in any situation giving rise to a duty of care are that there should exist between the party owing the duty and the party to whom it is owed a relationship characterised by the law as one of proximity or neighbourhood and that the situation should be one in which the court considers it fair, just and reasonable that the law should impose a duty of a given scope on the one party for the benefit of the other . . . the concepts of proximity and fairness . . . are not susceptible of any such precise definition as would

> be necessary to give them utility as practical tests, but amount in effect to little more than convenient labels to attach to the features of different specific situations . . . I think the law has now moved in the direction of attaching greater significance to the more traditional categorisation of distinct and recognisable situations as guides to the existence, the scope and the limits of the varied duties of care which the law imposes.

Finally, it should noted that in *Murphy v Brentwood District Council* [1990] 2 All ER 908 the House of Lords overruled *Anns v Merton*. (See 'Economic loss', p. 58.)

The present position

It can be seen from the above extracts that there are now four requirements for the existence of a duty of care. These are: foresight of damage, proximity, policy and whether it is just and reasonable to impose a duty. A court will not necessarily refer to them all in the same case.

Before looking at these concepts it is necessary to note the major change that has taken place. Instead of applying the two stage test to the facts of the case, the court will look at the particular relationship between plaintiff and defendant in the context of the type of damage caused (i.e. whether it is physical damage or economic loss).

An example could be given of an accountant who negligently prepares a firm's accounts. He could of course be liable for breach of contract to the firm but could he be liable to a third party in negligence? The court will start by looking at the relationship between the accountant and the third party. Was it reasonably foreseeable that this party would suffer financial loss as a result of the negligently prepared accounts? If it was not foreseeable that the third party would see the accounts (e.g. if they were leaked) then no duty is owed. The next stage is to determine whether there is proximity between the parties. Various factors will go towards this element, such as whether it was reasonable of the plaintiff to rely on the accounts and whether he was entitled to do so in the circumstances in which he received the information. Would it be just and reasonable to impose a duty? The court might take into account any other (e.g. statutory) obligation which the defendant might be under. Finally the court could deny the existence of a duty on policy grounds.

It should be noted that the courts concern is with attempts to extend duty areas into new relationships and types of loss, particularly economic loss. Where a duty, such as that between highway users, has been traditionally recognised, this will be unaffected.

Proximity and foreseeability

Foreseeability means that the defendant must have foreseen some damage to the plaintiff at the time of his alleged negligence. The important factor is that the plaintiff has to establish that the duty was owed to him. He cannot build on a duty owed to another.

Bourhill v Young [1943] AC 92

The plaintiff was descending from a tram when she heard a motor accident. She did not see the accident but later saw blood on the road and suffered nervous shock. It was reasonably foreseeable that some people would suffer damage as a result of the defendant's negligent driving, but the plaintiff was not foreseeable as she was so far from the accident and was owed no duty of care. The test for foreseeability is an objective one, it is the foresight of the reasonable man that counts, not the foresight of the defendant.

It can be seen from the extracts above that there was for a time some confusion as to whether there was any distinction between foresight and proximity. It can equally be seen that this problem has been resolved. The two are distinct although foresight of damage is a necessary ingredient of proximity.

What will constitute proximity will vary from case to case. Where the case is a road accident and physical damage is caused to the plaintiff, then mere foreseeability of damage will be sufficient to establish proximity. If the plaintiff is not struck by the vehicle but suffers nervous shock as a result of witnessing the accident, then factors such as the relationship between the plaintiff and the person placed in physical danger, and the closeness of the plaintiff to the scene of the accident, will determine proximity.

Proximity is clearly a complex idea and will be developed in later chapters as specific examples of negligence are looked at.

Just and reasonable and policy

The basis of any decision as to duty of care will be policy. It can therefore fairly be asked whether there is any difference between proximity, just and reasonable, and policy. Would a court be prepared to find that there was proximity and then say it was not just and reasonable to impose a duty or vice versa?

No clear answer can be given to this question as yet. But the indication in *Caparo* v *Dickman* was that proximity could be used as a comprehensive term embracing all three.

The expression policy appears to have changed in meaning with the recent cases. Under the old *Anns* v *Merton* test, policy had a broad meaning which encompassed proximity, fair and reasonable and public policy in the narrow sense in which it is now used.

This can best be explained through the so-called 'floodgates' problem. This is a difficulty which the courts have grappled with in this area for a long time. The accepted definition of 'floodgates' was given by Cardozo CJ in the US case of *Ultramares Corp.* v *Touche* (1931) 174 NE 441 at 444 as: the undesirability of exposing defendants to a potential liability 'in an indeterminate amount for an indeterminate time to an indeterminate class'. Take two examples of this problem, one involving physical damage and the other economic loss.

Example A

Arthur drives his car negligently with th[e] result that he crashes into a group of small children waiting to cross the road outside a prim[ar]y school at 9 a.m. The injuries to the children struck by the car present no difficulties in ter[ms] of duty of care. The neighbour test can be applied. The problem will come from persons w[ho] suffer nervous shock as a result of witnessing the accident. This may include parents, te[ac]hers, school crossing patrol and strangers who just happen to be passing. These will make [u]p Cardozo's 'indeterminate class'. The common law needs to draw a line limiting those wh[o c]an recover. The old law would have asked whether nervous shock was reasonably forese[e]able to a particular person and then whether there were any 'policy' grounds why that per[so]n should not be owed a duty. The 'new' law will ask the four questions. But a duty could b[e] denied on any of these grounds. Assume that it is reasonably foreseeable that anyone [wo]uld suffer nervous shock at the sight of a horrific accident. Does it make any difference [wh]ether the court denies a duty on the grounds of lack of proximity between Arthur and the [pl]aintiff; that it would not be just and reasonable to impose a duty; or that a duty should no[t b]e imposed on the grounds of public policy?

Using the term policy in its narrow modern sense, there are no policy grounds for denying liability for nervous shoc[k] generally. It may not be just and reasonable to impose a duty because of the bu[r]den that would fall on Arthur (or rather his insurers) but the reason that would [b]e given by the court would be that there was no proximity between the plaintiff an[d] Arthur. It could well be argued here of course that there are no grounds for den[yi]ng a claim to anyone who suffers identifiable nervous shock. Opponents of the f[lo]odgates theory argue that it should not be used to deny a claim to a large but f[or]eseeable class of persons in cases of physical damage.

Example B

Arthur fails to have his car serviced [an]d as a result, it breaks down in the Mersey Tunnel causing an enormous traffic jam. As a [r]esult, large numbers of people are late for work and lose wages. Others are on their way [to] business meetings and lose contracts as a result of being held up. This loss may continue [to] ripple down a chain. The late employee may cause his firm to lose business etc. No duty [of] care is owed by Arthur in respect of these claims for economic loss. The number of claim[s would] be indeterminate as it would depend on what time of day the car broke down. The [ex]tent of the claims would also be indeterminate, as it would depend upon who was stuck t[he]re. Finally, if a duty was recognised, where would it end? With the people in the tunnel? W[ith] the people with whom they had or expected to have contractual relations?

The same question may be asked [ag]ain. On what grounds should the courts deny a duty of care. If you say that the[re] is no proximity between Arthur and persons suffering economic loss, you can [se]e that this may introduce elements of just and reasonableness and perhaps publi[c p]olicy.

The conclusion to be drawn is t[ha]t the headings indicated by the appellate courts are not watertight and run into [e]ach other. In fact, it could even be said, with respect, that the courts have rep[la]ced the old uncertain terminology with new, equally uncertain terminology.

4 | Nervous shock

INTRODUCTION

Claims in this area are typically where a person suffers a reaction when they witness an accident in which a loved one is injured. No damages are recoverable for the ordinary grief, sorrow or distress which is suffered. Before a person can claim they have to establish, on the basis of medical evidence, that they suffered a definite and identifiable psychiatric illness.

Lawyers have traditionally used the expression nervous shock to describe this condition. However, the Court of Appeal has indicated that the expression psychiatric damage is preferable (*Attia* v *British Gas plc* [1987] 3 All ER 455 at 462). Whatever expression is used, the plaintiff must establish harm over and above ordinary grief and distress.

The problem raised by the expression nervous shock is that the term has a different meaning according to whether a lawyer or doctor is using it. In medical terms nervous shock means the primary response to traumatic stimulus. This response is short in duration and too transient to be compensated in damages. It is the secondary response caused by an individual's failure to deal adequately with a traumatic event that is referred to as nervous shock by lawyers and is compensated by damages. This secondary response is relatively rare but when it occurs will take the form of reactive depression, anxiety neurosis, post-traumatic stress disorder or other recognisable psychiatric disorder.

PROBLEMS RAISED

Nervous shock is dealt with separately from ordinary physical damage for a number of reasons. Initially, the courts had difficulty in identifying a genuine claim from a fictitious one. Advances in psychiatry in the twentieth century mean this is no longer a major problem and it is rarely referred to by the courts.

There is a problem in placing a monetary value on this type of harm. A successful plaintiff will recover for pecuniary losses, such as loss of earnings, in the normal way. But damages for non-pecuniary loss have to be assessed by the court. However, this is a problem which they have to deal with in all personal injuries claims. Is it any more difficult to assess these damages in nervous shock cases than in, e.g., paralysis cases?

The major difficulty is the floodgates problem. Ordinary physical damage caused by negligent conduct will by its nature be limited to those within the range of impact. Nervous shock is not so limited, as persons not within the range of impact may be affected. The courts have been conscious of this problem as they developed the law and have imposed restrictions on those who can recover.

HISTORICAL DEVELOPMENT

The initial response of the common law to claims for nervous shock was to deny liability until the early part of the twentieth century.

Dulieu v White & Sons [1901] 2 KB 669

The plaintiff, who was pregnant, was working behind the bar of a public house when the defendant's servant negligently drove a horse van into the public house. The plaintiff suffered shock resulting in the premature birth of her child. The plaintiff was entitled to recover as the shock was due to fear for her own personal safety. Shock suffered as a result of fear for the safety of another would not be compensated.

Hambrook v Stokes Bros [1925] 1 KB 141

The defendants left a lorry unattended at the top of a hill with the brake off. The lorry ran down the hill and eventually crashed. The plaintiff's wife had just left her children round a bend in the road. She saw the lorry and feared for the safety of her children. She was told that a girl with glasses had been injured and thinking it was her daughter she suffered nervous shock leading to her death. Damages were awarded although she was not within the foreseeable area of impact and the shock was suffered as a result of fear for another's safety. A new limitation was imposed, that the shock should occur as a result of what the plaintiff witnessed as a result of her own unaided senses, rather than as a result of what others later told her.

Following this case two factors became important in determining whether a person owed a duty not to cause nervous shock. One was the closeness of the plaintiff to the accident and whether the defendant was aware of the plaintiff's presence. The other was the relationship between the person suffering nervous shock and the person placed in danger. It became apparent that close family ties such as parent–child or spouse, would suffice. However other relationships were also recognised.

Chadwick *v* British Railways Board [1967] 1 WLR 912

A serious train crash occurred as a result of the negligence of a train driver. The plaintiff attended the scene and helped with the rescue work. As a result of what he saw he suffered from nervous shock. It was held that a duty was owed to rescuers and that as nervous shock was foreseeable in these circumstances the defendants were liable.

Dooley *v* Cammell Laird & Co Ltd [1951] 1 Lloyds Rep 271

The plaintiff was operating a crane belonging to the defendants when a sling broke and the crane's load dropped into the hold of a ship. The plaintiff's fellow employees were working in the hold and the plaintiff suffered nervous shock at the thought that they might have been injured. The plaintiff recovered damages.

PRESENT LAW

The question of the requirements for a duty of care in nervous shock cases was taken to the House of Lords in 1983. At this time the law could be stated as being that a duty was owed if the plaintiff had a sufficiently close relationship with the person placed in danger and witnessed the accident with their own unaided senses. If both these requirements were satisfied then there would be proximity between the parties.

McLoughlin *v* O'Brian [1983] AC 410

At the time of a road accident involving her family, Mrs McLoughlin was at her home two miles away. An hour later she was informed of the accident and driven to a hospital where her family had been taken. She saw her daughter covered with dirt and oil and with her face cut. Her husband was in a similar condition and her son very badly injured and screaming. Her other daughter had died almost immediately. What she saw caused her to suffer from organic depression and a personality change. Negligence proceedings were brought against the defendants who had negligently caused the accident.

The House of Lords unanimously held that the plaintiff was owed a duty of care by the defendants. This clearly involved some extension of the existing law as Mrs McLoughlin was not at the scene of the accident. However the reasoning of their Lordships varied.

Lords Bridge and Scarman adopted a test based on foreseeability alone. In assessing reasonable foreseeability: space, time, distance, the nature of the injuries and the relationship to the victim were factors to be weighed, but not legal limitations. Policy was rejected as inappropriate for the court and any floodgates problem dismissed.

Lords Edmund-Davies and Wilberforce were of the opinion that policy issues were justiciable by a court. Lord Wilberforce stated that there were three elements in a claim. The first was the relationship between the plaintiff and the person suffering injury. Persons with close family ties would satisfy this test. Mere bystanders at an accident would be owed no duty. Relationships in between would have to be scrutinised on a case by case basis. The second factor was that the plaintiff had to be proximate to the accident in terms of time and space. To be successful the plaintiff had to be within sight or sound of the accident or come upon its immediate aftermath. (As Mrs McLoughlin did.) Thirdly, shock resulting from being told by a third party of the accident would not be compensated. The question of whether simultaneous television would suffice as sound or sight was left open.

McLoughlin left the law in an uncertain state. If Lord Wilberforce's restrictions were seen as immovable restrictions, then a plaintiff who fell on the wrong side of the line would fail. The reasonable foresight test adopted by Lords Bridge and Scarman gave more scope for justice while eschewing certainty. One uncertainty can be illustrated by a point that Lord Bridge made. He gave the example of a person reading of an accident in the paper and suffering nervous shock. He would be prepared to grant a remedy in such circumstances but Lord Wilberforce would not.

Case law subsequent to McLoughlin indicated that the reasonable foreseeability approach would be adopted: e.g. liability was extended to where the shock was caused by the sight of property damage when the plaintiff's house burned down as a result of the defendant's negligence (*Attia* v *British Gas plc* [1987] 3 All ER 455).

It should also be noted that in applying a foreseeability test the court will take into account the egg-shell skull principle, that the defendant must take the plaintiff as he finds him as regards physical characteristics.

Brice *v* Brown [1984] 1 All ER 997

A nine year old girl and her mother were involved in an accident in the taxi in which they were travelling. The girl suffered slight injuries but the mother, who was emotionally unstable, suffered serious and long lasting nervous shock. The court applied a test of whether the person of customary phlegm would have suffered shock in these circumstances. If not, then the plaintiff would have no claim. If yes, then the plaintiff could recover for the full extent of her shock, even if the person of customary phlegm would not have suffered shock to that extent. (See remoteness of damage for the egg-shell skull rule.) It is not clear whether the claim of a person who is employed to perform rescue work would be accepted by the courts. However, the claims of the firemen who attended the Kings Cross fire have been settled.

Further development and controversy in the law has been provided by the terrible tragedy at the Hillsborough football ground.

THE HILLSBOROUGH LITIGATION

Jones *v* Wright [1991] 2 WLR 814; (first instance) [1991] 3 All ER 88 (Court of Appeal)

On 15th April 1989 the F.A. Cup semi-final was due to be played between Liverpool and Nottingham Forest at Hillsborough stadium in Sheffield. The match was a sell out and television cameras were at the ground to record the football for transmission later that evening. The match was halted after six minutes as the weight of numbers of people in the Leppings Lane pens had created such pressure that spectators were being trapped against the wire separating the pens from the pitch. Some ninety-five people died from their injuries and another four hundred needed hospital treatment. Thousands witnessed the horrific events from other parts of the ground and millions more witnessed what was happening on live television broadcasts or heard the news on radio. Many of those watching or listening had loved ones at the match. Inevitably a large number of people suffered psychological disorders and some cases within well accepted categories of nervous shock were settled. Sixteen test cases were brought to determine whether the defendant (the Chief Constable of the police force responsible for policing the ground) owed them a duty of care. These cases were representative of one hundred and fifty similar claims.

Four of the plaintiffs had actually attended the match and witnessed the events and had friends or relatives in the Leppings Lane pens. One plaintiff was outside the ground and watched the events on television in a coach. He later identified the body of his son-in-law in a mortuary. Nine of the plaintiffs witnessed the disaster on television and had loved ones at the match. One plaintiff heard the news on the radio and later saw recorded highlights on television. The final plaintiff heard the news while out shopping, heard the news on the radio some two hours later and at 10 p.m. saw recorded television.

The plaintiffs had all been examined by the same medical expert and the trial judge accepted his evidence that they were all suffering from at least one psychiatric illness.

The issue for the court was therefore whether the defendant owed each plaintiff a duty of care. Two issues were pertinent as to proximity. First, the necessary degree of relationship between the plaintiff and the person in danger. Second, the question of geographical proximity to the accident. The question of simultaneous television transmission arose for decision for the first time.

On necessary relationship, the first instance judge held that parents, spouses and siblings of a victim had a close enough relationship to be foreseeable. The Court of Appeal was split on this point. Stocker LJ and Nolan LJ were prepared to accept that a person who fell outside the accepted categories of parent–child, spouse or rescuer, could claim, provided they could establish a sufficient degree of relationship and care. Parker LJ agreed that the claim was based on relationship and care. On this basis the accepted categories had a presumptive claim, but the presumption could be rebutted if the necessary degree of care was not present. Thus spouses who were separated and hated each other could have the presumption in their favour defeated. The result in the instant case was that all persons who did not fall within the parent–child or spouse categories had their claims rejected as no evidence had been led to establish the necessary degree of care required. An example of such a relationship would be where a grandparent had brought up a child from being a baby.

On the question of geographical proximity, the trial judge considered that all persons in, or immediately outside the stadium were sufficiently proximate in terms of time and space. Those persons who witnessed the scenes on television and had the necessary degree of relationship could also claim. Plaintiffs who were told of the disaster or heard it on the radio had no claim. The Court of Appeal, however, took the view that those persons who suffered shock as a result of watching live television had no claim. While it was reasonably foreseeable that television pictures would be broadcast, the intervention of a third party between the accident and the plaintiff meant that television was not equivalent to sight or sound of the accident.

The Court of Appeal also took a narrow view of the immediate aftermath test. They regarded the events in *McLoughlin* as being equivalent to viewing the accident. Stress was placed on the fact that the family were still in the same state as they had been at the time of the accident. In cases where plaintiffs had viewed the corpse of a loved one some hours after the disaster, this was not regarded as the immediate aftermath.

Alcock & Others v Chief Constable of the South Yorkshire Police [1991] 4 All ER 907

Ten of the original plaintiffs appealed to the House of Lords and the House unanimously dismissed their appeals.

Counsel for the plaintiffs based his case on the argument that the sole test for duty in nervous shock cases was whether such illness was reasonably foreseeable. The House rejected this, in line with Lord Wilberforce's point in *McLoughlin* that foreseeability alone did not give rise to a duty.

The requirements for a duty of care in nervous shock cases were stated by the House of Lords to be:

(a)   A sufficiently close relationship of love and affection with the primary victim to make it reasonably foreseeable that the plaintiff might suffer nervous shock if he apprehended that the primary victim had been injured or might be injured.

      This means that the potential duty is not restricted to particular relationships such as spouses or parent–child. In spouse and parent–child cases there would appear to be a rebuttable presumption of such a relationship. In other relationships, such as siblings or engaged couples, it will be necessary for the plaintiff to lead evidence to prove the existence of such a relationship.

      Curiously, Lords Ackner, Keith and Oliver were not prepared to rule out even a bystander where the accident was particularly horrific and a reasonably strong-nerved person would have been affected. The example given was where a petrol tanker crashed into a school playground, caught fire and caused serious injuries to children.

      A duty will continue to be owed to rescuers on policy grounds. The case of *Dooley* v *Cammell Laird* is only mentioned by Lord Jauncey, who upholds it on the grounds that the crane driver was intimately involved in, but in no way responsible for the accident.

(b)   Proximity to the accident, or its immediate aftermath, was sufficiently close in terms of time and space.

      Sight or sound of the accident will continue to suffice. The House refused to lay down a strict definition of immediate aftermath. Lord Keith appeared to approve the Australian case of *Jaensch* v *Coffey* (1984) 54 ALR 417, where the aftermath of the accident continued as long as the victim remained in the state produced by the accident, up to and including immediate post-accident treatment. Lord Ackner viewed *McLoughlin* as being on the boundaries of what was acceptable. All judges were agreed that identifying a corpse in the mortuary eight hours after the accident was not within the immediate aftermath.

(c)   He suffered nervous shock through seeing or hearing the accident or its immediate aftermath.

      A person who was informed of the accident by a third party would have no claim. A person watching simultaneous television would normally have no claim as the broadcasting guidelines prevent the showing of suffering by recognisable individuals. If such pictures were shown, then the transmission would normally be regarded as a *novus actus interveniens*. There may be cases, however, where viewing simultaneous television may be treated as equivalent to sight and sound of the accident. An example is given of a televised hot-air ballon event with children in the balloon, which suddenly bursts into flames.

Further reading

Gearty, C [1984] CLJ 238
Teff, H (1983) 99 LQR 100
Trinidade, F A [1986] CLJ 476

5 | Economic loss

INTRODUCTION

Pure economic loss unaccompanied by physical damage presents a particular problem in negligence as negligence has traditionally operated in a protective manner to compensate people for loss caused by negligently inflicted physical damage.

Where a person has suffered economic loss their redress has traditionally been in contract law. The justification for this was the doctrine of consideration. Where a person had entered a bargain promise and provided consideration, this would justify the court protecting his expectation interest in a breach of contract action. Damages for breach of contract are to put the plaintiff in the position he would have been in if the contract had been performed. Contrast this with the tortious objective of damages, to put the plaintiff in the position he would have been in if the tort had not been committed. This protects the status quo interest.

Example

Take the facts of Donoghue v Stevenson. *The duty of care owed by the defendant was a duty not to cause physical damage, in this case personal injuries to the plaintiff caused by a contaminated drink. If the plaintiff had been sick over her clothes as a result of drinking the contaminated ginger beer, she would have had a claim for damage to property. Both the claim for personal injuries and the claim for property damage are status quo claims. But she could not have claimed for the cost of the ginger beer. This is regarded as a claim for economic loss and as the plaintiff had no contract, she had no claim. In this particular area (defective products) a distinction is drawn between providing a dangerous product (tort) and a defective product (contract).*

A further objection to allowing economic loss claims in negligence is that it would involve the courts in having to assess quality. Where the claim is brought in contract, the quality is fixed by the contract. In the above example, the legally required quality of the ginger beer. But this problem is somewhat exaggerated in consumer claims such as *Donoghue*. Had the purchaser of the ginger beer brought an action in contract, the quality of the drink would actually have been fixed by statute rather than by the contract (Sale of Goods Act 1979, ss. 14(2)).

The floodgates problem is often raised as a barrier to bringing an economic loss action in negligence. Economic loss is said to have a ripple effect which is not present in physical damage claims. No floodgates problem exists in contract as the doctrine of privity limits an action to those persons who have provided consideration and are therefore parties to the contract. However, there are economic loss claims which cannot be explained on floodgates grounds as the defendant's negligent conduct could only cause economic loss to the plaintiff.

HISTORICAL DEVELOPMENT

In cases of physical damage, the neighbour test provided a springboard for the development of a general principle of liability. Modern orthodoxy holds that there was no claim for economic loss. The next case is often cited to support the point.

Cattle *v* Stockton Waterworks Co (1875) LR 10 QB 453

The defendants negligently burst a water main. This added to the plaintiff's expense in building a tunnel. The plaintiff was under contract with a third party to build the tunnel. The plaintiff was unable to recover this expense as it was pure economic loss.

This case illustrates a recurrent problem. A makes a contract with B. C acts negligently. This makes it more expensive for A to complete his contract.

There were cases however where the decision had gone in favour of recovery.

Morrison Steamship Co Ltd *v* Greystoke Castle [1947] AC 265

Ships A and B collided. There was no damage to the cargo of ship A. Under maritime law, the owners of the cargo on ship A became liable to pay a sum of money to the owners of A. The cargo owners successfully sued the owners of ship B for negligence in causing the collision although the plaintiffs' loss was purely economic.

The recent trend against recovery of economic loss has led to this case being either ignored or explained away on the basis that it is peculiar to maritime law.

Where a person makes a negligent statement, the loss that will follow will normally be economic rather than physical. It was thought that the House of Lords decision in *Derry* v *Peek* (1889) 14 App Cas 337, precluded any action for negligent statements causing economic loss. Liability for statements would only arise where they were contractual, where there was a fiduciary duty, or in deceit. This position was restated by the Court of Appeal.

Candler *v* Crane Christmas & Co [1951] 2 KB 164

The defendant accountants prepared a company's accounts. They knew that these were to be given to the plaintiff to persuade him to invest money in the company. The plaintiff did invest money and suffered loss as the accounts had been negligently prepared and gave a false impression of the company. The plaintiff sued the defendants in negligence. The Court of Appeal held that no duty of care arose in these circumstances in the absence of a contractual relationship.

Denning LJ gave a powerful dissenting judgment. He argued that the defendants owed a duty of care to their:

> employer or client, and . . . any third person to whom they themselves show the accounts, or to whom they know their employer is going to show the accounts so as to induce them to invest money or take some other action on them. I do not think, however, the duty can be extended still further so as to include strangers of whom they have heard nothing and to whom their employer without their knowledge may choose to show their accounts.

A major change in the law on economic loss came with the House of Lords decision in the following case.

Hedley Byrne & Co Ltd *v* Heller & Partners Ltd [1964] AC 465

The appellants were advertising agents who became doubtful about the financial position of one of their clients, E Ltd. The appellants bankers enquired from E Ltd's bankers (the respondents) as to the financial position of E Ltd. The defendants replied that E Ltd was a respectably constituted company, considered good for its ordinary business engagements. The advice was given without responsibility by the respondents. Relying on this advice the appellants lost over £17,000 when E Ltd went into liquidation. An action was brought alleging that the advice had been given negligently by the respondents.

The appellants' action failed as the House of Lords held that the without responsibility clause amounted to a disclaimer of liability and no duty of care was owed.

The importance of the case lies in the fact that the House of Lords stated that in appropriate circumstances a duty of care could arise to give careful advice and that failure to do so could give rise to liability for economic loss caused by negligent advice.

The appellants in *Hedley Byrne* had to overcome two barriers (apart from the disclaimer clause). The first was the supposed bar on claims for negligent statements arising from *Derry* v *Peek*. It was this aspect of the law that the House of Lords concentrated on. The second barrier was the one against recovery of economic loss. This received little attention. The result was that the decision had the effect of allowing actions for economic loss caused by words but not economic loss caused by acts. This unfortunate distinction has been followed by the courts since. The remainder of this chapter will therefore be split into statements and acts.

ECONOMIC LOSS CAUSED BY NEGLIGENT STATEMENTS

The possibility of such claims was opened up by *Hedley Byrne* v *Heller*. The House of Lords was concerned with the floodgates problem and on this basis rejected the neighbour test as being inappropriate to deal with the problems raised by negligent statements.

If a defective product is put into circulation, then any damage caused will probably be limited to a small group of people and occur on only one occasion. However, once a negligent statement is put into circulation, a large number of people could be affected for a lengthy period of time. One example is that of the marine hydrographer who negligently made a shipping chart. Such charts generally have a long life span and large amounts of ships could sink as a result of the chart.

Having rejected reasonable foreseeability of damage alone as a sufficient criterion for imposing a duty, the House of Lords stated that for a duty to arise in giving advice there had to be a 'special relationship' between the giver and the recipient of the advice.

Lord Morris stated:

> My Lords, I consider that it follows and that it should now be regarded as settled that if someone possessed of a special skill undertakes, quite irrespective of contract, to apply that skill for the assistance of another person who relies on such skill, a duty of care will arise. Furthermore, if in a sphere in which a person is so placed that others could reasonably rely on his judgment or his skill or upon his ability to make careful inquiry a person takes it upon himself to give information or advice to, or allows his information or advice to be passed on to, another person who, as he knows, or should know, will place reliance upon it, then a duty of care will arise.

Since *Hedley Byrne* the courts have been attempting to construct a theory of liability in this area. The expressions used have changed, but for the sake of convenience we will continue to use the expression special relationship to describe the necessary ingredients of the duty. What then is required for there to be a special relationship?

Special skill

The defendant must be possessed of a special skill in giving this sort of advice.

Mutual Life and Citizens Assurance Co *v* Evatt [1971] AC 793

The Privy Council held by a majority of three to two that an insurance company did not owe a duty of care in giving investment advice. The majority held that a duty only arose when the defendant was in the business of giving that advice or had held himself out as competent to do so. The minority (Lords Reid and Morris) held that a duty would arise only where the plaintiff made it clear that he was seeking considered advice and intended to act on it in a specific way.

It is the minority view that has gained acceptance in English law. (See *Esso Petroleum Co v Mardon* [1976] QB 801.)

The purpose of this requirement is to exclude liability where advice is given informally. A person will not be liable for incorrect advice given when 'somewhat the worse for wear' at a party or for a conversation with a stranger in a railway carriage. A duty will not be owed where advice is given on a social occasion.

Chaudhry v Prabhaker [1988] 3 All ER 718

The plaintiff had asked a friend who had some knowledge of cars to find a suitable one that had not been involved in an accident. The defendant found a car and recommended it. The plaintiff bought it, however, it was found to have been involved in an accident. Counsel for the defendant had conceded that his client owed a duty of care as he was a gratuitous agent. The appeal was brought on the ground of whether the defendant had been in breach of duty. The Court of Appeal found that he had and as duty had been conceded the plaintiff's action succeeded.

Should the duty have been conceded? See May LJ at 725, Stuart-Smith LJ at 721 and Stocker LJ at 723.

Reasonable reliance

The advice must be given in circumstances in which the reasonable person in the defendant's position would appreciate that his advice would be likely to be relied on. Reliance in this area is used in the narrow sense that the words or conduct of the defendant imply an undertaking to an identifiable plaintiff to act in a certain way.

This requirement has caused a number of problems as the tide of judicial opinion has ebbed to and fro. A number of expressions have been used, such as 'equivalent to contract' and 'voluntary assumption of responsibility'. None of these expressions is particularly helpful when determining whether the courts are likely to find a duty and the latter expression was rejected by the House of Lords in *Smith* v *Bush* [1990] 1 AC 831 at 862. The House of Lords has also warned against trying to find any general principle:

> circumstances may differ infinitely and . . . there can be no necessary assumption that those features which have served in one case to create the relationship between the plaintiff and the defendant on which liability depends will necessarily be determinative of liability in another case. (*Caparo Industries plc v Dickman* [1990] 1 All ER 568 at 587 per Lord Oliver.)

Given this approach, the only feasible way to approach the point is to look at pockets of cases where a particular type of advice is given.

Surveyors and valuers

The problem arises where a surveyor is asked to value a house by a building society or other mortgage lending institution. The valuation will be shown to the prospective purchaser and he may (probably will) rely on it in deciding whether to purchase the property. If the valuation was negligently carried out and the house is worth less than was paid for it, does the surveyor owe the purchaser a duty of care?

If we look at this situation in diagrammatic form, we can see that there are contracts between the surveyor and the building society and between the building society and the purchaser. Despite the fact that the purchaser pays for the valuation, there is no contract between him and the surveyor.

Surveyor------------Building Society--------------Purchaser

Yianni *v* Edwin Evans & Sons [1982] QB 438

A house was valued for the plaintiffs by the defendants at £12,000. Relying on this valuation, the plaintiffs borrowed £12,000 by way of a mortgage from the building society who had arranged for the valuation. The plaintiffs later discovered that the house needed £18,000 worth of repairs doing. Park J found that the defendant owed a duty of care to the plaintiffs. The basis of his decision was that a large proportion of house buyers rely completely on the valuation and do not have a full structural survey carried out. This fact is known to surveyors who carry out this type of work.

Not surprisingly, the decision was not welcomed by surveyors. The practice commenced of placing disclaimers in valuations. The issue of whether a duty of care was owed by surveyors and the standing of the disclaimers came to the House of Lords in two linked cases.

Smith *v* Eric S Bush; Harris *v* Wyre Forest DC [1989] 2 All ER 514

In both cases valuations had been carried out for the plaintiffs by the defendants and disclaimer clauses inserted in the valuation. For example, valuation is confidential and is intended solely for the information of Wyre Forest District Council in determining what advance, if any, may be made on the security and that no responsibility whatsoever is implied or accepted by the Council for the value or condition of the property by reason of such inspection and report.

Three questions had to be answered in relation to each appeal.

(a) *Was a duty of care owed to the plaintiff?* The House of Lords unanimously held that a surveyor or valuer was capable of owing a duty to take reasonable care to a prospective purchaser. The decision in *Yianni* was upheld. Proximity arose from the surveyor's knowledge that the purchaser would probably rely on his valuation. It was just and reasonable to impose a duty as the advice was given in a professional rather than a social context. The extent of the duty was limited to the purchaser of the house. It did not extend to subsequent purchasers.

(b) *Did the disclaimers fall within the ambit of the Unfair Contract Terms Act 1977?* Section 1(1)(b) states that 'negligence' means the breach of any common law duty to take reasonable care. One of the arguments put forward by the surveyors was that the disclaimer of liability would at common law have prevented any duty arising and the Act therefore had no application. However, s. 11(3) states: 'the requirement of reasonableness under this Act is that it should be fair and reasonable to allow reliance on it, having regard to all the circumstances obtaining when the liability arose or (but for the notice) would have arisen'.

Section 13(1) states: 'sections 2 and 5 to 7 also prevent excluding or restricting liability by reference to terms and notices which exclude or restrict the relevant obligation or duty. The House of Lords interpreted these sections as meaning that the existence of a common law duty of care had to be judged by considering whether it would exist 'but for' the notice excluding liability. Any other interpretation would result in removing all liability for negligent misstatements from the ambit of the Act'.

(c)   *Did the notice satisfy the requirement of reasonableness imposed by s. 2(2) of the Act?* The meaning of reasonableness is dealt with by s. 11(3). The House considered that certain factors should be taken into account in determining reasonableness. Were the parties of equal bargaining power? Would it have been reasonably practicable to obtain the advice from an alternative source? How difficult is the task being undertaken for which liability is being excluded? What are the practical consequences of the decision on the question of reasonableness?

The conclusion was that the risk should fall on the surveyor rather than the purchaser and the disclaimer was unreasonable in the circumstances. A caveat was added to the effect that the houses in these cases were of modest value and that the risk might fall on the purchaser in cases involving the purchase of industrial property or expensive houses.

The end result of this litigation is that a purchaser of a house of 'modest value' now knows that they can rely on the valuation given for mortgage purposes. If this valuation is carried out negligently, then the purchaser can recover the difference between what the house was said to be worth and what it was actually worth, from the surveyor. The surveyor cannot rely on a disclaimer clause in the valuation. It was forecast that the cost of such valuations would probably increase to meet the surveyor's potential liability. It appears that what has happened, is that purchasers are being offered a choice of surveys between a full structural one and a valuation.

Accountants and auditors

When an accountant produces a report on the affairs of a company, to whom does he owe a duty of care? He will be in a contractual relationship with his client and a duty will accordingly be owed in contract. But the report might be seen and relied on by other people and for various purposes. The difference between these cases and the surveyor cases is that the communication of the advice is not made to an identified person (the purchaser) but to a class of persons. The position is further complicated by the fact that the company may be under a statutory duty to have an annual audit of their accounts prepared and the contents of the audit may also be laid down by statute.

JEB Fasteners v Marks Bloom & Co [1983] 1 All ER 583

Defendant accountants prepared accounts for their client and negligently overstated the value of the stock. The defendants were aware that the client was in financial difficulties and was seeking financial support. The plaintiff then took over the company after seeing the accounts. He then brought an action in negligence against the defendants. It was held that a duty of care was owed to the plaintiff but the action failed on the grounds of causation. The reason the plaintiff took over the company was to acquire the expertise of the directors. He was not concerned with the value of the stock.

In the late 1980s there was a large amount of litigation against accountants, much of it in connection with the take-over boom of this period. The question of the accountant's liability eventually arrived at the House of Lords.

Caparo Industries plc v Dickman [1990] 1 All ER 568

The case involved a public company. The appellants had audited the accounts of the company. The annual audit of a public company is regulated by statute and the Companies Act 1985 laid down in detail what the statutory accounts had to contain. The respondents had owned shares in the company and in reliance on the accounts purchased further shares and made a successful takeover bid for the company. The respondents alleged that the accounts were inaccurate and negligently prepared and that they had suffered loss as a result. The issue was whether the appellants owed a duty of care to the respondents in the preparation of the accounts. The House of Lords held that in preparing the accounts a duty of care was owed to members of the company (shareholders). But this duty was a limited one. It was to enable the members to exercise proper control over the company. In this sense the interest of the member was identical to that of the company. If a director had misappropriated funds this could be recouped by an action in the name of the company. But no duty was owed to an individual member in connection with a decision to buy additional shares based on reliance on the accounts. Whether such a duty existed in connection with a decision to sell shares was left open by the House.

The effect of the decision was to prevent companies contemplating a takeover bid from relying on the annual audited accounts to determine the amount of their bid. The bidder would have to make his own inquiries.

The basis of the decision was that anyone who makes an investment or lending decision in reliance on an unqualified opinion will not be able to sue the auditors for any losses suffered as a result. This applies to shareholders, investors or institutional lenders.

Cases subsequent to *Caparo* have been concerned with the purposes for which company accounts are prepared.

Morgan Crucible Co plc v Hill Samuel Bank Ltd [1991] 1 All ER 148

Directors and financial advisers of a target company in a takeover bid had made statements regarding the accuracy of financial statements and profit forecasts, intending that a bidder should rely on those forecasts. The bidder did rely and alleged that he suffered loss as a result. The original statement of claim was drafted on the basis of a duty of care based on reasonable foreseeability. Following *Caparo*, the plaintiffs applied for leave to amend the statement of claim to one based on an identified bidder. At first instance leave was refused and the plaintiff appealed. The Court of Appeal granted leave to amend as there was an arguable case and *Caparo* could be distinguished. The distinction was that here, assuming the facts pleaded were correct, express representations had been made to it after it had emerged as an identifiable bidder.

James McNaughton Paper Group Ltd v Hicks Anderson & Co [1991] 1 All ER 134

Accountants who drew up, at short notice, draft accounts of a company for the company's chairman, owed no duty of care to a bidder who took over the company after inspecting the accounts. The accounts had been drawn up for the benefit of the chairman and not of the plaintiffs and as they were draft accounts and not final accounts, the auditors could not have been expected to foresee reliance on them. Certain criteria were identified by the Court of Appeal as being important in determining whether a duty of care arises:

(a)   The purpose for which the statement was made.
(b)   The purpose for which the statement was communicated.
(c)   The relationship between the adviser, the advisee and any relevant third party.
(d)   The size of any class to which the advisee belonged.
(e)   The state of knowledge of the adviser (*JEB Fasteners?*).
(f)   Reliance by the advisee.

It is evident from *Morgan Crucible* that the question of an auditor or other financial adviser's negligence liability is far from settled. *Caparo* may have been intended to impose a *caveat emptor* regime on financial advice but it may not be successful in doing so. An interesting prospect lies on the horizon with the EC 5th Directive on the Harmonisation of Company Law. Article 62 of the Directive imposes liability on auditors to third parties where loss is caused through the auditor's wrongful acts.

Other problem situations

Pre-contractual statements

Where a statement is made in the course of pre-contractual negotiations a duty of care may arise. The plaintiff in these circumstances may have a choice of actions. If the statement amounts to a misrepresentation, i.e. if it is an untrue statement of fact which induces the contract, then the plaintiff may have an action for damages under the Misrepresentation Act 1967. The same statement may give rise to a duty of care under the *Hedley Byrne* v *Heller* principles (*Esso Petroleum Co Ltd* v *Mardon* [1975] QB 819).

There are differences between the two actions which may affect the plaintiff's decision as to which to frame his action in.

An action for damages for misrepresentation under s. 2(1) Misrepresentation Act 1967 means that the plaintiff must show that the statement was followed by a contract between the maker and the recipient of the statement. In a negligence action the plaintiff must show that there was a special relationship between the parties.

Misrepresentation is attended by technical rules to the effect that the plaintiff must show that it was a statement of fact as opposed to opinion. This distinction has not been introduced into negligence actions.

The burden of proof is also different. Once the plaintiff has established a misrepresentation, it is up to the defendant to show that it was not made negligently. In the negligence action, the burden of proof is on the plaintiff to show that the defendant made the statement negligently.

Cases where there is no reliance by the plaintiff

In this situation B relies on a statement made by A and loss is caused to C as a result. It is difficult to fit these cases into the *Hedley Byrne* v *Heller* framework, as there is no reliance by the plaintiff on the defendant's advice.

Ministry of Housing and Local Government v Sharp [1970] 1 All ER 1009

A planning charge was registered in the local land charges registry (A). This meant that anyone undertaking development on the land would have to repay the Ministry (C) the compensation it had paid out for refusing development permission. Two years later planning permission was granted and a search of the registry requested by a prospective purchaser (B). Due to the carelessness of a clerk in the registry, the charge did not appear on the certificate issued after the search. This meant that the purchaser was not liable to pay the Ministry. The Court of Appeal held that the clerk's employers were vicariously liable for his negligence.

Ross v Caunters [1980] Ch 297

The defendant solicitors had prepared a will but failed to warn the testator that it should not be witnessed by the spouse of a beneficiary. The will was witnessed by the husband of the plaintiff beneficiary with the result that her legacy was rendered void. The defendants admitted negligence but argued that the only duty that they owed was to the testator. Megarry VC held that a duty of care was owed to the plaintiff as a sufficient relationship of neighbourhood or proximity existed between the parties.

It would appear that these two cases survive *Caparo* v *Dickman*, as only one person could have suffered damage in either case. There was therefore no danger of liability to an indefinite class. The fact that neither of them can be brought within the specific *Hedley Byrne* principles is not a problem, as these are only a part of the wider tort of negligence.

ECONOMIC LOSS CAUSED BY ACTS

Introduction

Since the decision in *Hedley Byrne* v *Heller*, liability for economic loss in negligence has developed in two broad areas: economic loss caused by statements and economic loss caused by acts. There was no logical reason why this should have happened and the ensuing distinction has had some unfortunate results.

Economic loss suffered by the plaintiff as a result of damage to property of a third party

This situation occurs where the defendant negligently damages property belonging to a third party on which the plaintiff relied in some way. A simple example of this situation is the cable cases.

Spartan Steel & Alloys Ltd v Martin & Co Ltd [1973] QB 27

The defendants negligently severed an electricity cable, causing the plaintiff's factory to shut down. The plaintiffs claimed damages under three heads.

(i)   Damage to goods in production at the time of the power cut (physical damage).
(ii)   Loss of profit on (a). (consequential economic loss).
(iii) Loss of profit on goods which could not be manufactured due to the power cut (pure economic loss).

The Court of Appeal held by a majority (Edmund-Davies LJ dissenting) that (a) and (b) were recoverable but (c) was not. If such claims were allowed then the potential losses were enormous. In this case only the plaintiff's factory had suffered the power cut but an entire estate of factories could have been affected. The court thought that it was better to let the loss lie where it fell and for factories to take out insurance against interrupted production. To shift the loss to the defendant might be to impose a crippling financial burden.

Subsequent cases have raised more complex factual situations in the area of shipping.

Candlewood Navigation Corpn Ltd v Mitsui OSK Lines Ltd (*The Mineral Transporter*) [1986] 1 AC 1

The first plaintiffs were the owners of a ship which was damaged by the negligence of the defendants. The first plaintiffs had chartered the ship to the second defendants and the effect of the charter was to put the second defendants in possession of the ship. The ship was then re-let by the second plaintiffs to the first plaintiffs on a time charter, which does not confer possession. The first plaintiffs claimed for the hire fees they had to pay while the ship was inoperative, and loss of profits for that period. The claim failed, although the plaintiffs were owners, both items of loss were suffered in their capacity as charterers, not as owners. The Privy Council refused the claim on floodgates grounds, the ripple effect which might be created if claims were allowed when a person's contractual relations had been made less profitable as a result of physical damage to the property of a third party.

Leigh & Sillivan Ltd v Aliakmon Shipping Co Ltd (*The Aliakmon*) [1986] 1 AC 785

The plaintiff suffered economic loss when goods which he had contracted to purchase were damaged at sea. At the time of the damage the risk but not the ownership of the goods had passed to the plaintiff. The plaintiff claimed that he was owed a duty of care by the defendants who had damaged the goods. The loss was classified as economic loss rather than physical damage because at the time of the damage the goods belonged to a third party. There was no floodgates risk in this case but the House of Lords held that no duty was owed. Lord Brandon stated:

> where a general rule, which is simple to understand and easy to apply, has been established by a long line of authority over many years, I do not think the law should allow special pleading in a particular case within the general rule to detract from its application . . . certainty of the law is of the utmost importance, especially but by no means only in commercial matters. (At 816–17)

The 'general rule' referred to by Lord Brandon is that the plaintiff may only sue in negligence for damage to property or any loss consequential on that damage, if he was the owner of the property or in possession at the time of the damage. The fact that he has other contractual rights in the property which become less valuable, or a contractual obligation in respect of the property becomes more expensive, does not entitle him to sue. It was pointed out by Lord Brandon that if the law was certain then people would protect themselves by other methods, e.g. contractual protection of their position.

Acquisition of defective property

A person who acquires defective property will have a primary claim in the law of contract. The friend who purchased the ginger beer in *Donoghue* v *Stevenson* could have sued the cafe owner for the cost of the ginger beer. In such consumer cases the Sale of Goods Act 1979 implies conditions of merchantable quality and fitness for the purpose, into the contract. Such an action depends on a contractual relationship existing, the defendant being solvent and there being no exclusion clause in the contract. The contractual chain can be illustrated:

Manufacturer————Wholesaler————Retailer————Purchaser— — — Gift

In theory any legal problems could be solved by a chain of contract actions but in practice there are problems. Insolvency by anyone in the chain could lead to the chain breaking down as it is not generally worthwhile suing an insolvent party. Attempts have therefore been made to bring negligence actions to circumvent this problem.

If the retailer is insolvent, could the purchaser sue the manufacturer in negligence for supplying a defective (as opposed to a dangerous) product? (See *Muirhead* v *Industrial Tank Specialities Ltd* below.)

The recipient of a gift has of course no contractual protection as they have no contract with anyone. If the product causes physical damage then they will have a tort action against the manufacturer. But do they have any remedy if the product is simply of defective quality? Such a claim would be a claim for pure economic loss.

In the case of realty, the common law historically provided little protection to the purchaser. (See 'Defective Premises', p. 121, for details.) The purchaser of a new house obtained limited contractual protection but the financial instability of the building trade sometimes rendered this of no value. Purchasers of old houses obtained virtually no contractual protection because of the doctrine of *caveat emptor*.

Sub-contractor————Builder————P1————P2

P1 would have a contract with the builder, but if the builder became insolvent and the damage had been caused by the negligence of a sub-contractor, P1 has no contractual remedy.

The local authority may also have a part to play in the construction by approving plans and checking the progress of buildings under construction. This work is done on the basis of statutory powers rather than contract. If the work is carried out negligently, would a person affected have a tort claim against the local authority?

P2 only has a contract with P1 and this is subject to the principle of 'let the buyer beware'.

Where businessmen embarked on a tripartite venture such as a building contract, protection was given by contract law. Problems of insolvency could give rise to attempts to circumvent the contractual chain by bringing an action in negligence.

Client————Main contractor——————Sub-contractor 1————Sub-contractor 2

Two common problems arise. The first is where the completed building is defective and the main contractor has become insolvent. The defect is due to sub-contractor 1's negligence. Sub-contractor 1 cannot be sued for breach of contract by the client unless the client has taken out a collateral contract or warranty with him. A similar situation would arise where the defect is due to sub-contractor 2's negligence and sub-contractor 1 has become insolvent. The main contractor cannot perform his contract with the client and has no contractual action against sub-contractor 2.

In the 1970s and early 1980s the common law began to provide protection in tort for the purchasers of defective realty. A duty of care would be owed by anyone involved in the building process to avoid a risk of physical damage to the health or safety of the occupier of the house. The damages in such cases were the cost of making the building safe (*Anns v Merton* [1978] AC 728). Actions were brought against builders and also against local authorities. No floodgates problem existed in such cases, as only a residential owner could bring a claim and the extent of the claim was reasonably foreseeable.

The highpoint of recovery of economic loss was reached in 1983 when the House of Lords upheld a claim that a duty of care was owed by a sub-contractor to the client.

Junior Books Ltd *v* Veitchi Co Ltd [1983] AC 520

The plaintiffs had contracted with the main contractors for the construction of a factory. The defendants were specialist flooring sub-contractors. They were nominated by the plaintiffs but had no contract with them. The floor was defective and had to be re-laid. The plaintiffs brought an action in negligence against the sub-contractors, claiming the cost of re-laying the floor and loss of profit while this was being done. The House of Lords held that because of the close proximity between the parties, a duty of care was owed to the plaintiff. The key factor was that the plaintiff had nominated the defendants as sub-contractors.

At the time the decision was thought to mark the end of the distinction between contract and tort actions. But the decision has not proved popular with the judiciary and although it survives as a precedent on its own particular facts, it has not been followed. After this case the courts retreated from protecting economic loss caused by negligent acts. A logical extension of *Junior Books* would have been to apply it to the purchaser of defective property, provided there was sufficient proximity between manufacturer and purchaser. But in *Muirhead* v *Industrial Tank Specialities Ltd* [1986] QB 507 the Court of Appeal held that there was insufficient proximity between an ordinary purchaser of goods and the manufacturer of those goods to impose a duty of care in respect of economic loss.

In the area of tripartite business arrangements the courts have consistently refused to allow a negligence action for economic loss.

Simaan General Contracting Co v Pilkington Glass Ltd [1988] QB 758

The plaintiffs were the main contractors on a building project in Abu Dhabi. It was a term of the contract with the building owner that the curtain glass walling be a particular shade of green, as green is the colour of peace in Islam. The plaintiff engaged a firm to obtain and erect the glass. This firm ordered the glass from the defendants. The glass was of the wrong colour and this caused extra expense to the plaintiff in his performance of his contract with the building owner. The glass erectors went into liquidation, which prevented a contract action against them. The plaintiffs sued the defendants in negligence. The action failed as the plaintiffs were unable to show that the defendants had assumed any responsibility to them. The absence of a contract between plaintiff and defendant was fatal.

Greater Nottingham Co-operative Society v Cementation Piling and Foundations Ltd [1988] 2 All ER 971

The plaintiffs entered a contract to have their premises extended. The defendants were nominated sub-contractors for the pile-driving. There was a contract between the plaintiffs and the defendants in respect of materials and design. The defendants carried out the work negligently with the result that the plaintiff suffered economic loss. The contract did not cover the way in which the loss came about and the negligence action failed as the contract was conclusive as to the parties rights.

Pacific Associates Inc v Baxter [1990] 1 QB 993

The plaintiff successfully tendered for dredging and reclamation work. The work was to be supervised by an engineer retained by the employer. The contractor would be paid when the work was certified by the engineer. The contract stated that the contractor was entitled to extra payment if he encountered hard material which could not have been reasonably foreseen. The engineer rejected claims for such payments on the ground that the hard materials should have been foreseen. The contractor sued the engineer in negligence for £45 million. The Court of Appeal held that there was no duty owed by the engineer. The engineer was retained by the employer and was not employed to exercise due care on behalf of the contractor and had not assumed responsibility to do so. There was therefore no action based on *Hedley Byrne* grounds. The court also rejected an argument based on close and direct proximity as there was insufficient proximity.

Major statements of principle came from the House of Lords in the building cases as they tried to rein in the development unleashed by *Anns* v *Merton*.

D&F Estates Ltd *v* Church Commissioners for England [1988] 2 All ER 992

The House of Lords held that a builder was not liable in negligence to a building owner for defects of quality. The builder was only liable where the defect caused personal injuries or damage to other property. Lord Bridge stated that economic loss would only be recoverable in a negligence action under the *Hedley Byrne* principles or where the unique proximity of *Junior Books* applied.

Murphy *v* Brentwood District Council [1990] 2 All ER 908

A seven judge House of Lords was assembled and they overruled their own previous decision in *Anns* v *Merton*. The narrow ratio of the case was that a local authority is not liable in negligence to a building owner or occupier for the cost of remedying a dangerous defect, which resulted from the negligence of the authority in not ensuring that the building was erected in accordance with the building regulations. (See 'Defective Premises', p. 124.)

The wider importance of the case is that it marks a contraction in the scope of duty of care in economic loss cases. Beyond this it is difficult to extract any general principles from the judgments. The case will however provide a benchmark for some time to come in economic loss claims. Any plaintiff arguing for a duty to be owed in respect of economic loss which does not fall within *Hedley Byrne* principles, will face a difficult task.

Where does this leave *Junior Books*? In *Murphy*, the House of Lords cleared away the *Anns* v *Merton* precedent but left *Junior Books*. A number of judicial attempts have been made to explain away the case. In *Tate & Lyle Industries Ltd* v *Greater London Council* [1983] 2 AC 509, it was treated as a case of physical damage. In *D&F Estates* Lord Bridge thought that the case rested on unique proximity. Lord Oliver was of the opinion that it rested on the *Hedley Byrne* principle of reliance.

It would appear that the complex problem of economic loss has not yet been solved. Whether a solution is found in contract or tort remains to be seen.

Further reading

Cooke, Sir R (1991) 107 LQR 46
Fleming, J G, (1990) 106 LQR 349
Markesinis, BS (1987) 103 LQR 354
Stapleton, J (1991) 107 LQR 249
Weir, T [1990] CLJ 212

6 | Omissions

INTRODUCTION

One of the characteristics of a negligence action is that it is a method of compensating for wrongfully caused harm. Harm can be caused either by a positive act (misfeasance) or by omitting to act (nonfeasance).

Traditionally, negligence only protected against the former. If you wanted someone to take positive action on your behalf you had to pay them and thereby obtain contractual protection. Exceptions to this have always existed. Where there is a particular relationship between the parties, such as parent and child, then there may be a duty to act positively for the benefit of the child. The question could then be posed as to whether the parent was also liable for damage inflicted on other persons by the child.

LIABILITY FOR OMISSIONS

In *Donoghue* v *Stevenson*, Lord Atkin referred to 'acts or omissions which you can reasonably foresee would be likely to injure your neighbour'. The reference to omissions here was to an omission in the course of positive conduct, e.g., if a person is driving a car and omits to apply the brakes. At this time the conventional view was that there was no liability in negligence for a simple failure to act for another person's benefit.

Example

X has fallen into a river and is drowning. X calls out for help. Y is walking along the river bank and hears X. There is a lifebelt provided on the bank but Y walks past and does nothing. In these circumstances there is no liability on Y as he does not owe X a duty of care, unless there is a relationship between X and Y which gives rise to a duty to act positively.

What would be the position if Y embarked on a rescue attempt and then withdrew, making X's position worse? By embarking on a positive act, does Y undertake a duty? Would it be strange to say that the person who does nothing has no liability, whereas the good samaritan could be sued?

The principles on liability for omissions were laid down by the House of Lords.

Smith *v* Littlewoods Organisation Ltd [1987] 1 All ER 710

L bought a cinema in Dunfermline with the intention of demolishing it and building a supermarket. The cinema was empty and a fire was started by unknown children. The fire spread to the appellant's land and damaged his buildings. Fires had previously been started in the building but this fact was not known to L. The appellant's action in negligence against L failed.

Lord Goff stated that there was a general principle that no duty existed to prevent persons deliberately inflicting damage on another person. There were four exceptions to this principle.

(a)   Where there was a special relationship between the parties such as a contractual relationship. An example of this arose in *Stansbie* v *Troman* [1948] 1 All ER 599. A decorator working on the plaintiff's premises was told to lock up if he went out. He did not and a thief entered the house and stole money. The decorator was held liable for the loss.

(b)   Where there was a special relationship between the defendant and the third party. In *Home Office* v *Dorset Yacht Co Ltd* [1970] 2 All ER 294, boys escaped from a borstal due to the negligence of the appellant's employees. The boys caused damage to the respondent's property. The defendants were responsible for controlling the third party (the boys) and were held to owe a duty of care to the respondents.

(c)   Where the defendant negligently causes or permits a source of danger to be created, which is then interfered with by third parties. In *Haynes* v *Harwood* [1935] 1 KB 146 a horse was left unattended in a busy street. Children threw stones at the horse and it bolted. A policeman was injured in attempting to stop the horse. The defendant was held to owe a duty of care to the policeman.

(d)   Where the defendant knew or had means of knowledge that a third party was creating a danger on his property and failed to take reasonable steps to abate it. Examples of this kind of liability usually arise in nuisance. See e.g. *Goldman* v *Hargrave* [1966] 2 All ER 989. There was no liability under this head in the present case as the defendants had no means of knowing that the building represented a fire hazard.

It should be pointed out that Lords Brandon, Griffiths and Mackay decided the case on its own facts. They did not rule out liability on the basis of any general rule of no liability. It is therefore possible that liability could be developed from these speeches.

LIABILITY FOR THE ACTS OF THIRD PARTIES

This subject is closely related to the question of liability for omissions. The question is: when will A be liable to B for the negligent act of C? Any question of A's liability will normally concern his omission to exercise control over C.

Carmarthenshire County Council *v* Lewis [1955] 1 All ER 565

A lorry driver was killed when he swerved to avoid a four year old child. The child had been left in a classroom at school while the teacher attended to another child. The child had wandered out onto the road and caused the accident. The defendants were held liable on the basis of their vicarious liability for the teacher's negligence. Duty was established on the basis of a reasonably foreseeable plaintiff. (See also *Home Office* v *Dorset Yacht Co* above.)

P Perl (Exporters) Ltd *v* Camden London Borough Council [1984] QB 342

The defendant council owned adjoining premises. One (142) was let to the plaintiff and the other (144) was divided into flats. There was no lock on the door of 144 and thieves entered and knocked a hole in the wall into 142. Property belonging to the plaintiff was stolen. The Court of Appeal held that the defendants were not liable as mere foreseeability of harm was not sufficient to establish a duty.

The issue of damage caused by third parties is closely connected with that of remoteness of damage. Once the courts have held that a duty exists it is very difficult for them to say that the damage is too remote.

A policy issue which exists in this area and which may partially explain the courts' reluctance to impose duties is insurance. In the cases of fire damage the plaintiff will normally have fire insurance and so will not be out of pocket. But in inner-city areas it may be difficult to obtain fire insurance.

Further reading

McClean, J (1988) 8 Oxford J Legal Stud 442
Markesinis, B S (1989) 105 LQR 104

7 | Breach of duty and proof of negligence

INTRODUCTION

Once the plaintiff has shown that the defendant owed him a duty of care it is necessary for him to prove that the defendant was in breach of that duty.

Until this century negligence cases were tried by jury and the question of negligence was for the jury to decide. During the nineteenth century, judges exercised increasing control over this decision and it was necessary to have a test to give to the jury to determine whether the defendant had been negligent.

Negligence cases are now tried by a judge alone. The standard of care expected of a particular defendant is usually set by law, but the question of whether the defendant fell below that standard is one of fact, to be determined by reference to all the circumstances of the case. In cases of negligent driving, for instance, the standard of care is that of the reasonable driver, not a perfect driver or a learner driver. Whether the defendant driver in the case in question has fallen below that standard is a question for the judge to decide based on the facts proved in evidence.

The standard set by the court may be affected by policy issues. For example, where the defendant has compulsory insurance, the court may be tempted to set a high standard as this means the plaintiff will be compensated. Where setting a high standard and imposing liability will affect scarce resources, the court may set a lower standard. This may be one of the factors affecting liability in medical negligence cases. To compensate one plaintiff may mean closing a ward and depriving a large number of patients of treatment.

It is up to the plaintiff to prove that the defendant was negligent and this may be his hardest task. The plaintiff may not know what happened and ascertaining the facts could be difficult and expensive. In practice, the success or failure of most negligence actions depends on the plaintiff's ability to prove negligence.

THE REASONABLE MAN TEST

As a subjective inquiry by the court into each person's capabilities would be impossible, an objective test was chosen. The standard of conduct to be attained is that of the reasonable man. The classic statement was given by Alderson B in *Blyth* v *Birmingham Waterworks Co* (1856) 11 Ex 781: 'Negligence is the omission to do something which a reasonable man, guided upon those considerations which ordinarily regulate the conduct of human affairs, would do, or doing something which a prudent and reasonable man would not do.'

Because the test is objective, no account is usually taken of individual disabilities or peculiarities.

Nettleship *v* Weston [1971] 2 QB 691

The plaintiff gave the defendant driving lessons. The defendant had been careful but on her third lesson the car struck a lamp post and the plaintiff was injured. It was held that the defendant, although a learner driver, would be judged by the standard of the average competent driver: 'The learner driver may be doing his best, but his incompetent best is not good enough. He must drive in as good a manner as a driver of skill, experience and care.'

Roberts *v* Ramsbottom [1980] 1 WLR 823

The defendant drove his car after he had unknowingly suffered a cerebral haemorrhage and was unfit to drive. He collided with a stationary van and then with a parked vehicle. It was held that he had continued to drive after he had suffered a seizure which affected his reactions and was negligent in doing so. The court stated that a person might escape liability if his actions at the relevant time were wholly beyond his control, so as to amount to automatism. The fact that his consciousness was impaired due to brain malfunction did not amount to automatism. The reasonably prudent person would have stopped driving in such circumstances.

There are two circumstances where subjective factors may be taken into account.

In the case of children, there is a dearth of authority, but in *McHale* v *Watson* [1966] ALR 513, it was held that the standard to be expected of a child defendant was that to be expected of a child of the same age, intelligence and experience. This appears to indicate that the age of the child will be taken into account. There is no equivalent English case but the cases on contributory negligence indicate that a similar approach would be taken.

Secondly, where a person acts in an emergency, this will be taken into account when assessing the standard of behaviour to be expected: *Jones* v *Boyce* (1816) 171 ER 540.

The test is that of the reasonable man placed in the defendant's position.

Glasgow Corpn *v* Muir [1943] AC 448

The appellants allowed a church picnic party to use their tea room on a wet day. Members of the party had to carry the tea urn through a passage where children were buying ice creams.

For an unexplained reason the urn was dropped and children were scalded by the tea. The House of Lords held that judged by the standards of the reasonable man there was no liability: 'Legal liability is limited to those consequences of our acts which a reasonable man of ordinary intelligence and experience so acting would have in contemplation.' There was no reason why the defendants would anticipate the event happening as a result of granting permission. The urn was in the care of responsible people who took due care for the safety of the children.

Roe v Minister of Health [1954] 2 QB 66

The plaintiff was paralysed after receiving an injection in hospital. Phenol had leaked into the syringe and caused the paralysis. At this time it was not known that phenol could get into the syringe through invisible cracks. The defendants were not negligent, as judged by the standard of the reasonable person at the time of the accident, they could not have avoided the accident. The court will not condemn a defendant with 'the benefit of hindsight'.

FACTORS DETERMINING NEGLIGENCE

The reasonable man is a fictional character and the decision as to negligence is a value judgment made by the judge.

One way of establishing negligence might be to show a failure to conform to standard practice. But it would be dangerous to use this as an infallible guideline and would abdicate the court's responsibility. If all drivers regularly break the speed limit on a certain road, a judge is unlikely to accept this fact as evidence that the defendant was not negligent. The test is how the defendant ought to have behaved. Similar reasoning might be applied to a factory owner who speeds up his production line to a point where it is dangerous for his employees and argues that all his competitors do the same.

In some areas standard practice will carry great weight and in cases of medical negligence conformity with standard practice will nearly always result in a finding of no negligence.

Provided the defendant has complied with the required standard for that profession there is no negligence.

Luxmoore-May v Messenger May and Baverstock [1990] 1 All ER 1067

It was alleged that the defendant auctioneers had negligently failed to identify two paintings as those of a famous painter. They were sold at auction for £840 and a few months later sold again for £88,000. The Court of Appeal likened the skill to be expected of a provincial auctioneer to that of a general medical practitioner. On the facts, the defendants had not been negligent, as differing views on the painter could have been held by experts. The auctioneer's duty was to do his job with honesty and due diligence.

Failure to conform with standard practice is usually good evidence that the defendant has been negligent but this is not conclusive.

Brown v Rolls-Royce Ltd [1960] 1 WLR 210

The plaintiff contracted dermatitis at work. The defendant employers had provided washing facilities at work but did not supply a barrier cream which was supplied by other employers in the same type of work. There was conflicting evidence as to how effective this cream was. The plaintiff was unable to prove that if the cream had been supplied she would not have suffered dermatitis. The defendants were held not to have been negligent in failing to supply the cream.

A judge is likely to take a number of factors into account in determining negligence:

The skill which the defendant professes to have

Where a person has held himself out as having a particular skill, he is required to show the skill normally possessed by persons doing that work. A solicitor will be required to show the skill of the average solicitor and a plumber that of the average plumber. The fact that that person is in his first day in the job is irrelevant, as the test is objective.

If a layman attempts a specialised task then all the circumstances of the case will need to be looked at.

Wells v Cooper [1958] 2 All ER 527

The defendant fixed a door handle onto a door. He did the job as well as an ordinary carpenter would do it. The handle came off in the plaintiff's hand and he was injured. It was held that the defendant had exercised such care as was required of him and was not liable. The degree of skill was not to be measured by the skill which the defendant actually possessed but by the skill which a reasonably competent carpenter would have.

If a person acted in an emergency then he would be judged by the standards of a reasonable person, not a specialist. A climber who was required to treat an injured fellow climber would not be judged by the standards of a doctor. The dearth of authorities on this point perhaps suggests an inherent decency on the part of those so treated!

The degree of probability that damage will be done

Care must be taken in respect of a risk that is reasonably foreseeable. Nearly all human actions involve some risk of damage but not every risky act will result in liability.

Bolton v Stone [1951] AC 850

The plaintiff was injured on the highway by a cricket ball hit from the defendant's ground. The ball had been hit 100 yards and cleared a 17 foot fence which was 78 yards from the batsman. The evidence showed that the ball had only been hit out of the ground six times in the previous 30 years. The defendants were found not to have been negligent, as the risk was so small that the reasonable man would have been justified in disregarding it.

This case was also argued in nuisance but counsel conceded that if he could not succeed in negligence, he could not succeed in nuisance.

Hilder v Associated Portland Cement Manufacturers Ltd [1961] 1 WLR 1434

The plaintiff's husband was riding his motor cycle along a road beside a piece of open land occupied by the defendants. Children were permitted to play football on the land. A ball was kicked onto the road causing a fatal accident. As there was a strong possibility of injury to road users, the defendants were negligent, as they had taken no additional precautions to ensure the safety of road users.

It should be remembered that the test is reasonable care in all the circumstances of the case. The plaintiff may have characteristics which render the likelihood of harm greater and therefore increase the risk.

Haley v London Electricity Board [1965] AC 778

The defendants left a hammer on the pavement to warn people of excavations. The plaintiff, who was blind, tripped over the hammer and was injured. It was held that although the warning was adequate for sighted persons, it was inadequate for a blind person. The number of blind people was sufficiently large to make them a class which the defendants ought reasonably to have had in contemplation. The cost of prevention in this case was low.

The courts also take the view that dealings with children demand a high degree of care. In *Yachuk* v *Oliver Blais* [1949] AC 386 the defendants sold petrol to a nine year old. The plaintiff was burned when the chilldren set fire to the petrol. The defendants were held liable for selling the petrol, although the child had said he needed it for his mother's car.

The magnitude of harm likely

The court will take into account not only the risk of any damage to the plaintiff but also the extent of the damage that is risked.

Paris v Stepney Borough Council [1951] AC 367

The plaintiff, who had one eye, was employed as a mechanic in the defendant's garage. Part of his job involved welding. It was not normal to supply goggles to men involved in such work. A piece of metal flew into the plaintiff's eye with the result that he became completely blind. The defendants were held liable, although they would not have been liable to a person with normal sight. The greater risk to the plaintiff meant that greater precautions than normal had to be taken.

Withers v Perry Chain Co Ltd [1961] 1 WLR 1314

The plaintiff was prone to dermatitis and was given the most grease free job available. Despite this she contracted dermatitis. The defendant employers were held not liable as they had done all that was reasonable, short of refusing to employ her at all.

The utility of the object to be achieved

The court may be called on to assess the social utility of the defendant's conduct in determining whether he was negligent. Asquith J stated in *Daborn* v *Bath Tramways* [1946] 2 All ER 333:

> If all the trains in this country were restricted to a speed of five miles per hour, there would be fewer accidents, but our national life would be intolerably slowed down. The purpose to be served, if sufficiently important, justifies the assumption of abnormal risk.

✓ **Watt v Hertfordshire County Council** [1954] 1 WLR 835

The plaintiff fireman was on duty when an emergency call was received. A woman had been trapped under a car and lifting equipment was required. A heavy jack was loaded onto a lorry which was not equipped to secure it. On the way to the accident the jack moved and injured the plaintiff, who sued his employers. The action failed, as in the circumstances, the risk involved was not so great as to prohibit an attempt to save life.

Other values may not be so easy to assess. What, for example, is the value of playing cricket? Was this a factor which influenced the decision in *Bolton* v *Stone*? It would clearly have made a difference if the plaintiff's injury had been caused by an unlawful activity.

The practicability of prevention

Once the court has identified a risk as reasonably foreseeable, the question is whether the defendants should have taken precautions against that risk. If the cost of eliminating the risk is out of proportion to the extent of the risk, then the defendant will not be obliged to take preventative measures. (See *Bolton* v *Stone*.)

✓ **Latimer v A.E.C. Ltd** [1953] AC 643

After a factory was flooded, the owner did all that he could to eliminate the effects of the flooding by using sawdust on the floors. Some areas of floor remained uncovered. The plaintiff fell on one of these areas and was injured. He sued his employer in negligence, alleging that the factory ought to have been closed. It was held that it was not necessary to take such a precaution as it was out of proportion to the risk involved.

It is not normally necessary to eliminate the risk altogether, as this would amount to insurance against the risk.

An economic formula?

Legal rules have been analysed by economists and tested aginst economic principles. It has been suggested that a defendant should be negligent if the likelihood of the injury multiplied by the gravity of the injury, exceeds the cost of taking adequate precautions.

The effect of a finding of negligence by a court is to shift the loss from the plaintiff to the defendant. Economists argue that, based on efficiency, this should only happen where the cost of avoiding the accident is less than avoiding the accident costs.

This formula omits one vital factor and that is the social utility of the defendant's conduct. There are also severe problems in assessing what the costs of an accident are.

PROOF OF NEGLIGENCE

Introduction

The most difficult task that a plaintiff faces in a negligence action is likely to be proving that the defendant was negligent.

The basic rule is that he who affirms must prove. It is therefore up to the plaintiff to prove, on the balance of probabilities, that the defendant was negligent.

This rule is relaxed in two instances.

Proof of criminal conviction

Section 11 of the Civil Evidence Act 1968, provides that the fact of conviction on a criminal charge is admissible in evidence in a civil case based on the same facts. Where the defendant has been convicted of a criminal offence in respect of conduct which is alleged to be negligent, a rebuttable presumption of liability is created. To escape liability the defendant must prove that he was not negligent.

If the defendant is sued for negligent driving and has been convicted of a criminal offence in respect of that driving, then the defendant must prove that he was not negligent. This is difficult but not impossible. To drive through a red traffic light is a criminal offence but it does not necessarily amount to negligence.

Res ipsa loquitur

The phrase *res ipsa loquitur* means the thing speaks for itself. Where the maxim applies, the court will be prepared to infer that the defendant was negligent without hearing detailed evidence from the plaintiff as to what the defendant did or did not do.

The origin of the phrase lies in the following cases.

Scott *v* London and St Katherine's Dock Co (1865) 3 H&C 596

The plaintiff was standing near the door of the defendant's warehouse when some bags of sugar fell on him. The first instance judge entered a verdict for the defendant as there was no evidence that he had been negligent. The Court of Appeal directed a new trial. Erle CJ stated:

> There must be reasonable evidence of negligence. But where the thing is shown to be under the management of the defendant or his servants, and the accident is such as in the ordinary course of things does not happen if those who have the management use proper care, it affords reasonable evidence, in the absence of explanation by the defendants, that the accident arose from want of care.

This maxim has since been referred to as *res ipsa loquitur*. The maxim is said to have three requirements.

(a)   That the thing causing the damage was under the exclusive control of the defendant.

This means that the very occurrence of the accident should point to negligence on the part of the defendant and to no-one else. The courts have been liberal in their interpretation of control. In defective products cases, control lies in the manufacturing process even though the damage is caused long after the product leaves the factory.

Gee v Metropolitan Railway (1873) LR 8QB 161

The plaintiff leaned against the door of a train shortly after it left the station. The door opened and the plaintiff fell out. As the door had recently been under the control of the defendants, there was evidence of negligence on their part.

Easson v London and North Eastern Railway [1944] 1 KB 421

The plaintiff, a four year old child, fell out of the door of a train. At the time of the accident the train was seven miles from its last stopping place. It was held that *res ipsa loquitur* was not applicable in these circumstances. The defendants did not have sufficient control over the door at the time. Any passenger on the train could have interfered with the door.

(b)   The accident must be of the sort that does not happen in the absence of negligence.

The facts in *Scott* v *London & St Katherine's Dock Co* illustrate this requirement. Bags of sugar do not normally fall out of the sky unless someone has been negligent.

The maxim has been invoked in medical negligence actions.

Mahon v Osborne [1939] 2 KB 14

The plaintiff entered hospital for an abdominal operation. He later died and a swab was found in his body. The plaintiff was entitled to call expert evidence to show that the accident would not have occurred without negligence.

In medical cases the plaintiff may not be able to show who was negligent. In such cases the maxim of *res ipsa loquitur* will be available to make the employing health authority vicariously liable.

(c)   There must be no explanation for the accident.

Res ipsa loquitur is only available where there is no explanation for the accident. If all the facts are known, then the only question is whether or not negligence can be inferred.

Barkway v South Wales Transport Co Ltd [1950] 1 All ER 392

The plaintiff was injured in a road accident when the bus he was travelling in burst a tyre and crashed. The reason for the burst tyre was a defect in its wall which could not have been discovered beforehand. It was held that *res ipsa loquitur* was inapplicable. The defendants were found liable because they had not instructed their drivers to report heavy blows to tyres. This was sufficient to establish negligence.

If the defendant successfully negatives any of the conditions required for *res ipsa loquitur*, the plaintiff must prove, by affirmative evidence, that it was the defendant's carelessness that caused his damage: *Ng Chum Pui* v *Lee Chuen Tat* [1988] RTR 298.

What is the effect of the maxim?

Once the ~~defendant~~ *plaintiff* has successfully raised *res ipsa loquitur*, the evidential burden of proof shifts to the defendant. What the defendant has to prove to avoid liability is a matter of controversy. Does he have to prove that he was not negligent, or is it sufficient if he raises an alternative explanation for the accident which does not connote negligence on his part?

Colvilles v Devine [1969] 1 WLR 475

A pipe carrying oxygen exploded. The defendants suggested that this could have been caused by particles igniting. This would have provided a non-negligent explanation for the explosion. The court held that the defendants did not have to prove this. On the facts, the defendants were held liable, as they had not proved that filters to prevent particle entry were effective or had been checked.

The result in this case appears to be consistent with the view that the defendant must prove no negligence, but some of the views expressed in the judgments appear sympathetic to the alternative explanation theory.

Ward v Tesco Stores Ltd [1976] 1 WLR 810

The plaintiff slipped on some yoghurt on the floor of the defendant's supermarket. This was all she could prove, except to show that three weeks later orange juice remained on the floor of the same supermarket for fifteen minutes. The defendants gave evidence that the floor was brushed five or six times a day and that if staff saw a spillage they were instructed to stay there and call someone to clean it up. The Court of Appeal held that the plaintiff's evidence constituted a prima facie case of negligence. The floor was under the defendant's control and the accident was of the kind that does not normally happen if reasonable care is taken. The defendants were therefore obliged to take reasonable care. They had failed to do this and the plaintiff succeeded.

Henderson v H.E. Jenkins & Sons [1970] AC 282

The plaintiff's husband was killed when the brakes on a lorry failed on a steep hill. The defendants pleaded that the failure resulted from a latent defect in a brake pipe. They advanced evidence to show that they had cleaned and visually inspected the pipe and that the cause of failure was corrosion. The corrosion could only be detected by removing the pipe, a practice which was not recommended by the manufacturers or Ministry of Transport. The House of Lords held that the plaintiff had raised an inference of negligence and the defendants had failed to rebut this. They should have gone on to show that nothing in the vehicle's life would have caused abnormal corrosion or called for special inspection. Again this case would appear to support the view that the defendant must prove that he was not negligent.

Within the cases cited above there is disagreement among the judiciary as to the precise effect that raising the maxim of *res ipsa loquitur* has. There is much abstruse discussion on whether the legal burden of proof or the evidential burden, shifts to the defendant. The latter is undoubtedly correct. Once the plaintiff has satisfied the points required to raise *res ipsa loquitur*, there is an inference of negligence, which the defendant must displace. What he has to do to displace the inference will vary from case to case. In some cases he will have to prove he was not negligent. In others, raising a plausible alternative non-negligent explanation will suffice.

Further reading

Atiyah, P S (1972) 35 MLR 337
Millner, M (1976) 92 LQR 131
Stapleton, J (1988) 104 LQR 213

8 | Causation and remoteness of damage

INTRODUCTION

The third element in the plaintiff's case in negligence is damage. This is an essential ingredient of the tort as it is not actionable *per se*.

The plaintiff must prove that his damage was caused by the defendant's breach of duty and that the damage was not too remote. The first element is sometimes called causation in fact, and the latter causation in law.

Causation in fact deals with the question of whether as a matter of fact the damage was caused by the breach of duty.

Example

A railway company has instructed its engine drivers that before they go over a crossing, they must sound their whistle, to give warning to anyone crossing. One morning a person is found dead on the crossing as a result of being run over by a train. During the night a train has failed to sound its whistle. All the elements of negligence are present. The railway company owes a duty of care to crossing users. There has been a breach of duty by an engine driver in failing to sound his whistle. There is damage. But as yet there is no negligence action. It is necessary for the plaintiff to establish that the train that caused the damage was the train that failed to sound its whistle.

The question of remoteness of damage arises where causation in fact is established, but the court holds that as a matter of law the damage is too remote. The court will not want the defendant to be liable indefinitely for damage and will impose a cut off point beyond which the damage is said to be too remote.

Example

The defendant drove negligently on the motorway and his car swerved and left the road. The car landed on a railway line. A mainline railway train was derailed by the car. The train struck a dam, which burst, flooding a small town.

On this kind of scenario the bill for damages potentially runs into millions of pounds. What the defendant has done is to set in motion a chain of events. This will establish factual causation. The court will probably wish to terminate the defendant's liability at a particular point. This may be after the damage to the train. Any damage beyond this point is too remote.

An event which occurs after the breach of duty and which contributes to the plaintiff's damage, may break the chain of causation, so as to render the defendant not liable for any damage beyond this point. Where this occurs the event is known as a *novus actus interveniens*.

FACTUAL CAUSATION

The but for test

The starting point for assessing whether the defendant's breach of duty is a factual cause of the plaintiff's damage is the but for test. This basic test is whether the damage would not have occurred but for the breach of duty.

Barnett v Chelsea and Kensington Hospital Management Committee [1969] 1 QB 428

The plaintiff's husband attended the defendant's hospital and complained of vomiting. The doctor in casualty refused to examine him and he was told to see his own doctor in the morning if he still felt unwell. Five hours later he died of arsenic poisoning. The defendants owed the deceased a duty of care which they had breached by failing to examine him. They were held not liable, as the evidence established that even if he had been examined, he would have died before diagnosis and treatment could have been carried out. As the deceased would have died regardless of the breach of duty, the breach was not a cause of his death.

In most cases the but for test presents no difficulties. However there are areas where the test presents problems. These are in relation to the degree of probability of damage occurring, negligent omissions and multiple causes of harm.

Degree of probability of damage

If there is uncertainty as to whether the defendant's negligence has caused the damage, it has to be determined what degree of probability of damage occurring has to be established by the plaintiff.

Where the injury is traumatic, such as a person being struck by a car or having a hand cut off in a machine, there is usually no difficulty. The presence of the car on the road or the existence of the machine will be treated as a cause.

But where a disease is contracted by the defendant, more intractable difficulties arise. Medical science may not be able to specifically pinpoint the cause of the disease or link negligent conduct to its appearance.

McGhee v National Coal Board [1973] 1 WLR 1

The plaintiff worked in the defendant's brick kilns. Conditions were very hot and dusty. He had to cycle home unwashed as no washing facilities were provided at work. The plaintiff contracted dermatitis, a skin disease. He argued that if the defendant had provided washing facilities he would not have caught the disease. The medical evidence did not establish that the plaintiff would not have caught the disease if washing facilities had been provided. The House of Lords held that the plaintiff could succeed on the ground that the defendant had materially increased the risk of the plaintiff contracting the disease. The defendants (who had admitted negligence) had increased the risk of particular damage occurring and that damage had occurred.

The *McGhee* decision has proved to be controversial as the plaintiff never established that the defendant was a cause of his damage. It can perhaps best be viewed as a policy decision. Where the defendant has created a risk of particular damage and that damage has occurred, the defendant should not be allowed to escape liability because the medical evidence is inconclusive. The case has been subjected to analysis by the House of Lords in the more unfriendly climate of the 1980s.

Wilsher v Essex Area Health Authority [1988] 1 All ER 871

The plaintiff was born prematurely and suffered from an oxygen deficiency. Due to the admitted negligence of a doctor, the plaintiff was given excessive oxygen. The plaintiff suffered from deteriorating eyesight and became almost blind. The allegation was that the excess oxygen negligently administered had caused the blindness. The medical evidence showed that excessive oxygen was a cause of blindness in premature babies but it was not the only factor which caused blindness. The House of Lords held that the plaintiff had to establish, on the balance of probabilities, that the defendant's breach of duty was a cause of the injury. A retrial of the action was ordered.

The House considered the decision in *McGhee* and stated that the judgment of Lord Wilberforce in that case was a minority one and did not represent the law. Lord Wilberforce had said that where a person created a risk and injury occurred within that area of risk, the burden of proof was reversed and the defendant had to prove that his negligence was not a cause. The House held that the burden of proof of causation remained on the plaintiff throughout the case. The plaintiff had to prove that the breach of duty was at least a material contributory cause of the harm.

The House also distinguished *McGhee*, as in that case the plaintiff's injury was caused by the brick dust. The only question was whether earlier washing would have prevented the dermatitis. In *Wilsher* there were a number of different possible causes of the plaintiff's blindness and the plaintiff had not been able to establish the defendant's negligence as the cause. What the defendants had done, was not to enhance the risk that the known factors would lead to blindness, but to add to the list of factors which might lead to blindness.

If the plaintiff cannot establish that the breach of duty was a material contributory cause of his damage, could the question be approached on the basis of loss of chance? Instead of taking an all or nothing approach based on causation, look at the question in terms of measure of damages and award a percentage. This approach was taken by the Court of Appeal in the following case but failed on the facts in the House of Lords.

Hotson *v* East Berkshire Area Health Authority [1987] 2 All ER 909

The plaintiff fell and was taken to hospital, where his knee was X-rayed. A hip injury was not diagnosed. Five days later he returned to hospital, when the hip injury was discovered. By this time the hip injury had resulted in a deformity of the hip joint. The defendants argued that deformity would have occurred as a result of the injury, whether or not it had been properly diagnosed on the first trip to hospital. The trial judge found that the delay denied the plaintiff a 25% chance of avoiding the hip deformity and awarded 25% of the damages he would have awarded had the injury been solely caused by the delayed diagnosis. This approach was approved by the Court of Appeal. The plaintiff's claim was for loss of the benefit of timely treatment rather than the chance of successful treatment. The House of Lords held that the issue was one of causation, not quantification of damage. As the plaintiff had failed on balance of probabilities to prove that the delayed treatment had at least been a material contributory cause of the deformity, the plaintiff's action failed. The House did not, unfortunately, deal with the question of whether a claim framed as a loss of chance claim was acceptable.

The burden of proof to establish causation therefore rests on the plaintiff throughout the case. If he fails to establish, on the balance of probabilities, that the defendant's negligence was a material contributory cause of his damage, his action fails. Where there is only one possible cause of the damage and the defendant's breach of duty has exposed the plaintiff to the risk of damage which has materialised, then causation is established. It is not yet known whether a claim in tort can be framed in terms of loss of chance.

Negligent omissions

The but for test also presents problems where the breach of duty consists of an omission to act. This is apparent in the cases on industrial safety equipment.

McWilliams *v* Sir William Arrol & Co Ltd [1962] 1 WLR 295

The plaintiff was a steel erector who fell to his death at work. When the accident occurred he was not wearing a safety belt. The defendants were in breach of their statutory duty in failing to provide safety belts but advanced evidence to show that the plaintiff would not have worn one if it had been provided. The defendants were held not liable, as it was probable that the plaintiff would not have worn a safety belt and would therefore have fallen, even if one had been provided. The burden of proof is on the plaintiff to show that the defendant's breach of duty is a cause and this had not been established. The decision in *Wilsher* would appear to be consistent with this reasoning.

More than one cause

Where the plaintiff's damage is the result of more than one cause, the but for test does not appear to provide an answer to causation problems.

Example

A and B simultaneously fire guns and C is struck by bullets from both guns. An application of the but for test will mean that neither A nor B will be liable. This would be clearly unjust so A and B will both be held liable.

If C was struck by only one bullet but could not prove whose gun the bullet came from, a Canadian case has held that both A and B were liable (Cook v Lewis [1952] 1 DLR 1). The reason for the decision was that the burden of proof lay on the defendants to prove that they had not been negligent and they had failed to discharge this burden. How do you think an English court would decide this case?

Multiple causes may be either successive or concurrent. Where the causes are successive and the second defendant's breach of duty has caused the same damage as that of the first defendant, the but for test will exonerate the second defendant.

Performance Cars v Abraham [1962] 1 QB 33

The second defendant negligently collided with the plaintiff's Rolls-Royce. The car had previously been in a collision caused by the negligence of the first defendant. The second defendant damaged the same part of the car as the first defendant. The court held that the second defendant was not liable for the cost of a respray, as at the time of the accident the car was already in need of one.

What is the position when the first defendant is sued and the second defendant has caused similar or greater damage?

Baker v Willoughby [1970] AC 467

The plaintiff suffered injuries to his left leg as a result of the defendant's negligence. The plaintiff went to work in a new job after the accident and while at work he was shot in the left leg during an armed robbery. As a result, the plaintiff's leg had to be amputated. The armed robber, needless to say, did not stay around to be sued. The defendant argued that any liability which he had, extended only from his breach of duty until the armed robbery. At this point the effects of his negligence were overtaken by the effects of the second tort (the armed robbery). Applying the but for test would have produced this result. But the House of Lords refused to apply the but for test. Firstly, the plaintiff was compensated for the loss he suffered as a result of the injury, not for the injury itself. The second tort had not reduced the plaintiff's suffering or his reduction in earning capacity. Secondly, even if the plaintiff could have sued the armed robbers, they would only have been liable for depriving the plaintiff of a damaged left leg. So if the defendant's argument succeeded, the plaintiff would be left under-compensated.

Jobling v Associated Dairies [1982] AC 794

The plaintiff suffered an injury to his back at work in 1973, caused by the defendant's breach of duty. The injury reduced the plaintiff's earning capacity by 50%. Before the trial of the action in 1979 the plaintiff was discovered to be suffering from a back disease, unrelated to the injury, which rendered him totally unfit for work by 1976. The House of Lords applied the but for test to restrict the defendant's liability for loss of earnings to the period before the onset of the disease.

The House of Lords criticized the reasoning in *Baker*, but the decision survives. Where there are two successive torts, the first tortfeasor's liability is unaffected by the second tort. Where the tort is followed by a disabling illness, this must be taken into account in assessing the tortfeasor's liability.

Both the above cases are personal injury cases and tort damages are not the only form of compensation available. *Baker* is based on a policy of not under-compensating the plaintiff. *Jobling* is based on not over-compensating the plaintiff. The House of Lords pointed out in *Jobling*, that the plaintiff in *Baker* would have been entitled to compensation from the Criminal Injuries Compensation Scheme and there was therefore a danger of over-compensation. This is not entirely correct, as the only compensation would have been for the damage caused by the armed robbery. Had the defendant been found not liable in *Baker*, the plaintiff would still have remained uncompensated for his original injuries.

In *Jobling*, the plaintiff might have been able to claim social security benefits to partially compensate for his losses. But it is still possible to fall between tort damages and entitlement to social security.

The distinctions between the two cases are not convincing and the apparent conflict and the difficulties posed by causation in the medical negligence cases show the drawbacks of using the tort system as a method of compensating for personal injuries.

REMOTENESS OF DAMAGE

Introduction

Damages may be denied even where the plaintiff is able to establish a factual link between the breach of duty and his damage. This will be on the ground that the breach of duty was not the legal cause of the damage and will be expressed by saying that the damage was too remote. This area of law is affected by policy considerations, as the court will not wish to impose too heavy a burden on the defendant or his insurers.

The basic test for remoteness of damage remained the same until 1961 and was then changed by a Privy Council decision. The earlier test will be considered here for reasons of comparison and because it still provides the basis of the remoteness test in some other torts.

The direct consequence test

This is the test for remoteness of damage that held sway until 1961. It was laid down by the Court of Appeal in the following case.

Re Polemis and Furness, Withy & Co [1921] 3 KB 560

Charterers of a ship loaded it with benzine. The benzine leaked and this caused the ship's hold to fill with vapour. A stevedore negligently dropped a wooden plank into the hold of the ship. This caused a spark, which ignited the vapour, causing an explosion which destroyed the ship. The Court of Appeal held that the stevedore's employers were vicariously liable for the stevedore's negligence and that the damage was not too remote. The test for remoteness of damage in negligence actions was stated to be whether the damage was a direct consequence of the breach of duty. An indirect consequence was damage due to the operation of independent causes having no connection with the negligent act, except that they could not avoid its results.

It is important to note that in order for the defendant to be liable at all, he must owe the plaintiff a duty of care. For a duty to arise, some damage to the plaintiff must be reasonably foreseeable. In *Polemis* some damage was foreseeable as a result of the plank being dropped. Duty was therefore established. The explosion was a direct consequence of the breach of duty, therefore the damage was not too remote, although the kind of property damage that occurred could not have been foreseen.

Reasonable foreseeability test

The test for remoteness of damage was changed by the Privy Council in 1961.

Overseas Tankship (UK) Ltd v Morts Dock & Engineering Co (The Wagon Mound No 1) [1961] AC 388 (Hereafter *Wagon Mound 1*)

The defendants negligently discharged fuel oil into Sydney Harbour. The oil spread to the plaintiff's wharf where welding was taking place. The plaintiffs were assured that there was no danger of the oil catching fire on water and continued welding. Two days later the oil caught fire and the wharf and ships being repaired there were damaged by the fire. There was also some damage by fouling to the wharf. The trial judge found that it was not foreseeable that fuel oil on water would catch fire but there was some foreseeable damage in the fouling. This was sufficient to establish duty and as the fire damage was a direct consequence of the breach of duty, the defendants were also liable for the fire damage.

On appeal, the Privy Council held that the defendants were not liable for the fire damage. The test for remoteness of damage was whether the kind of damage suffered by the plaintiff was reasonably foreseeable by the defendant at the time of the breach of duty.

Is there any difference between *Polemis* and *Wagon Mound*? Reasonable foreseeability is always a necessary ingredient of a negligence action as it is required to establish duty of care. What needs to be reasonably foreseeable for this purpose, is a broad type of damage such as personal injuries or property damage. The key to the

Wagon Mound test is what is meant by a kind of damage. If this is taken in a very broad sense, then there is no difference between the direct consequence and the reasonable foreseeability test. But if kind is interpreted more narrowly, then it will have the effect of limiting the defendant's liability. In *Wagon Mound* the kind of damage that needed to be foreseeable was fire damage. This is clearly narrower than property damage. Had the reasonable foreseeability test been used in *Polemis*, it is likely that the defendants would have been not liable. Damage by explosion was probably not a foreseeable kind of damage.

It is now necessary to see how the courts have interpreted the reasonable foreseeability test.

Kind of damage

A number of principles have emerged on remoteness of damage.

(a)   If the kind of damage suffered is reasonably foreseeable, it does not matter that the damage came about in an unforeseeable way.

Hughes v Lord Advocate [1963] AC 837

The defendant's employees erected a tent over a manhole and surrounded the tent with paraffin lamps. The hole was left unguarded while the men were on a tea break. The ten year old plaintiff dropped one of the paraffin lamps down the hole and due to an unusual combination of circumstances there was an explosion and the plaintiff was badly burned. The defendants argued that they were not liable, as the way in which the damage came about was not foreseeable and the damage was therefore too remote. This was rejected by the House of Lords. They asked what kind of damage was foreseeable as a result of the breach of duty. The answer was burns. What kind of damage had occurred. The answer was burns. The damage was therefore not too remote. The fact that the burns had come about in an unforeseeable way did not render the damage too remote.

However, the plaintiff friendly approach in *Hughes* can be contrasted with the approach in the next two cases.

Doughty v Turner Manufacturing Co Ltd [1964] 1 QB 518

A workman at the defendant's factory dropped an asbestos cover into some molten liquid. The asbestos reacted with the liquid, there was an eruption and the plaintiff was burned. The court held that the damage to the plaintiff was too remote. Damage by eruption was not foreseeable in the circumstances but damage by splashing was.

Did the court ask the right question on kind of damage here? Or should the kind of damage have been burns? Does this case contradict *Hughes*? One view of this case is that no damage to the plaintiff was foreseeable because of the angle at which the cover fell into the molten liquid. The decision could be supported on this basis.

Tremain v Pike [1969] 1 WLR 1556

The plaintiff was employed by the defendant as a herdsman. He contracted Weil's disease, a rare disease contracted from rat's urine. The defendant had allowed the rat population on his farm to grow too large. The court held that the damage suffered by the plaintiff was too remote as Weil's disease was unforeseeable, although it was foreseeable that the plaintiff would have suffered damage from rats.

It is thought that this decision is doubtful in view of the Court of Appeal decision in *Parsons* v *Uttley Ingham & Co* [1978] QB 791.

(b)   Provided the the kind of damage is reasonably foreseeable, it does not matter that it is more extensive than could have been foreseen.

Vacwell Engineering Co Ltd v BDH Chemicals Ltd [1971] 1 QB 88

The defendants supplied a chemical to the plaintiffs but failed to warn that it was liable to explode on contact with water. A scientist working for the plaintiffs placed the chemical in water. This caused a violent explosion resulting in extensive damage. The defendants were held liable. Some property damage was foreseeable and the fact that it was more extensive than might have been foreseen did not matter.

The extent of damage principle is also illustrated by the 'egg shell skull rule'. This states that the defendant must take the plaintiff as he finds him, as regards his physical characteristics.

Smith v Leech Brain & Co [1962] 2 QB 405

The plaintiff suffered a burn on his lip as a result of the defendant's negligence. The burn caused the plaintiff to contract cancer, as the tissues of his lips were in a pre-malignant state. He died three years after the accident. The defendants argued that they were not responsible for his death, as it could not have been foreseen. The court stated that they had to take the plaintiff as they found him. The question for remoteness was whether the defendants could have foreseen a burn, not whether they could have foreseen cancer. The defendants were held liable.

The principle also applies where the plaintiff's damage is a combination of the defendant's negligence and medical treatment to which he was allergic.

Robinson v Post Office [1974] 1 WLR 1176

The plaintiff was employed by the defendant. He fell down a ladder as a result of the defendant's negligence and cut his leg. The doctor gave him an anti-tetanus injection to which the plaintiff was allergic. As a result he contracted encephalitis, an inflammation of the brain. The defendants were held liable for both the original injury and the encephalitis, as it was foreseeable that the plaintiff would be given an anti-tetanus injection.

If the medical treatment was given negligently, i.e. if the doctor should have been aware that the plaintiff was allergic, then it is likely that the court would treat the medical negligence as a *novus actus interveniens* which broke the chain of causation.

There is no case in civil law which extends the egg shell skull rule beyond physical characteristics. This could arise if the plaintiff suffered negligently inflicted injuries and then refused to have a blood transfusion because of his religious beliefs. If the plaintiff died, the court would then have to determine whether the defendant was liable for the death.

Degree of probability of damage

There has been little discussion on the necessary degree of probability of a kind of damage occurring.

In cases of personal injury it has been seen that the courts generally take a broad view of the question of kind of damage and also of the degree of foreseeability necessary. The egg shell skull rule and rule on extent of damage make the remoteness rules plaintiff friendly where personal injuries are suffered. Broadly speaking, provided the plaintiff can establish that personal injury was reasonably foreseeable as a real risk, the damage is not too remote.

In property damage cases the courts have generally been more restrictive. We have seen that in *Wagon Mound* they did not define the kind of damage necessary as property damage but distinguished between damage by fouling and fire damage.

The Wagon Mound (No 2) [1967] 1 AC 617

This case was concerned with the same facts as *Wagon Mound (No 1)* and the same defendants. The action was brought by the owners of the two ships which were being repaired at the time of the fire and were damaged. The action was brought in negligence and nuisance. The trial judge found that there was a bare possibility of fire damage but that this was so remote it could be ignored. The Privy Council reversed the decision, stating that provided fire damage was foreseeable as a kind of damage, the degree of likelihood was irrelevant to the question of kind of damage suffered. The reason for the different decisions in the two cases was the different finding of fact at first instance.

The Privy Council held that the test for remoteness of damage in nuisance was the same as that in negligence.

The narrower approach to remoteness of damage in property damage cases could be explained on the grounds that the plaintiff is likely to be insured against such damage and that the extent of the damage in such cases could be great.

Impecuniosity

The plaintiff's initial loss may be made greater by his financial inability to take steps to minimise his loss. Is such loss too remote or not?

The Liesbosch Dredger [1933] AC 448

A dredger was sunk due to the defendant's negligence. The owners of the dredger required it to complete a contract which contained an onerous penalty clause. The plaintiffs could not afford to buy a new dredger and had to hire one. The question was whether the cost of hire was recoverable or was too remote. The House of Lords held that the cost of hire was an indirect consequence (note the date of the case) and therefore too remote.

This decision has not proved popular and has frequently been distinguished. Where the plaintiff delayed having his car repaired until he knew the defendants would pay the cost, the cost of hire of a replacement car was recoverable (*Martindale* v *Duncan* [1973] 2 All ER 355).

Torts where Wagon Mound *does not apply*

The *Wagon Mound* test is now established as the remoteness test for negligence and nuisance. There are torts where a different test is used.

If the defendant intends to do harm, e.g. in trespass, then liability will be more extensive than where he is negligent. Policy factors which restrict liability in negligence cases do not apply in intentional torts. The defendant will generally be liable for all damage flowing from the tort once factual causation has been established. In deceit cases the defendant will be held liable for all the loss flowing from the fraudulent statement (*Doyle* v *Olby (Ironmongers) Ltd* [1969] 2 QB 158).

The reasonable foreseeability test should not apply in strict liability torts as foresight of damage is not generally required to establish liability. It must be said that the position is far from clear in torts such as *Rylands* v *Fletcher*.

NOVUS ACTUS INTERVENIENS

Introduction

The defendant's breach of duty may be a cause of the plaintiff's damage in the sense that it satisfies the but for test, but some other factual cause, intervening after the breach, may be regarded as the sole cause of some, or all, of the plaintiff's damage. Where this happens the intervening cause is known as a *novus actus interveniens* and breaks the chain of causation between the defendant and plaintiff. Any damage occurring after the *novus actus interveniens* will be regarded as being too remote.

Example

A negligently runs over B, who is then run over by C. C's action is unlikely to break the chain of causation, as this is a risk to which A's negligence exposed B. But if C stole B's wallet, the court would be unlikely to find A liable, as this was not a risk to which A had exposed B.

The law in this area is far from clear. One of the difficulties is created by the courts obscuring policy factors with legalistic reasoning. The problem is not unique to this area but is particularly acute here. The key policy factor is the court's determination of where the loss should lie.

The legal (formalistic) tests used can be demonstrated by two cases.

Home Office *v* Dorset Yacht Co Ltd [1970] AC 1004

Due to the negligence of the defendant's employees, borstal trainees escaped and caused damage to neighbouring property. The majority of the House of Lords treated the case as being concerned with duty of care. Lord Reid considered that the case was one of remoteness of damage. He considered whether the boys' acts broke the chain of causation. In order to do this they had to be something very unlikely to happen or they would not be regarded as a *novus actus interveniens*. As it was very likely that if the boys escaped, nearby property would be damaged, the boys' acts did not break the chain of causation. The escape took place in Dorset and the damage occurred nearby. Had the boys boarded a train to Carlisle and caused damage there, this might have been regarded as too remote.

Lamb *v* Camden Borough Council [1981] QB 625

The defendants negligently broke a water main. The water damaged the plaintiff's house and caused it to be left empty. Squatters broke in and caused damage. The question was whether the defendants were liable for the damage caused by the squatters or whether the squatters' actions amounted to a *novus actus interveniens*.

Lord Oliver took up and modified Lord Reid's test. If the act should have been foreseen by a reasonable man as likely, it would not break the chain of causation. He found that the squatters' actions were not foreseeable in this sense and therefore did amount to a *novus actus interveniens*.

Lord Denning decided the case on the basis of policy. He thought that as the plaintiff was more likely to be insured against the risk, then the loss should lie with the plaintiff. This illustrates one of the problems of judges making policy decisions. In fact, the defendants were more likely to be insured on an all risks policy for council employees. As the plaintiff had ceased to occupy the house, it was likely that she was not covered by insurance.

A *novus actus interveniens* may take one of three forms.

(a) A natural event

The courts will generally be reluctant to find that a natural event breaks the chain of causation as the plaintiff has no-one else to sue if the defendant is exonerated. If the defendant negligently starts a fire and strong winds then cause the flames to spread to the plaintiff's property, the court will not find that the winds break the chain of causation.

However, if the natural event causes damage simply because the breach of duty has placed the plaintiff or his property in a position where the damage can be caused, the chain of causation will be broken, unless the natural event was likely to happen.

Example

The plaintiff is injured in a road accident caused by the defendant's negligence. An ambulance is called to take the plaintiff to hospital. On the way a strong wind gets up and blows a tree down. The tree lands on the ambulance and causes further injuries to the plaintiff. The defendant will not be liable for the injuries caused by the tree. This will be treated as a novus actus interveniens *which breaks the chain of causation.*

What would the position be if there was an exceptionally strong gale blowing at the time of the original road accident? Should the defendant have foreseen damage caused by a falling tree?

This principle is illustrated in relation to property damage by the following case.

Carslogie Steamship Co *v* Royal Norwegian Government [1952] AC 292

The plaintiff's ship was damaged in a collision for which the defendant's ship was responsible. After temporary repairs the ship set out for the United States on a voyage it would not have made had the collision not occurred. The ship suffered damage due to heavy weather conditions. The storm damage was not treated as a consequence of the collision but as an intervening event in the course of an ordinary voyage. It is important that the decision of the ship's owners to put to sea was voluntary.

(b) Intervening act of a third party

Where the defendant's breach of duty is followed by a third party act which is also a cause of the plaintiff's damage, the court has to determine the extent of the defendant's liability. If the third party act is held to be a *novus actus interveniens*, then the defendant is not liable for any damage occurring after the act.

Where the defendant's duty was to guard the plaintiff or his property from a third party, then the third party act will not relieve the defendant from the consequences of his negligence.

Stansbie *v* Troman [1948] 2 KB 48

The defendant was employed as a decorator by the plaintiff. He was told to lock the door if he went out. He failed to do this and a thief (third party) entered the house and stole property belonging to the plaintiff. The defendant was held liable for the loss, as the thief's act did not break the chain of causation.

Recent cases in this area have tended to concentrate on the aspect of duty rather than remoteness. (See 'Liability for omissions and third parties', pp. 58–61.)

Where there is no duty to guard the plaintiff or his property, the situation is more difficult.

In order to break the chain of causation the third party act must be independent of the breach of duty.

The Oropesa [1943] P 32

A collision at sea was caused by the negligence of the *Oropesa*. The captain of the other ship put out a boat to discuss salvage. At the time there were very heavy seas. The boat overturned and a sailor was drowned. The question was whether the captain's decision to put out the boat amounted to a *novus actus interveniens*. The court held that the action of sending the boat out was caused by and flowed from the collision. As this act was not independent of the defendant's negligence it did not break the chain of causation and the defendants were liable for the sailor's death.

The third party act must be voluntary in order to amount to a *novus actus interveniens*. The captain's action in *The Oropesa* was not voluntary in this sense.

Where the third party act is negligent, it may or may not break the chain of causation.

Rouse *v* Squires [1973] QB 889

The negligence of the first defendant caused an accident. The second defendant also drove negligently and collided with the vehicles that had been involved in the first accident, killing the plaintiff. The court held that the first defendant's negligence was a cause of the death and he was held 25% responsible. The second accident did not break the chain of causation as it was a natural consequence of the first accident.

Knightley *v* Johns [1982] 1 WLR 349

The negligent driving of the defendant caused an accident and blocked a road tunnel. A police officer negligently sent the plaintiff, another police officer, into the tunnel, against the traffic flow. The defendant was held not liable for the injury to the plaintiff. The court stated that 'negligent conduct is more likely to break the chain of causation than conduct which is not'. Stephenson LJ stated that the courts sought refuge in 'common sense rather than logic on the facts and circumstances of each case'.

Where the third party act consists of deliberate wrongful conduct the courts will use the tests set out in *Home Office* v *Dorset Yacht* and *Lamb* v *Camden* (see above).

(c) Act of the plaintiff

Cases where the plaintiff's conduct is called into question are normally concerned with contributory negligence. Where the plaintiff has been found to have been contributorily negligent, his damages will be reduced by the proportion that he is found to be to blame for his damage. However, the defendant may allege that the plaintiff's conduct breaks the chain of causation, so as to render the defendant not liable for some, or all, of the plaintiff's damage.

The test applied by the courts in these cases is whether the plaintiff was acting reasonably in the circumstances.

McKew *v* Holland & Hannen & Cubbitts (Scotland) Ltd [1969] 3 All ER 1621

The plaintiff injured his leg as a result of the defendant's negligence. As a result of his injury he sometimes lost control of his leg. He attempted to descend a steep staircase which had no handrail, whilst holding a small child by the hand. His leg gave way and he pushed the child to safety. He then jumped to avoid falling and broke his ankle. The defendants were held not liable for this injury, as the plaintiff's unreasonable conduct broke the chain of causation. It was not the decision to jump that was unreasonable, it was placing himself unnecessarily in a position where he might be confronted with such an emergency.

Weiland *v* Cyril Lord Carpets Ltd [1969] 3 All ER 1006

The plaintiff was unable to adjust her bi-focal spectacles as a result of a neck injury inflicted by the defendant's negligence. She was worried about catching public transport in such a condition and went to her son's office to ask him to drive her home. On the way into the office she fell down a flight of stairs and was injured. On these facts the plaintiff was held to have acted reasonably and the defendant was liable for her injuries.

CONCLUSION

It can be seen that this area raises many difficult issues for the courts to decide. The factual circumstances that can arise are infinite and the judges rely on a mixture of legal principle, policy and common sense to guide them through the maze.

An illustration of the problems and possible solutions is provided by the following example. This also highlights the way in which a court may choose from a number of doctrines in coming to a solution.

Example

Fred received head injuries at work as a result of his employer's negligence. As a result of his injuries Fred became depressed and two years after the accident committed suicide as a result of his depression. The medical evidence establishes that but for the accident, Fred would probably not have committed suicide.

Legally there are a number of ways in which the court could approach this, but the basic question is whether the court wishes to compensate the estate and dependants of a suicide. This is the policy issue. Factual causation based on the but for test is established.

The court could determine that the death was too remote.

Pigney *v* Pointer's Transport Services Ltd [1957] 1 WLR 1121

The plaintiff's husband was injured in an accident at work. The injuries led to anxiety neurosis and depression, as a result of which the defendant hanged himself. The claim by the widow was allowed by the court applying the direct consequence test for remoteness.

This case was decided under the *Polemis* test. Would the death be reasonably foreseeable? If the deceased was prone to depression, the court could treat it as an example of the egg shell skull rule.

Meah *v* McCreamer [1985] 1 All ER 367

The plaintiff suffered severe head injuries in a car accident caused by the negligence of the defendant. As a result he underwent a personality change and started to attack women. Two of his victims successfully sued him and the plaintiff then tried to recover the damages from the defendant. The action failed as the damage claimed was too remote and on policy grounds it would not be right to allow an indemnity for the consequence of a criminal act. The court considered *Pigney* and distinguished it. There the widow was recovering damages for the death of the original victim of the defendant's negligence.

An attempt was made by Lord Denning to avoid giving damages following a suicide (*Hyde* v *Thameside Area Health Authority* (1981) 2 PN 26). However, consider the following case.

Kirkham *v* Chief Constable of the Greater Manchester Police [1989] 3 All ER 882

The action was brought against the police on the grounds that they failed to inform the prison authorities of the deceased's suicidal tendencies. The deceased had committed suicide at a remand centre. It was held:

(a)   When the police took the deceased into custody they assumed certain responsibilities, including that of passing on information which might affect his well being when he was transferred to the prison authorities.

(b)   As the deceased had been suffering from clinical depression which impaired his judgment, his act had not been voluntary and the defence of *volenti* failed.

(c)   The defence of *ex turpi causa* would not apply having regard to the changing public opinion of suicide.

(d)   Suicide was not too remote a consequence of the breach of duty.

(e)   The suicide did not amount to a *novus actus interveniens*.

9 | Defences to negligence

INTRODUCTION

It is traditional to find a chapter on defences at the end of a tort textbook. However the development of negligence doctrines means that it is convenient to consider certain defences which have particular relevance to negligence at this stage.

There are three defences to a negligence action. *Volenti non fit injuria* means that the plaintiff voluntarily agrees to undertake the legal risk of harm at his own expense. This is a complete defence to an action. Contributory negligence is where the plaintiff's fault has contributed to his damage and the damages awarded are reduced in proportion to his fault. *Ex turpi causa* means that from a bad cause no action arises. A person who is involved in a criminal act at the time he is injured may be denied an action.

Example

John and Brian had been drinking together. John offered Brian a lift home and Brian accepted. Due to John's negligent driving the car crashed and Brian was injured. Brian was not wearing a seat belt, was thrown forward and hit his head on the windscreen.

If Brian sued John for negligence he could be met with the defences of volenti *non fit injuria and contributory negligence. The defence of* volenti *would fail as Brian may be aware that John is drunk but he did not consent to him driving negligently. Knowledge of a risk does not equal consent to run that risk. There is also a statutory provision which prevents* volenti *operating in these circumstances. Brian would have his damages reduced for contributory negligence in riding with a driver who he knew was drunk and in failing to wear a seat belt.*

If Brian and John were engaged in a get-away from the scene of a crime at the time of the accident, John could also raise the defence of ex turpi causa *(illegality) to the action.*

VOLENTI NON FIT INJURIA

Introduction

The requirements for a defence of *volenti non fit injuria* in a negligence action are a matter for some controversy. It must be shown that the plaintiff acted voluntarily in the sense that he could exercise a free choice. Some judges are of the opinion that there must be an express or implied agreement between the parties before the defence can operate. The other view is that where the plaintiff comes across a danger which has already been created by the defendant the defence can operate. If the defence is successful then the plaintiff will recover no damages at all. This was also the case where contributory negligence was established before 1945. In cases before that date there was no practical difference for the plaintiff in being found to be *volenti* or contributorily negligent. The pre-1945 cases must be read with this in mind.

Before this defence has any role to play it must be shown that the defendant has committed a tort.

Wooldridge *v* Sumner [1963] 2 QB 43

The plaintiff was a professional photographer. During a horse show he positioned himself at the edge of the arena. He was knocked down and injured by a horse when the rider lost control while riding too fast. The Court of Appeal held that the defendant rider's failure to control his horse was simply an error of judgment which did not amount to negligence. The standard of care owed by a competitor to a spectator was not to act with reckless disregard for the spectator's safety. As this duty had not been broken there was no room for the defence of *volenti non fit injuria* to operate.

The standard of care laid down in this case has been doubted in subsequent cases. (See e.g. *Condon* v *Basi* [1985] 2 All ER 453 where a standard of reasonable care was applied to participants in a football match.)

The defence applies in cases of intentional and negligent infliction of harm, although it operates in different ways.

In intentional torts the defence operates in the form of consent. Where the plaintiff has consented to the defendant's act he will have no action. So a boxer who is struck by his opponent cannot sue him for battery. A patient who signs a consent form for a surgical operation cannot later sue the surgeon for battery.

Where the harm was negligently inflicted the defence gives rise to greater difficulties. The defendant has to show that the plaintiff assumed the legal risk of injury in circumstances where the defendant's act would otherwise amount to negligence. The effect of the defence is that the plaintiff consents to exempt the defendant from a duty of care which would otherwise have been owed.

There are certain requirements before the defence will apply.

Voluntary

The plaintiff must have had a genuine freedom of choice before the defence can be successfully raised against him.

> A man cannot be said to be truly willing unless he is in a position to choose freely, and freedom of choice predicates, not only full knowledge of the circumstances on which the exercise of choice is conditioned, so that he may be able to choose wisely, but the absence from his mind of any feeling of constraint so that nothing shall interfere with the freedom of his will (Scott LJ in *Bowater* v *Rowley Regis Corporation* [1944] KB 476).

The approach to this point in employer–employee cases has changed. In the early part of the nineteenth century employees were assumed to consent to the risks in the work that they did. The courts did not accept that the employer–employee relationship was not an equal one and that an employee might have continued to work in the face of danger for fear of losing his job. At the end of the nineteenth century judicial attitudes changed.

Smith *v* Baker [1891] AC 325

The plaintiff was employed by the defendants on the construction of a railway. While he was working, a crane moved rocks over his head. Both he and his employers knew there was a risk of a stone falling on him and he had complained to them about this. A stone fell and injured the plaintiff and he sued his employers for negligence. The employers pleaded *volenti non fit injuria* but this was rejected by the court. Although the plaintiff knew of the risk and continued to work, there was no evidence that he had voluntarily undertaken to run the risk of injury. Merely continuing to work did not indicate *volens*.

The approach in this case has been continued by the courts and it is very rare for a *volenti* plea to succeed in an employee–employer case. Such a plea might be successful where the employee had been paid danger money to undertake precisely that risk. The defence has also succeeded where the employee was under no pressure to take a particular risk but deliberately chose a dangerous method of working.

ICI Ltd *v* Shatwell [1965] AC 656

The plaintiff and his brother were both experienced shotfirers employed by the defendants. They jointly chose to ignore their employer's orders and statutory safety regulations, by testing detonators without taking shelter. There was an explosion and the plaintiff was injured. He sued the defendants on the grounds of their vicarious liability for his brother's negligence and breach of statutory duty. The question for the House of Lords was whether an employer who was under no statutory duty could be vicariously liable for an employee's breach of statutory duty to another employee. Had the plaintiff acted on his own, rather than in combination with his brother, no action would have lain. The House held that the plaintiff was *volens* to the risk of harm and his action therefore failed. Had the plaintiff sued his brother then the action would have failed on the grounds of *volenti*. There had been no pressure brought by the employers to adopt that method of working. Therefore there was no reason why *volenti* should not succeed for the employer.

There is a difficult problem posed by a person who commits suicide. Is he acting voluntarily or not? It has been held that *volenti* will provide a complete defence in actions against the police or hospital authorities where the deceased was of sound mind. If the deceased's judgment was impaired by mental illness and he was incapable of coming to a balanced decision, his act is not voluntary and *volenti* will not apply (*Kirkham* v *Chief Constable of Greater Manchester Police* [1990] 3 All ER 246). This approach seems to beg the question as to whether a suicide can ever be regarded as being in their right mind.

The issue of voluntariness also arises in the rescue cases. A rescuer who acts to save a person in danger and is injured, cannot be said to exercise the free choice which is necessary for *volenti*. (See under 'Rescue cases', p. 103.)

Agreement

Where the parties have reached an express agreement that the plaintiff will voluntarily assume the risk of harm and this agreement is made before the negligent act, then the defence will operate.

This point is subject to any statutory restriction which is placed on the parties' freedom to agree. If the agreement is subject to the Unfair Contract Terms Act 1977, then it is important that it does not contravene its provisions: e.g. in certain circumstances it is not possible to exclude liability for death or personal injuries at all. The defendant will not be allowed to get round the Act by saying that the plaintiff was *volenti*. (See s. 2(1), s. 2(3).)

In limited circumstances the courts may be prepared to imply the agreement to run the risk (e.g. *ICI* v *Shatwell*). The reluctance of the courts to imply an agreement can be seen in the cases where the plaintiff has accepted a lift with the defendant who is incapable of driving.

Dann *v* Hamilton [1939] 1 KB 509

The defendant drove the plaintiff and her mother to London to see the Coronation lights. They visited several public houses and the defendant's ability to drive was clearly impaired. One passenger decided that the driver was drunk and got out of the car. The plaintiff said she would take the risk of an accident happening. A few minutes later there was an accident and the plaintiff was injured. It was held that *volenti* did not apply on these facts as the plaintiff had not consented to or absolved the defendant from subsequent negligence on his part.

Asquith J stated that the defence of *volenti* was applicable where the plaintiff came to a situation where the danger had already been created by the defendant's negligence.

Nettleship *v* Weston [1971] 2 QB 691

The plaintiff gave the defendant driving lessons. On the third lesson the defendant drove negligently and hit a lamp post. The plaintiff was injured and sued in negligence. The action was successful and the defence of *volenti* failed. The plaintiff had not consented to run the risk of injury as he had checked on whether the car was covered for passenger's insurance.

Lord Denning stated: 'Nothing will suffice short of an agreement to waive any claim for negligence. The plaintiff must agree, expressly or impliedly, to waive any claim for any injury that may befall him due to the lack of reasonable care by the defendant.'

Owens _v_ Brimmell [1977] 2 WLR 943

The plaintiff and defendant spent the evening on a pub crawl together. The plaintiff accepted a lift home with the defendant although he knew the defendant was drunk. The defendant drove negligently and the plaintiff received serious injuries in a crash. The defence of _volenti_ was held to be inappropriate but the plaintiff's damages were reduced for his contributory negligence in riding with a drunken driver and failing to wear a seat belt.

In these cases the plaintiff is aware of the risk but does not consent to the act of negligence that causes his injury. It was pointed out in _Dann_ v _Hamilton_ that the defence could apply in cases where: 'the drunkenness of the driver at the material time is so extreme and so glaring that to accept a lift from him is like engaging in an intrinsically and obviously dangerous occupation, intermeddling with an unexploded bomb or walking along on the edge of an unfenced cliff'.

Morris _v_ Murray [1990] 3 All ER 801

The plaintiff went for a ride in a private plane piloted by the defendant, despite the fact that he knew the defendant was drunk. The plane crashed and the plaintiff was injured. It was held by the Court of Appeal that the pilot's drunkenness was so extreme and obvious that participating in the flight was like engaging in an intrinsically and obviously dangerous occupation. The defence of _volenti_ succeeded. Accepting lifts with drunken pilots is more dangerous than with drunken drivers.

The position with drunken drivers is affected by a statutory provision. The Road Traffic Act 1988, s. 149 provides that _volenti_ is not available where a passenger in a car sues the driver in circumstances where insurance is compulsory. At one time it was thought that the section only applied to express agreements and not to an implied agreement. This view has now been rejected by the Court of Appeal.

Pitts _v_ Hunt [1990] 3 All ER 344

The plaintiff was a pillion passenger on a motor bike driven by the defendant. The defendant was drunk, had never passed a driving test, was uninsured and drove dangerously. The plaintiff encouraged him in this behaviour. The statutory provision was held to prevent the defendant from relying on any form of the _volenti_ defence. Had it not been for the section, the court was of the view that the claim would have been defeated by _volenti_.

The plaintiff's claim was held to have been defeated by the maxim of _ex turpi causa_. This would appear to defeat the intention of the statutory provision.

Problem

Is it necessary for the defendant to prove that the plaintiff agreed to waive his legal rights in order for him to succeed in a _volenti_ plea?

Judicial views on whether an agreement that the plaintiff will waive any claim against the defendant is necessary, are mixed. At one extreme Diplock LJ stated in _Wooldridge_ v _Sumner_: 'The defence of _volenti_ in the absence of express contract, has no application to negligence simpliciter where the duty of care is based solely on proximity or "neighbourship" in the Atkinian sense.'

Where there is an express agreement to such effect there is little difficulty. Whether the agreement takes the form of a contract term or notice, it will be regulated by statute. Such waivers are probably covered by the Unfair Contract Terms Act 1977. An express agreement by a passenger in a car to waive his rights to sue the driver for negligently inflicted injuries is, as we have seen, negated by statute.

Slightly less extreme was Lord Denning's view in *Nettleship* v *Weston*: 'Nothing will suffice short of an agreement to waive any claim for negligence. The plaintiff must agree, expressly or impliedly, to waive any claim for any injury that may befall him due to the lack of reasonable care by the defendant.'

The courts are understandably reluctant to imply an agreement. It is necessary that there should be some kind of previous relationship between the parties. We have seen this in cases such as *Dann* v *Hamilton*. However, in *Morris* v *Murray* the Court of Appeal held that the defence of *volenti* should have succeeded. This was on the basis that the act of the plaintiff relied on as consent preceded, and licensed in advance, a possible subsequent act of negligence. The plaintiff had waived the defendant's duty to take care. A similar view may be taken where the parties embark on a criminal act together and the plaintiff is injured as a result of the defendant's negligence. The trend in such cases is, however, to apply the maxim *ex turpi causa*.

Can *volenti* be raised where the plaintiff encounters a risk which has already been created by the defendant's negligence?

Baker *v* T E Hopkins & Son Ltd [1959] 1 WLR 966

The defendant's employees had been placed in danger by being required to work in a confined space with a petrol driven engine producing poisonous fumes. A doctor attempted to rescue the men and was killed by the fumes. He was aware of the danger at the time he attempted the rescue. *Volenti* was held to be inapplicable as the doctor could not be said to have agreed to the risk. He had only become involved after the defendant's negligent act.

This case can perhaps be explained on policy grounds as the plaintiff was a rescuer and the courts do not wish to deter rescue. It could also be argued that the doctor was not acting voluntarily.

Judicial support for the view that *volenti* can be raised in these circumstances exists in *Dann* v *Hamilton*, *Morris* v *Murray* and *Pitts* v *Hunt*. This presents certain problems. The fact that the plaintiff chose to run the risk should not give rise to *volenti*, as knowledge of the risk is not sufficient. In these circumstances the plaintiff's conduct amounts to contributory negligence as he acted negligently. This confuses the two defences which have different outcomes. *Volenti* operates to defeat the claim completely. Contributory negligence reduces the plaintiff's damages.

Statutory provisions also exist which suggest that a *volenti* plea can succeed in the absence of agreement. These provisions are the Occupier's Liability Act 1957, s. 2(5), Animals Act 1971, s. 5(2), Unfair Contract Terms Act 1977, s. 2(3). However, these provisions could be viewed as one off examples of voluntary acceptance of risk.

Knowledge

In order for *volenti* to operate, the plaintiff must have knowledge of the existence of the risk and its nature and extent. The test for knowledge is subjective. If the plaintiff should have been aware of the risk but was not, the defence will fail (*Smith v Austin Lifts Ltd* [1959] 1 WLR 100). This raises problems where the plaintiff was drunk at the time. If he was so drunk that he could not appreciate the nature of the risk, he will not be *volenti*.

The relationship between *volenti* and exclusion clauses

In cases where *volenti* is based on agreement, that agreement may amount to an exclusion clause. If it does, then it will be subject to the provisions of the Unfair Contract Terms Act 1977. Attempts to exclude liability for negligence are governed by s. 2. This section operates where the clause attempts to exclude or restrict business liability as defined in s. 1(3).

Section 2(1) will operate to defeat any attempt to exclude or restrict liability for death or personal injuries caused by negligence.

Section 2(2) applies a test of reasonableness to other types of damage caused by negligence.

Section 2(3) states: 'Where a contract term or notice purports to exclude or restrict liability for negligence a person's agreement to or awareness of it is not of itself to be taken as indicating his voluntary acceptance of any risk.'

As any agreement between the parties will be covered by the rest of the section, this subsection will only apply where there is no agreement between the parties and the plaintiff comes upon an already existing risk.

CONTRIBUTORY NEGLIGENCE

Introduction

This defence will apply where the damage which the plaintiff has suffered was caused partly by his own fault and partly by the fault of the defendant. In order to establish the defence, the defendant must prove that the plaintiff failed to take reasonable care for his own safety and that this failure was a cause of his damage. If contributory negligence is established, the modern position is that the plaintiff will have his damages reduced by the court in proportion to his fault. If he would have received £10,000 but was found to be 25% contributorily negligent, his damages will be £7,500.

This was not always the case. At common law, if the court found that the plaintiff was partially to blame for his injuries, he received nothing at all. Contributory negligence operated as a complete defence.

Butterfield v Forrester (1809) 11 East 60

The plaintiff rode his horse violently and collided with a pole which the defendant had negligently left in the road. It was held that if the plaintiff had used ordinary care the accident would not have happened. The plaintiff was therefore guilty of contributory negligence and could recover nothing.

This rule proved too severe for the courts and exceptions were developed to it. One of these was the rule of lost opportunity or effective last chance.

Davies v Mann (1842) 10 M & W 546

The plaintiff negligently fastened his ass up on the highway. The defendant drove his wagon too fast and collided with the ass, which was killed. The defendant was held liable as if he had driven more slowly he could have avoided the accident.

After this the law became increasingly convoluted as the courts tried to escape the rigours of a rule which meant that the court had to make a finding in favour of one party or the other. The rule was all or nothing.

In 1911 courts were given a statutory power to apportion damages in cases of collision at sea (Maritime Conventions Act 1911). In 1945 a general power to apportion damages was given to the courts by the Law Reform (Contributory Negligence) Act 1945. Section 1(1) provides:

> Where any person suffers damage as the result partly of his own fault and partly of the fault of any other person or persons, a claim in respect of that damage shall not be defeated by reason of the fault of the person suffering the damage, but the damages recoverable in respect thereof shall be reduced to such an extent as the court thinks just and equitable having regard to the claimant's share in the responsibility for the damage.

The scope of the 1945 Act

The Act will only apply where a person has suffered damage. Damage is defined by s. 4 as including loss of life and personal injury. Property damage would appear to be included as this was the case before the Act was passed. Whether economic loss is included is unknown but it would be logical if it were.

The Act will only apply where the damage was caused partly by the fault of the defendant and partly by the fault of the plaintiff. In the absence of fault the court therefore has no power under the Act to apportion damages.

Fault is defined by s. 4: 'negligence, breach of statutory duty or other act or omission which gives rise to a liability in tort or would, apart from the Act give rise to the defence of contributory negligence'.

It must be remembered that fault is referred to in two contexts, the fault of the defendant and the fault of the plaintiff. Fault of the defendant means negligence, breach of statutory duty or other act or omission which gives rise to a liability in tort. This causes no problem, as the defendant can be said to be at fault whenever he commits a tort. The fault of the plaintiff means an act or omission which would, apart from the Act give rise to the defence of contributory negligence. This causes problems of interpretation.

A narrow view would be that if contributory negligence was not a defence at common law, then it will not be available under the Act. This would mean that the defence was not available for torts such as deceit and intentional trespass to the person.

The other view is that where the conduct of the plaintiff would have given rise to the defence at common law if he was suing for negligence, the defence is applicable.

What is clear is that the Act does not apply to conversion or intentional torts against goods by virtue of of the Torts (Interference With Goods) Act 1977, s. 11.

The Act does apply in negligence, nuisance, and actions under the rule in *Rylands* v *Fletcher*. The Act does not apply to actions in deceit. It is unclear whether the Act applies to trespass to the person but apparently it does.

Barnes v Nayer, *The Times* 19 December 1986

The defendant was convicted of the manslaughter of the plaintiff's wife. A civil action for trespass to the person followed. The defendant raised contributory negligence as a defence (amongst others), on the grounds that he had been provoked. The Court of Appeal considered that the defendant's response was out of all proportion to the alleged provocation but on appropriate facts contributory negligence could be relied on as a defence to battery.

Elements of contributory negligence

The defendant must prove that the plaintiff failed to take reasonable care for his own safety and that this failure was a cause of his damage.

It is not necessary for the plaintiff to owe the defendant a duty of care:

> Although contributory negligence does not depend on a duty of care, it does depend on foreseeability. Just as actionable negligence requires the foreseeability of harm to others, so contributory negligence requires the foreseeability of harm to oneself. A person is guilty of contributory negligence if he ought reasonably to have foreseen that, if he did not act as a reasonable, prudent man, he might be hurt himself; and in his reckonings he must take into account the possibility of others being careless (Denning LJ in *Jones* v *Livox Quarries Ltd* [1952] 2 QB 608).

A motorcyclist does not owe a duty to other road users to wear a crash helmet but in failing to do so he is guilty of contributory negligence if he suffers head injuries in an accident. He should foresee harm to himself, although there is no risk of harm to anyone else.

The plaintiff's conduct

In considering whether the plaintiff was contributorily negligent the court will take into account factors similar to those which would render the defendant negligent. The test is basically an objective one, although subjective factors are introduced when looking at child defendants and persons under a disability.

The plaintiff's failure to take care for his own safety may be a cause of the accident which results in his damage. This occurs where two motorists are held to be equally to blame for a collision and the plaintiff is injured. A person who plies a driver with drinks and then accepts a lift and is injured will also be liable under this head.

Alternatively, a person may place himself in a dangerous position which exposes him to the risk of involvement in the accident in which he is harmed.

Davies v Swan Motor Co (Swansea) Ltd [1949] 2 KB 291

The plaintiff's husband rode on the offside step of a dust-cart. He was aware of the danger of such a practice. The dust-cart was being overtaken by one of the defendant's buses when a collision occurred the husband was killed. The driver of the dust-cart, the driver of the bus, and the husband were all held to have been negligent, the husband because of the dangerous manner in which he was riding on the dust-cart. He was therefore held to have been guilty of contributory negligence and the widow's damages reduced.

Jones v Livox Quarries Ltd [1952] 2 QB 608

The plaintiff was riding on the tow bar at the back of a traxcavator on his way back to the canteen. Another vehicle was driven negligently into the back of the traxcavator, causing injury to the plaintiff. The plaintiff's damages were reduced on the grounds of his contributory negligence. Lord Denning said that the result would have been otherwise if the plaintiff had been e.g. hit in the eye by a shot from a negligent sportsman.

Similar reasoning could be applied where the plaintiff puts himself in a position which is not dangerous in itself but he is aware of circumstances which make it more likely that he will suffer harm. This would explain the cases where the plaintiff accepts a lift with a driver whom he knows is drunk. In these circumstances the courts will find that the plaintiff was guilty of contributory negligence but not *volens* to the risk (*Owens* v *Brimmell* [1977] QB 859).

The third possibility is that the plaintiff may take up a position which is not in itself dangerous but where his failure to take precautions increases the risk of the extent of harm which he may suffer.

Froom v Butcher [1976] QB 286

The plaintiff's car was in a collision with the defendant's car caused by the defendant's negligence. At the time of the accident the plaintiff was not wearing a seat belt. His injuries were worse than they would have been if he had been wearing a seat belt. It was held by the Court of Appeal that his damages should be reduced by 20%. The standard of care was to be judged objectively and the prudent man would wear a seat belt unless there were exceptional circumstances.

Since this case it has been made a criminal offence not to wear a seat belt in the front seat of a car. There are certain exceptions to this such as pregnant women.

There are a number of areas where problems are caused in trying to ascertain the appropriate standard of care for the plaintiff.

Children

The traditional view is that there is no age below which a child cannot be held to be guilty of contributory negligence. This view has been challenged by Lord Denning.

Gough v Thorne [1966] 1 WLR 1387

The plaintiff was aged 13 years. A lorry driver signalled to her to cross the road. She did so without stopping to see if the road was clear. She was run over by a car travelling at excessive speed and overtaking on the wrong side. It was held that the plaintiff was not guilty of contributory negligence. If she had been an adult the position would have been different. Lord Denning stated:

> A very young child cannot be guilty of contributory negligence. An older child may be; but it depends on the circumstances. A judge should only find a child guilty of contributory negligence if he or she is of such an age as reasonably to be expected to take precautions for his or her own safety; and then he or she is only to be found guilty if blame should be attached to him or her.

Yachuk v Oliver Blais [1949] AC 386

A nine year old child bought petrol from the defendants after falsely stating that his mother needed it for her car. The child used the petrol for a game in which he was burned. The defendants were held to have been negligent in selling the child the petrol but the child was not contributorily negligent. He did not know and could not have been expected to know the qualities of petrol.

Dilemma

When assessing the plaintiff's conduct the court will make allowance for the fact that the defendant's negligence has placed the plaintiff in a dilemma. If the plaintiff chooses a course which carries a risk of harm in order to avoid a reasonably perceived greater danger he will not be contributorily negligent.

Jones v Boyce (1816) 1 Stark 493

The plaintiff was a passenger on the defendant's coach. A coupling rein broke loose and thinking that the coach was about to crash, the plaintiff jumped out and broke his leg. The coach did not in fact crash and if he had remained on it he would have suffered no harm. As his actions were those of a prudent and reasonable man, he was not contributorily negligent.

Where the defendant's negligence has placed a person in danger and the plaintiff has attempted a rescue, the court will be slow to find the rescuer contributorily negligent. (See 'Rescue cases', p. 103.)

Workmen

In cases where an employee sues his employer for breach of statutory duty, the court will be slow to find that the employer was guilty of contributory negligence. Regard must be had to the fact that the employee's sense of danger will have been dulled by familiarity, repetition, noise, confusion, fatigue and preoccupation with work (*Caswell* v *Powell Duffryn Associated Collieries Ltd* [1940] AC 152). The reason for this lenient approach is that the court will not want to undermine the statutory regulations which are often designed to protect workmen from the consequences of their own carelessness.

The courts will hold employees liable for their contributory negligence however.

Jayes *v* IMI (Kynoch) Ltd [1985] ICR 155

The plaintiff, an experienced workman, was cleaning a machine when his hand was pulled into the machine and he lost the tip of a finger. The machine had had its safety guard removed. The plaintiff, in an action under the Factories Act 1961, s. 14, was held to have been 100% contributorily negligent after he admitted that what he had done had been extremely foolish.

Whether this lenient approach applies in actions for negligence is not clear but the employer's personal non-delegable duty to the employee to take into account the possibility of the employee's carelessness for his own safety is relevant in such a calculation.

Causation

In order for contributory negligence to constitute a defence, the plaintiff's fault must be a legal and factual cause of the harm suffered. It is not necessary that the plaintiff's fault be a cause of the accident itself.

In *Jones* v *Livox Quarries*, the plaintiff's position on the traxcavator was held to be one of the causes of his damage, although the most obvious risk to the plaintiff was that he would fall off. His action in riding on the tow bar had sufficient causal potency to be regarded as a cause of his injuries. Factual causation was established and the damage was not too remote. Had the plaintiff been shot, then this would have been too remote a consequence and causation not established.

In the seat belt cases the plaintiff's failure to take precautions for his own safety is regarded as a contributing cause of his injuries, but it is necessary for the defendant to prove that the failure to wear a seat belt was a cause of the injuries. If the plaintiff was thrown forwards and injured, then clearly failure to wear a seat belt is contributory negligence. But for the failure, either the plaintiff would not have been injured or his injuries would not have been so severe. However, if something enters the vehicle and crushes the plaintiff backwards against the seat, the failure to wear the seat belt would appear to be irrelevant and fail the test of causation. The plaintiff would have suffered the injuries even if he had been wearing a belt.

The first test that must be passed is the but for test for factual causation. Would the alleged consequence have occurred but for the negligent cause. If the plaintiff's alleged contributory negligence fails this test it is not necessary to go any further (s. 1(1)).

The Act itself does not change the rules on causation, so it is still necessary to use common law rules. This can give rise to some difficult problems.

Stapley Gypsum Mines Ltd [1953] AC 663

Two miners had been instructed to bring down an unsafe part of the roof which presented a danger to the miners. They disobeyed instructions by continuing to work when they had failed to do this. The roof collapsed and one of the men was killed. His widow sued the defendants for negligence. The court had to decide whether the damage was solely as a result of the negligence of the plaintiff's husband or whether the negligence of his workmate was also a factor. The House of Lords approached the question in a commonsense manner and held the actions of both workmen were causes. The plaintiff's action succeeded but his damages were reduced by 80% on the grounds of contributory negligence.

It is important to remember that if one act is held to be the sole cause of the damage and that act is one of the plaintiff, then the plaintiff will recover nothing. The act could be regarded as a *novus actus interveniens*. See e.g. *McKew v Holland Hannen & Cubbitts*.

Apportionment

The Law Reform (Contributory Negligence) Act, s. 1(1) directs the court to reduce the plaintiff's damages to the extent that the court thinks just and equitable having regard to the claimant's share in the responsibility for the damage.

There are two possible ways of assessing the claimant's share in the responsibility for the damage, causation and blameworthiness.

If a test of causative potency is used then logically every case should end with a 50/50 apportionment, as each of the plaintiff's and defendant's conduct is a cause. The courts however take a commonsense view, rather than a philosophical view, and arrive at apportionments other than 50/50. (See *Stapley v Gypsum Mines Ltd.*)

Where the comparative blameworthiness or culpability of the parties is taken into account, then the test is an objective one of deviating from the standard of behaviour of the reasonable man. It is not a moral test. The reasonable man, for example, would wear a seat belt.

The requirement that the reduction should be just and equitable means that there is no single test for determining the level of reduction of damages. The courts treat it as a question of fact and take an *ad hoc* approach.

Can there be a 100% reduction for contributory negligence? If there can be then there is no practical difference between this defence and *volenti*, as the plaintiff receives no damages. In *Pitts v Hunt* [1990] 3 All ER 344, the trial judge felt he was unable to apply *volenti non fit injuria* because of the statutory provision. However, he held the plaintiff to be 100% contributorily negligent. The Court of Appeal stated that it was impermissible to make a finding of 100% contributory negligence, as the Act states that the plaintiff must suffer damage partly as a result of his own fault and partly as a result of the defendant's fault. The trial judge must therefore apportion blame between the parties. A finding of 100% contributory negligence does not do this.

Multiple defendants

Difficulties arise where there is more than one defendant. In cases where the plaintiff was not at fault, he can recover his full loss against any of the defendants. That person will then have to seek a contribution from the other defendants under the Civil Liability (Contribution) Act 1978.

Where the plaintiff was at fault and contributed to his own injuries, is it necessary to balance the plaintiff's contributory negligence against each defendant separately?

Fitzgerald v Lane [1988] 2 All ER 961

The plaintiff stepped out into the traffic on a busy road. He was struck by a vehicle driven by the first defendant. This pushed him into the path of an oncoming vehicle driven by the second defendant. Both defendants were accepted to be negligent and the plaintiff was contributorily negligent. At first instance the three parties were held equally to blame and the plaintiff's damages were therefore reduced by one-third. This was held to be the wrong approach by the House of Lords. It was necessary to distinguish two questions. First, the contributory negligence of the plaintiff and the amount by which his damages should be reduced. Second, the amount of contribution recoverable between the two defendants. The plaintiff's culpability was in setting the scene for the accident. The response of the defendants then had to be looked at. The plaintiff's conduct and the totality of the tortious conduct of the defendants were compared. As the plaintiff was as much to blame for his injuries as the defendants, his damages were reduced by 50%.

One final point to be remembered about contributory negligence is that it differs in effect from a finding of negligence. The latter does not usually directly affect the defendant's pocket as he will be insured. A finding of contributory negligence on the other hand has a direct financial effect on the plaintiff. He gets less in damages.

EX TURPI CAUSA

The court may deny an action to a plaintiff who suffered damage while participating in a criminal activity. In negligence actions the court may find that no duty of care was owed in the circumstances. The defence may be referred to as illegality or *ex turpi causa non oritur actio*. This means that an action cannot be founded on a bad cause.

Pitts v Hunt [1990] 3 All ER 344

(For facts see *volenti non fit injuria*). Beldam LJ reviewed the authorities and stated that deciding whether the defence applied involved answering two questions. First, had there been any illegality of which the court should take note. Second, would it be an affront to the public conscience to allow the plaintiff to recover. A robust approach should be taken to these questions. The fact that there had been unlawfulness should not mean that a remedy should be denied. Taking account of the view of drunk driving, the plaintiff should be precluded on grounds of public policy from recovering compensation.

A different approach was taken by Dillon and Balcombe LJJ. Dillon LJ dismissed the conscience approach as it would be difficult to apply and would inevitably be affected by emotional factors. This would lead to a graph of illegalities graded according to moral turpitude. Dillon and Balcombe LJJ agreed that a preferable approach would be to deny a duty of care in certain cases of joint illegal enterprises. The defence would have this effect where first, the plaintiff's action is directly connected with the joint illegal enterprise and not merely incidental to it. Second, the circumstances of the illegal venture must be such that the court cannot determine the standard of care to be observed.

An objection to the use of the defence in this case was that it enabled the court to evade the statutory prohibition on applying *volenti non fit injuria*. This cannot have been the intention of Parliament when it prevented drivers from contracting out of their liability to a passenger.

The first point raised by Dillon and Balcombe LJJ can be illustrated as follows. Two safebreakers are on their way to open a safe and they have a fight. One is injured. *Ex turpi causa* would not provide a defence. (But see *Murphy* v *Culhane* [1977] QB 94 for a case involving a criminal affray where the plaintiff got more than he bargained for and it was stated that the defence could apply.) If the safebreakers were actually trying to open the safe and one was injured by the other's negligent use of explosives, then the defence could apply.

The second point is shown by cases where two criminals are engaged in attempting a getaway from the scene of the crime. The car is driven negligently at speed and the passenger is injured. The court would be unwilling or unable to determine what speed would be expected from a competent getaway driver. (See *Ashton* v *Turner* [1980] 3 All ER 870.)

Which test will be followed remains to be seen. Despite the criticism levelled at the public conscience test it has been used in a number of cases. For example in *Kirkham* v *Chief Constable of the Greater Manchester Police* [1990] 3 All ER 246, the court refused to bar the claim on the grounds of suicide. This was no longer an affront to the public conscience, where the suicide resulted from mental instability.

The test of difficulty in setting the appropriate standard of care poses problems. One is that the defence applies in torts other than negligence. A second is that cases arise where there is no doubt about the appropriate standard.

Rance *v* Mid-Downs Health Authority [1991] 1 All ER 801

The allegation of negligence was that the defendant had failed to observe a foetal abnormality during pregnancy and the plaintiff had been denied the possibility of an abortion. Such an abortion would have been illegal under the then existing law. There would have been no difficulty in establishing the appropriate standard of care for the medical defendant. It was held that there had been no negligence, but on grounds of public policy the court would not award compensation where the plaintiff would have had to have broken the law.

It is not clear what kind of conduct will bar an action. The fact that a tort was committed is not sufficient. A duty of care can be owed to a trespasser (see 'Defective Premises', p. 116.) The conduct does not even have to be illegal. The decision in *Kirkham* leaves open the possibility that a suicide in their right mind could be *ex turpi causa*. The conduct will usually be criminal but not all crimes will be sufficient to raise the defence. For example, a breach of statutory duty will not bar a claim.

THE RESCUE CASES

We have seen that issues of causation and blameworthiness raise problems for the courts when deciding whether the plaintiff's conduct was sufficiently serious to deserve a reduction in his entitlement to damages, or to deserve no damages at all. Public policy plays a part in a number of these decisions and a student could be forgiven for confusion at the complexity of the area and the number of legal doctrines used. This chapter will be concluded by looking at the so called 'rescue cases' and seeing how the various doctrines apply.

The public policy issue in these cases is that the courts do not want to deter rescue and it has been held that a duty of care is owed to rescuers (*Chadwick* v *British Railways Board* [1967] 1 WLR 912).

Example

A's negligence has placed B in danger and C is injured in attempting a rescue of B. C sues A in negligence. Assume that a duty of care is owed by A to C as a rescue was reasonably foreseeable in the circumstances.

There are three possible 'defences' that A can raise to C's action.

He could argue that C's action in attempting a rescue was a novus actus interveniens *of the plaintiff which broke the chain of causation. A's negligence would not then be a cause of C's injuries. The court will apply a test of whether the plaintiff's rescue attempt was likely as a result of the breach of duty and whether the plaintiff acted reasonably.*

Alternatively, A could argue that in attempting a rescue C was volens *to the risk of injury. Because of the nature of rescue cases, the danger will usually have been created by the defendant's negligence before the plaintiff comes on the scene. If the view is taken (see volenti) that an agreement is necessary for volenti, then it will usually be inapplicable in rescue cases. The courts do not always take this view.*

Finally, A could attempt to prove that C was contributorily negligent in that his fault was a cause of his injuries.

The courts will generally be reluctant to invoke any of these defences to deny the rescuer compensation.

Haynes *v* Harwood [1935] 1 KB 146

A horse van was left unattended by the driver in an area with three schools. There were always a number of children in the street. A child threw a stone at the horse, which bolted. The plaintiff, a police officer, saw that highway users were in danger and tried to stop the horse. He suffered personal injuries. The court held that *volenti non fit injuria* did not succeed as a defence as the plaintiff did not exercise the freedom of choice which was necessary. (There is also a problem as to whether the defence applies where the plaintiff encounters an already existing danger.) There was no *novus actus interveniens* as what occurred was a likely result of the original breach of duty by the defendants.

Contrast this case with *Cutler* v *United Dairies* [1933] 2 KB 297. Here a horse had bolted into a field. Nobody was in any danger from the horse but the plaintiff entered the field and tried to calm the horse and was injured. The plaintiff was *volenti* as he had freedom of choice as to whether to attempt a rescue and there was a *novus actus interveniens* as the danger had passed.

Harrison *v* British Rail Board [1981] 3 All ER 679

The defendant attempted to board a moving train. The plaintiff guard saw the defendant on the outside of the train and gave the incorrect signal to the driver. It should have been a signal to stop but was the accelerate signal. The guard attempted to pull the defendant into the train but both fell out and the guard was injured. The court held that where a person places himself in danger and it is foreseeable that another person may attempt a rescue, the rescued person owes a duty of care to the rescuer. However, the defendant was found to have been contributorily negligent in pressing the wrong signal and his damages were reduced by 20%.

The court pointed out that it was rare that a rescuer would be found to be contributorily negligent.

This case supports the view expressed in *Baker* v *Hopkins* that a person who places himself in danger may owe a duty of care to a rescuer. If a climber ignores safety advice and a member of the mountain rescue team is injured attempting a rescue, that person could sue the climber for negligence.

Would a rescuer be denied an action on the ground of *ex turpi causa*, e.g. if one burglar was injured attempting to assist another who had been placed in danger by the dangerous condition of the house they were breaking into? (See *Pitts* v *Hunt* for possible tests.)

Part III
SPECIFIC AREAS OF NEGLIGENCE AND BREACH OF STATUTORY DUTY

10 | Defective premises

INTRODUCTION

A specialised area of negligence is provided by liability for defective premises. This chapter is divided into three parts. First, the liability of an occupier of the premises to a visitor or trespasser to the premises. Second, the liability of a landlord for defects in the premises. Finally, the liability of a person involved in the construction process.

OCCUPIER'S LIABILITY

Introduction

Liability in this area is governed by two statutes. Where the plaintiff was a visitor to the premises, the Occupiers' Liability Act 1957 applies. Where the plaintiff was a trespasser, the Occupiers' Liability Act 1984 will be applied. The fact that the law is statute based means that attention must be paid to the wording of the relevant sections in answering questions.

A common factor in either action is the defendant, who will be the occupier of the premises. There is no statutory definition of occupier so it is necessary to turn to the common law. The term occupier is rather misleading, as it is the person who controls the premises, rather than the physical occupier, who is responsible.

Wheat v E Lacon & Co Ltd [1966] AC 522

The defendants were the owners of a public house which was run by a manager and his wife, who had a licence to live on the first floor and to take in paying guests. The manager occupied the premises on the basis of being an employee rather than a tenant. A paying guest was killed when he tried to get to the bar on the first floor by an emergency staircase. The House of Lords considered who was the occupier. They held that it was both the manager and the owners. Lord Denning stated:

> Wherever a person has a sufficient degree of control over premises that he ought to realise that any failure on his part to use care may result in injury to a person coming lawfully there, then he is an occupier and the person coming lawfully there is his visitor.

Lord Denning identified four categories of occupier:

(a)   A landlord who lets premises. The landlord has parted with control of the premises so the tenant will be the occupier.

(b)   The landlord lets part of a building but retains other parts such as a common staircase. The landlord remains as occupier for the parts of the building he has retained.

(c)   Where a landowner licenses a person to use premises and the owner has a right to enter on the premises to do repairs, the owner retains control and is the occupier.

(d)   Where independent contractors are employed to do work on premises, the owner will generally retain sufficient control to be an occupier. It is possible that the contractors will also be occupiers. This will depend on the amount of control which they have while the work is in progress.

In the event neither the manager nor the owners were held to be in breach of duty. There had been a bulb on the staircase but this had been removed by a stranger, for whose actions the defendants were not responsible.

The case established that there can be more than one occupier of the same premises, although the duty required of each might be different: e.g. a seaside promenade might be under the control of a local authority and the water authority as part of the sea defences. If a person was injured by broken glass left there, the relevant occupier would be the local authority. If the injury was due to the state of repair of the structure, the water authority would be the relevant occupier.

An estate in land is not necessary in order to be an occupier and neither is physical possession. The key factor is whether a person exercised a sufficient degree of control.

Harris v Birkenhead Corporation [1976] 1 WLR 279

A local authority issued a compulsory purchase order on a house and a notice of entry which enabled them to take over the premises after 14 days. The house was not vacated for several months. When it was vacated no steps were taken to have it boarded up by the local authority. The plaintiff, a four year old child, entered the house through an unsecured door and fell from a second floor window. The Court of Appeal held that actual physical possession was not necessary for there to be control. The fact that the local authority had the legal right to control the premises made them occupiers to the exclusion of the previous owners of the house. The local authority was in the best position to avoid accidents.

Once the relevant occupier or occupiers have been identified the next stage is to ascertain the status of the plaintiff. If he is a lawful visitor it is necessary to go to the 1957 Act. If the plaintiff was a trespasser, then the 1984 Act is appropriate.

Occupier's liability to visitors

The scope of the Occupiers' Liability Act 1957

At this stage it is necessary to make three points about the scope of the Act.

(a)   A plaintiff may claim for personal injuries and damage to property. The scope of property includes property of persons who are not themselves visitors (s. 1(3)(b)):

(b)   Before the Act, the courts had drawn a distinction between the occupancy duty and the activity duty. The former was concerned with dangers due to the state of the premises. The latter with dangers created by the occupier's activities on his premises, such as driving a vehicle. In cases of occupancy duty the special rules on occupier's liability applied. For activity duty the ordinary rules of negligence applied.

It is not clear whether this distinction has survived the Act. Section 1(1) refers to dangers due to the state of the premises or things done or omitted to be done on them. This could be interpreted as meaning that the Act applies to the activity duty. However s. 1(2) refers to harm suffered, in consequence of a person's occupation or control of premises. This only appears to include the occupancy duty. There is no conclusive case on the point but in *Ogwo* v *Taylor* [1987] 2 WLR, Brown LJ (*obiter*) was of the opinion that where a fireman was injured fighting a fire at the defendant's premises, which was not due to a defect in the premises, the Act had no application.

The distinction is unlikely to make much difference, as once a duty has been found to exist, the standard of care will be the same, reasonable care in all the circumstances of the case.

(c)   The Act applies not only to land and buildings but also to fixed and moveable structures, including any vehicle or aircraft (s. 1(3)(a)). The Act has been held to apply to a digging machine used to construct a tunnel (*Bunker* v *Charles Brand & Son Ltd* [1969] 2 QB 480).

Who is a visitor?

The duty of care under the 1957 Act is owed to visitors (s. 1(2)). All lawful visitors to the premises are covered by this term. It includes invitees and licensees and those who have a contractual right to enter, where there is no express contractual duty of care (s. 5(1)). Where a person enters under a contractual right, the common duty of care under the Act will be implied into the contract, unless the contract expressly provides for a higher standard of care.

A person who enters under a right conferred by law is treated as a visitor, whether or not they have the occupier's express permission to enter (s. 2(6)). Policemen, firemen and employees of public utility companies may come into such a category provided they do not exceed their power of entry.

Three problem areas arise with visitors:

(a)   Rights of way

Persons who lawfully exercise a private right of way are not treated as visitors and are therefore not covered by the 1957 Act (*Holden* v *White* [1982] 2 WLR 1030). Such people are now covered by the Occupiers' Liability Act 1984, s. 1(1)(a) and will be owed a duty of care under that Act.

Persons exercising a public right of way are not treated as visitors (*Greenhalgh* v *British Railways Board* [1969] 2 QB 286). Neither are they covered by the 1984 Act, as s. 1(7) of that Act specifically excludes them. Any duty owed to such a person would therefore have to be at common law.

(b)   Implied permission

A person who claims that he had implied permission to enter premises must prove that there was such permission.

There is implied permission for a person to enter premises and state their business to the occupier. If the occupier then asks them to leave, they must be allowed a reasonable time to leave, after which they will become trespassers. Reasonable force may then be used to eject them. This presumption can be rebutted by the occupier putting up a notice specifically excluding certain types of person, such as salesmen and politicians.

When the occupier's duty to a trespasser was a limited one of not intentionally or recklessly injuring the trespasser, the concept of implied permission was an important one. The success or failure of the action would depend on whether the plaintiff was classed as a trespasser or not. In deserving cases the courts would sometimes find implied permission.

Lowery *v* Walker [1911] AC 10

People regularly used the defendant's unfenced land to take a short cut. The defendant had taken no serious steps to prevent them as most were his customers. The defendant then allowed a wild horse on his land, which attacked the plaintiff. The plaintiff was held to have implied permission and therefore was not a trespasser.

The court's willingness to find an implied licence or permission was particularly strong in the case of children, especially where there was something attractive to children on the land.

The passing of the Occupiers' Liability Act 1984 means that there should now be an insignificant number of cases where the court is asked to find implied permission. There is little difference, for example, between the position of a child trespasser whom the occupier knows to be present and a child visitor.

(c)   Limitations on permission

The occupier may place limitations on the permission to enter. A person who is allowed to enter one part of a building only, will become a trespasser if he enters another part 'When you invite a person into your house to use the stairs you do not invite him to slide down the bannisters' (*The Calgarth* [1927] P 93 per Scrutton LJ). However, any usage incidental to that permitted will be covered. A person entering a public house will be allowed to enter the toilet.

If a person is given permission to enter a building at a particular time, then entry at another time may render him a trespasser. This is a question of interpretation. A visitor to a public house who is asked to stay on for a private party by the landlord will remain a visitor.

Finally, a person who is given permission to enter for a particular purpose will be a trespasser if he enters for a different purpose. The decorator who is given the keys for the purpose of working, will be a trespasser if he lets himself in in the middle of the night to watch a video.

(d)   It is possible for a person to be visitor in relation to one occupier and a trespasser to another

Ferguson v Welsh [1987] 3 All ER 777

The council owned land and employed demolition contractors to do work there. The contractors sub-contracted the work to another firm. An employee of the sub-contractors was injured during the demolition work. The cause of the accident was held to be the unsafe system of work used by the plaintiff's employers rather than use of the premises. As the sub-contracting was unauthorised, the plaintiff could have been a trespasser to the council.

What is the duty?

The occupier of the premises owes a common duty of care to all lawful visitors to the premises. The duty is in s. 2(2) of the Act:

> The common duty of care is a duty to take such care as in all the circumstances of the case is reasonable to see that the visitor will be reasonably safe in using the premises for the purposes for which he is invited or permitted to be there.

Whether the duty has been broken is a question of fact in each case. The factors which are applicable to the standard of care in common law negligence are applicable. However, the section makes two things clear.

It is the visitor and not the premises that have to be reasonably safe. The circumstances of the particular visitor have to be taken into account.

The duty only extends to the purpose for which the visitor was allowed entry. The Act gives specific guidance on certain points in relation to the duty of care.

(a)   Children

Section 2(3)(a) states: 'An occupier must be prepared for children to be less careful than adults. If the occupier allows a child to enter the premises then the premises must be reasonably safe for a child of that age.'

Glasgow Corporation v Taylor [1922] 1 AC 44

The plaintiff aged seven died after eating poisonous berries from a tree in a public park. The tree was not fenced and no warning was given. The defendants were held liable. The danger was not obvious to a child of that age.

Very young children present a problem in that there may be a question as to whether their parents should have exercised supervision over them. In such cases it may come down to allocating liability beween the parents and the occupier.

Phipps v Rochester Corporation [1955] 1 QB 450

The five year old plaintiff was injured while out with his seven year old sister. He fell into a trench on land which was used by children as a play area. The defendants were aware of this but took no steps to keep the children out. The defendants were held not liable on the facts. The court stated that reasonable parents will not send their children into danger without protection and that both the parents and the occupier must act reasonably.

(b)   Persons entering in the exercise of a calling

Section 2(3)(b) states: 'An occupier may expect that a person, in the exercise of his calling, will appreciate and guard against any special risks ordinarily incident to it, so far as the occupier leaves him free to do so.'

Roles v Nathan [1963] 1 WLR 1117

Two chimney sweeps were killed by carbon monoxide gas while attempting to seal a sweep hole in the chimney of a boiler. The defendant occupiers were held not liable, as they could assume that sweeps would be aware of this particular danger and also because the sweeps had been warned of the danger. Lord Denning stated that the position would have been different if the stairs leading to the basement had given way. That would not have been a risk incidental to the trade of chimney sweep.

General Cleaning Contractors v Christmas [1953] AC 180

The occupier was held not liable to a window cleaner who was injured when a defective window closed suddenly, causing him to fall. Defective windows were a risk which window cleaners should guard against.

The plaintiff did recover against his employer for using an unsafe system of work. (See 'Employer's liability', p. 152.)

The fact that the visitor has a specific skill is not in itself sufficient to absolve the occupier where he has not exercised the requisite degree of care. Firemen who exercise reasonable care in attempting to extinguish a negligently started fire will be able to recover against the occupier, if they are injured in the process of extinguishing the fire (*Salmon* v *Seafarers Restaurant* [1983] 1 WLR 1264; *Ogwo* v *Taylor* [1988] 2 WLR 988).

(c)   Independent contractors

Section 2(4)(b) states:

> Where damage is caused to a visitor by a danger due to the faulty execution of any work of construction, maintenance or repair by an independent contractor employed by the occupier, the occupier is not to be treated without more as answerable for the danger if in all the circumstances he had acted reasonably in entrusting the work to an independent contractor and had taken such steps (if any) as he reasonably ought in order to satisfy himself that the contractor was competent and that the work had been properly done.

A number of points need to be made about this section, which was passed to reverse a common law rule, which placed an occupier under a non-delegable duty to certain types of entrant. This duty could not be discharged by entrusting the work to an independent contractor.

(i)   The facts of the case must come within the section, which only applies to, the 'faulty execution of . . . construction, maintenance or repair . . .' Where a case falls outside the section the common law rule will apply.

(ii)   It must be reasonable for the occupier to entrust the work to an independent contractor. The more technical the work is, the more likely it will be reasonable to do so. The occupier must also be looked at. If the occupier is a layman with no technical skill then most jobs will be reasonably entrusted to contractors. The situation might be different with occupiers such as local authorities.

(iii)   The occupier must take reasonable steps to check that the contractor was competent to carry out the work. A lay person would appear to be able to do little in this direction, except perhaps check with local trade associations. Large corporate bodies and local authorities may have to take more exhaustive steps.

(iv)   The occupier must take reasonable steps to check that the work has been properly done. With technical work, the appointment of a competent contractor may be sufficient to discharge the duty.

Haseldine v Daw [1941] 2 KB 343

The plaintiff was killed when a lift fell to the bottom of its shaft. The occupiers had appointed a normally competent firm of engineers to maintain the lift. In doing so they had discharged their duty of care. The technical nature of the work meant that they could not be expected to check it had been satisfactorily done.

Woodward v Mayor of Hastings [1945] KB 174

The plaintiff child slipped on a snow-covered step at a school. The step had been negligently cleaned by a cleaner. There was some doubt as to whether the cleaner was an independent contractor, but the occupiers were held liable as they had failed to take reasonable steps to check that the work had been reasonably done: 'The craft of the charwoman may have its mysteries but there is no esoteric quality in the nature of the work which the cleaning of a snow covered step demands.'

If the section bars the plaintiff from suing the occupier, he may still be able to proceed against the contractor, either as an occupier, or under the common law negligence rules.

(d)   Warnings

Section 2(4)(a) states:

> Where damage is caused to a visitor by a danger of which he has been warned by the occupier, the warning is not to be treated without more as absolving the occupier from liability, unless in all the circumstances it was enough to enable the visitor to be reasonably safe.

The legal effect of a sufficient warning under this section is to discharge any duty of care which might have been owed by the occupier.

The mere fact that a warning has been given will not be sufficient to absolve the occupier. The warning must enable the visitor to take reasonable care for his own safety.

An example was given by Lord Denning in *Roles* v *Nathan*. Where a house has a river in front of it and a bridge across the river with a sign saying the bridge is dangerous, this is not an adequate warning, as any visitor has no choice as to whether to use the bridge. If there were two bridges and one of them said 'Danger use other bridge', then a person injured using the dangerous bridge would have no claim.

Where the danger is not obvious, then the warning must indicate its nature in sufficient detail for the visitor to take reasonable care for his own safety. A simple notice saying 'Danger' will not discharge the duty.

Defences

(a)   *Volenti*

A defence of *volenti non fit injuria* is provided by s. 2(5). 'The common duty of care does not impose upon an occupier any obligation willingly accepted as his by the visitor.'

This defence is covered by the general principles of *volenti*. (See defences to negligence.) The plaintiff must act voluntarily, so any person who has no choice as to whether they enter premises is not *volenti*.

Knowledge of the danger does not amount to the defence.

(b)   Contributory negligence

This defence will apply in actions under the Act, and a visitor who has failed to use reasonable care for his own safety and that failure was a cause of his damage will have his damages reduced. Section 2(3) provides that in considering the common duty of care, the circumstances include the degree of care and want of care which would ordinarily be looked for in such a visitor.

(c)   Exclusion

Section 2(1) states:

> An occupier of premises owes the same duty, the 'common duty of care' to all his visitors, except in so far as he is free to and does extend, restrict, modify or exclude his duty to any visitor or visitors by agreement or otherwise.

The reference to agreement or otherwise, means that the duty can be excluded etc. by means of a contract term or by a notice communicated to the visitor.

There are certain restrictions on the occupier's freedom to exclude etc.

(i)   The Unfair Contract Terms Act 1977. The Act will apply where the premises are being used for business purposes as defined in s. 1(3). It is the purpose that the premises are being used for, rather than the purpose of the visitor, that is important. Business will include professions, government and local authority activities. It does not include the granting of access for recreational or educational purposes, unless the granting of such access falls within the business purposes of the occupier (Occupiers' Liability Act 1984, s. 2).

The occupier cannot exclude liability for death or personal injuries caused by negligence (s. 2(1)). Any attempt to exclude liability for property damage will be subjected to a test of reasonableness (s. 2(2)).

The fact that a person was aware of an exclusionary term or notice does not in itself mean that he has voluntarily accepted the risk (*s. 2(3)*).

Example

Alan is a sales representative for a company. As part of his job he is required to visit building sites. He enters a site occupied by Bob. There is a notice on the gate which says: 'Danger, building sites are dangerous places. The occupier accepts no liability for injuries suffered by visitors or for damage to their property.' While on the site, a wall collapses on Alan, causing him injuries and damaging his car.

This notice could take effect in three ways. First, as a warning discharging the duty of care. As it fails to enable Alan to take reasonable care for his own safety it will not have this effect.

Secondly, to exclude the common duty of care. As Bob is using the premises for business purposes, the Unfair Contract Terms Act will apply. Section 2(1) means that the notice will fail to exclude Bob's liability for Alan's personal injuries. As regards Bob's liability for the damage to Alan's car, the exclusionary notice would be subjected to a reasonableness test.

Finally, if Bob claims that Alan was volenti *to the risk. The Unfair Contract Terms Act 1977, s. 2(3) will prevent any claim that Alan's awareness of the attempted exclusion rendered him* volens *to the risk. As Alan had to enter the site as part of his job, he lacked the necessary degree of voluntariness necessary for the defence.*

(ii)   It may not be possible for the occupier to exclude liability to a person who enters under a right conferred by law.

(iii)   If it is correct that the duty owed to trespassers is a minimum standard which cannot be excluded, then this minimum standard cannot be excluded against visitors. (See 'Liability to trespassers', p. 119.)

(iv) Section 3(1) provides that where an occupier is bound by contract to permit strangers to the contract to enter or use the premises, the duty of care owed to the stranger as a visitor cannot be restricted or excluded by the contract. A landlord who retains control over common parts of a building such as the stairs and puts an exclusion clause in the lease, cannot exclude liability to the tenant's visitors by virtue of this clause.

Liability to trespassers

Introduction

A trespasser is a person who goes onto land without an invitation of any sort and whose presence there is either unknown to the occupier, or if known, is objected to.

The common law was traditionally hostile to trespassers. The original duty owed was the basic one of not intentionally or recklessly injuring a trespasser known to be present (*Addie* v *Dumbreck Collieries* [1929] AC 358). This remained the law until 1972. The judiciary were forced to resort to legal fictions such as implied licences and allurements to turn trespassers into visitors in deserving cases, mainly involving children.

In *British Railways Board* v *Herrington* [1972] AC 877, the House of Lords introduced a new duty. The occupier owed a duty of common humanity to a trespasser known to be present. The duty was a subjective one, as in considering whether it had been broken, the court had to take account of the resources of the occupier.

The *Herrington* decision was subjected to a certain amount of criticism and was referred to the Law Commission, whose report (Law Commission No 75, Cmnd 6428) formed the basis of the Occupiers' Liability Act 1984.

The law on trespassers presents certain difficulties. To what extent should the occupier be aware of the presence of the trespasser? How can a distinction be made between trespassers of differing degrees of culpability, such as burglars and stray children? What standard of care should be owed and which defences should be applied? The Act attempts to answer these problems.

Scope of the Occupiers' Liability Act 1984

The Act will apply to persons other than visitors (s. 1(1)(a)). This covers trespassers; persons entering land under an access agreement or order under the National Parks and Access to the Countryside Act 1949; persons lawfully exercising a lawful right of way. The rest of this section will concentrate on the occupier's liability to trespassers.

The Act will apply in respect of any risk of their suffering injury on the premises by reason of any danger due to the state of the premises or to things done or omitted to be done on them (s. 1(1)(a)). The Act will therefore apply to the activity duty as well as the occupancy duty.

When is a duty owed?

Once the relationship of occupier and visitor is established, the occupier owes the common duty of care to the visitor. Once the relationship of occupier and trespasser is established, there is not automatically a duty. It is necessary to apply s. 1(3) which states:

> An occupier of premises owes a duty to another (not being his visitor) in respect of any such risk as is referred to in subsection (1) if –
> (a) he is aware of the danger or has reasonable grounds to believe it exists;
> (b) he knows or has reasonable grounds to believe that the other is in the vicinity of the danger concerned or that he may come into the vicinity of the danger (in either case whether the other has lawful authority for being in that vicinity or not); and
> (c) the risk is one against which, in all the circumstances of the case, he may reasonably be expected to offer the other some protection.

This section poses some problems. (c) is objective but (a) and (b) may be subjective. If the test is objective, then it is based on the beliefs of the reasonable occupier. If it is subjective, then it is based on the beliefs of the defendant.

A likely interpretation is that knowledge of the primary facts is subjective. Once it is established what the defendant knew, then the inference to be drawn from these primary facts is objective. Would a reasonable occupier have drawn the inference that there was a danger and that the presence of the trespasser was likely. This would mean that there is no duty on the occupier to inspect his premises for dangers or trespassers.

The content of the duty

Section 1(4) states that the duty is: 'to take such care as is reasonable in all the circumstances of the case to see that he does not suffer injury on the premises by reason of the danger concerned'.

This is the usual objective negligence standard. Unfortunately, the division of the test into whether a duty exists and whether it has been broken, means that the court will have to consider similar factors for both. The factors will be the age of the entrant, the nature of the premises, the extent of the risk and the practicability of precautions.

The Occupiers' Liability (Scotland) Act 1960 took the approach of imposing a duty of care on occupiers to all entrants. The standard of care varied according to the nature of the entrant. When Parliament was considering the 1984 Act they were only concerned with trespassers. The decision to split the test may have been a political one. The word trespasser has anti-social connotations, and to say that a duty was automatically owed to a trespasser but qualified by the standard, may have been too sophisticated.

The key factor would appear to be the age of the entrant. Between 1972 and 1984 there was no case where an adult trespasser succeeded. The rules on warnings and *volenti* give an indication why.

Warnings

Section 1(5) states:

> Any duty owed by virtue of this section in respect of a risk may, in an appropriate case, be discharged by taking such steps as are reasonable in all the circumstances of the case to give warning of the danger concerned or to discourage persons from incurring the risk.

Whether such a warning will discharge the duty of care will depend on the age of the entrant. In the case of an adult, a warning notice will normally discharge the duty. Almost any notice will be sufficient. With children there is a problem of their not appreciating the danger, or not being able to read. If the occupier has reason to anticipate the presence of a child trespasser he would do well to erect an obstacle to entry that is not in itself dangerous.

Volenti non fit injuria

Section 1(6) states:

> No duty is owed by virtue of this section to any person in respect of risks willingly accepted as his by that person (the question of whether a risk was so accepted to be decided on the same principles as in other cases in which one person owes a duty of care to another).

In the case of trespassers the courts have adopted an objective rather than a subjective test of agreement. Where the plaintiff is an adult, then knowledge of the risk accompanied by entry on the land will render the plaintiff *volenti* (*Titchener* v *British Railways Board* [1983] 3 All ER 770).

If this principle applies to the 1984 Act then it would mean that the defence of *volenti* will vary according to the category of entry. In the case of visitors, knowledge of risk plus entry is not sufficient to amount to *volenti*. The visitor must know enough to be reasonably safe.

Exclusion

The 1984 Act is silent on the question of exclusion, which means that any duty owed may or may not be excludable. There are three points in favour of any duty being unexcludable.

The Unfair Contract Terms Act 1977 does not apply to the 1984 Act as it only has application to common law duties and the statutory duty under the 1957 Act.

It was thought that the common law duty to trespassers was unexcludable as a minimum standard below which the law would not go. If this was the case and that principle was carried forward to the Act then the duty under the Act would be unexcludable. Against this is the fact that the standard under the Act is reasonable care, the normal negligence standard, whereas the common law duty was a lower one of common humanity.

The 1957 Act has specific provisions on its excludability whereas the 1984 Act is silent.

If the duty were held to be unexcludable, this would have the odd effect that a trespasser to premises not in business use could be better off than a visitor. The occupier could exclude his duty to the visitor but not to the trespasser.

Example

Charles is the owner of a piece of waste ground adjacent to his house. He has used the waste ground to dump old cars, which he intends to renovate. The waste ground is separated from a park by some old fencing which is in need of repair. Charles, who has just failed the first year of a law degree and is hard up, put up a notice on the fence: 'Danger – Keep Out – No Liability Accepted.'

Damian, an adult, entered the waste ground through a hole in the fence, intending to burgle Charles' house. On his way across the waste ground he tripped over some rusty car parts and was injured. His action would be determined by whether a duty was owed. One does not normally anticipate the presence of a burglar. If a duty was held to be owed, then it would probably be discharged by the warning notice. In any event Damian would probably be volenti *or the court could apply the maxim* ex turpi causa.

Elvis, an eight year old, entered the waste ground by a hole in the fence to explore. He was injured by drinking petrol from a can left in the boot of one of the cars. The court would have to consider whether a duty was owed. The key factor would be whether the presence of the trespasser should have been anticipated by Charles. Warning and volenti *would not appear to have any chance of success in this case. If the duty is unexcludable Elvis would appear to have a good chance of success.*

Floella, the child of an ex-friend of Charles, was left in Charles's care. She wandered into the waste ground to play and was injured by rusty metal. Floella is a visitor and would be owed the common duty of care. It appears likely on the facts that the duty would be broken. But if Floella's parents were aware of the notice, would Charles have succeeded in excluding liability?

LANDLORD'S LIABILITY

Introduction

The liability of a landlord to a person injured as a result of defective premises is complex. The tenant may have a remedy in contract based on the lease if he is injured and the landlord has broken a covenant to repair.

The landlord could be an occupier of part of the premises and be liable under the Occupier's Liability Acts. (See 'Occupier's liability', pp. 107–9, for the test for occupier.)

Normally the landlord will part with control of the premises after the lease and no occupier's liability action will be possible against him.

The common law was opposed to actions in tort and the landlord was immune from a tort action in respect of dangerous premises (*Cavalier* v *Pope* [1906] AC 428).

Liability in negligence

The immunity of a landlord from actions in negligence was confirmed by the Court of Appeal in 1984.

Rimmer *v* Liverpool City Council [1984] 1 All ER 930

The plaintiff was a tenant in a council flat designed and built by the defendants. He put his hand through a glass panel and was injured. He sued the council for letting a flat with a dangerous feature. It was held that there was no duty of care on landlords to ensure that premises were reasonably safe at the time of the letting.

It was held that the defendants owed a duty of care as designers and builders of the flat and were liable under that head.

Statutory liability

The Defective Premises Act 1972 contains two provisions in relation to the landlord's position.

Section 3

Section 3 states:

> Where work of construction, repair, maintenance or demolition or any other work is done on or in relation to premises, any duty of care owed, because of the doing of the work, to persons who might reasonably be expected to be affected by defects in the state of the premises created by the doing of the work shall not be abated by subsequent disposal of the premises by the person who owed the duty.

This section does no more than restate the common law position and could be considered superfluous. It does not apply to a failure to do work or to work carried out after the letting.

Section 4

Of more practical importance is s. 4.

> (1) Where premises are let under a tenancy which puts on the landlord an obligation to the tenant for the maintenance or repair of the premises, the landlord owes to all persons who might reasonably be expected to be affected by defects in the state of the premises a duty to take such care as is reasonable in all the circumstances to see that they are reasonably safe from personal injury or from damage to their property caused by a relevant defect.

(2) The said duty is owed if the landlord knows (whether as the result of being notified by the tenant or otherwise) or if he ought in all the circumstances to have known of the relevant defect.

For this section to apply, the landlord must be under an obligation to the tenant for the maintenance or repair of the premises, or he must have an express or implied right or power to enter the premises to carry out any description of maintenance or repair. The obligation may arise from an express term in the lease or may be implied by statute: e.g. the Landlord and Tenant Act 1985, ss. 11 and 12, which require the landlord to repair the exterior and structure of premises, where the lease of a dwelling house is for less than seven years. This provision cannot be contracted out of.

The duty will be owed where the landlord knows, or ought to have known, of a defect which would constitute a breach of his obligation to the tenant to repair the premises.

The duty will be owed to the tenant, residents, neighbours and passers-by on the highway. Whether a trespasser would be a foreseeable plaintiff is not known.

It should be noted that in the case of injury to neighbours and highway users there is an overlap between this section and the law of nuisance. (See 'Nuisance', p. 180.)

Example

Albert let a dwelling house on a monthly tenancy to Brenda. Due to high winds the chimney stack became unsafe. Brenda pointed this out to Albert, who took no remedial action. The chimney collapsed and fell to the ground.

Part of the chimney fell through the roof and injured Carol, Brenda's daughter. Albert is under a statutory obligation to repair the structure. He was aware of the need for repair and did nothing. He is therefore in breach of s. 4 and Carol would have an action under this section.

Donald was sitting in a deck chair in his garden next door, when part of the chimney fell on him. He would have an action under s. 4 and in private nuisance.

Edith was walking on the highway outside the house when she was injured. Edith would have an action under s. 4 and an action in public nuisance.

BUILDER'S LIABILITY

Introduction

The expression builder is used in the sense of all persons involved in the construction and sale of buildings. This includes developers, builders, sub-contractors, architects, surveyors, civil engineers and local authorities.

In a typical example, the land will be bought by a development company; a geological survey done by surveyors; plans drawn up by architects; the plans submitted to the local authority for approval and to check that they comply with the Building Regulations, which lay down minimum standards for public health and safety; a builder engaged to construct the houses, who may sub-contract certain aspects of the work to specialist firms. The builder and the development company may be the same entity. Each house will then be sold to a purchaser, (P1) who after a number of years may sell it to another purchaser (P2).

The house may show a defect a number of years after construction. A recurring problem is cracks caused by the fact that the foundations were of the wrong depth or made from the wrong materials. The house needs remedial action to make it safe, but who has to bear the cost of this work? If no work is done, then the house will eventually collapse and may cause personal injuries to the occupants.

Take an example. The house was built by B and completed in 1987. The plans were approved and work in progress inspected by LA. In 1987 the house was sold to P1. In 1989 P1 sold the house to P2. In 1990 a crack appeared in one of the walls. An engineer's report states that the foundations are defective and that the house will need underpinning and the foundations repaired. The cost of this work is £30,000.

What category does the damage fall into: physical damage or economic loss? The courts have taken the view that this is economic loss. If, for example, the house had collapsed and damaged an adjacent property, the damage to the adjacent property would be classed as physical damage, damage to *other* property.

In practical terms P2's most important protection would be the National House Building Council Scheme. This scheme applies to registered builders and developers. A purchaser of such a house obtains a House Purchaser's Agreement from the vendor. This provides that the house will be built in an efficient and workmanlike manner, with proper materials and be fit for human habitation. The vendor agrees to remedy any defects at his own expense in the first two years, where the defect arises from a breach of NHBC standards. Any major damage to the building which occurs within ten years is covered by an insurance policy. The agreement can be transferred with the house. If the house is covered by the scheme, then P2 may be able to have the work done on this basis.

If not, what legal remedies does P2 have? The diagram sets out the situation.

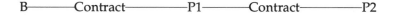

B————Contract————P1————Contract————P2

It can be seen that any contractual remedy that P2 has would be against P1. However, private sales of houses are subject to the doctrine of *caveat emptor* (let the buyer beware). P1 is not under a contractual duty to tell P2 of any defects he is aware of, unless P2 specifically asks. The defect in any case may not have been known at the time of the sale. The chances are that P2 will have no contract action against P1.

As P2 is not in privity of contract with B, he has no contract action against him. This leaves two possibilities.

Statutory liability

Parliament created a limited form of protection from builders with the Defective Premises Act 1972.

Section 1(1) imposes on builders, sub-contractors, architects and other professional persons a three part duty: that the work will be done in a workmanlike manner, proper materials will be used, and the house will be fit for human habitation.

The duty only applies in respect of dwellings and does not apply to commercial or industrial properties.

The duty is owed to the person to whose order the building is provided and to every person who acquires an interest in the dwelling. This means that the doctrine of privity of contract does not apply, and P2 in the example would have a theoretical claim against B.

Liability under the section is strict, in the sense that fault does not have to be proved against the builder. The duty cannot be excluded.

The limitation period is for six years from the date on which the dwelling was completed. P2 would therefore have until 1993 to commence proceedings under the section. In many cases of defective buildings, however, the defect does not become apparent until many years after the building was completed. By the time the occupier realises that there is an action he is statute barred.

The major drawback with the section is that it does not apply where the dwelling is protected by an NHBC scheme (s. 2). As the scheme applies to nearly all new dwellings, the Act is usually limited to alterations and conversions. If the house in the example was covered by the scheme, P2 would have no action under the section.

The Court of Appeal has recently held that the section applies to nonfeasance as well as misfeasance (*Andrews* v *Schooling* [1991] 3 All ER 723). A failure to carry out necessary work would give rise to liability. If the dwelling was without some necessary attribute such as a damp course or a roof, then it would be unfit for habitation, even though the problems resulting from the lack of the attribute had not then become apparent.

Negligence liability

In the 1970s the courts embarked on a massive extension of the builder's liability in negligence. They created a duty of care imposed on builders and owed to foreseeable victims of their negligence. As the loss to an owner-occupier was economic loss, the courts sidestepped the problems this presented by framing the duty in terms of not constructing a building which was a danger to the health and safety of the occupier (*Anns* v *Merton London Borough Council* [1978] AC 728).

In the example, P2 would have had a negligence action against B. The measure of damages would have been the amount required to make the house safe for occupation, i.e. £30,000. As the building trade is notoriously unstable financially and B might have gone out of business, many actions were brought against local authorities for negligently approving plans or negligent inspection of houses under construction.

From about 1983 the courts started to rein back the development they had unleashed. The specific reasons for this are not known but are connected with the wider trend of not allowing claims for economic loss in negligence actions. The courts may also have been influenced by the rising premiums which had to be paid by anyone involved in the construction of buildings. This rise was a result of successful actions being brought under the negligence principle.

The retrenchment by the courts took place in two House of Lords cases but it is unlikely that the problem has been solved.

D & F Estates Ltd v Church Commissioners for England [1988] 2 All ER 992

A firm of builders undertook construction work on a block of flats and sub-contracted the plastering work, which was carried out negligently. The result was that 15 years later the plaster was loose and needed replacement. The plaintiffs, who were lessees and occupiers of a flat in the block, sued the builders for the cost of remedial work already performed and the cost of future remedial work.

The House of Lords held that in the absence of a contractual relationship between the parties, the cost of repairing a defect in the structure, which was discovered before the defect had caused personal injury or physical damage to other property, was not recoverable in a negligence action. The cost of doing the repairs was economic loss which was not recoverable in a negligence action, except within the *Hedley Byrne* principle, or on the unique proximity of *Junior Books* v *Veitchi*.

A number of doubts were left by this decision. The idea of a complex structure was introduced. If the building is regarded as a complex structure, then damage to one part of the structure, caused by a hidden defect in another part, could be treated as damage to other property. The position of local authorities was also left unclear until the next case, which represents the present law.

Murphy v Brentwood District Council [1990] 2 All ER 908

The plaintiff purchased a pair of semi-detached houses from a construction company. The houses had been built on a concrete raft on an infilled site. The raft was defective and settlement occurred causing serious cracks to appear in the houses. It was alleged that the defendant council had negligently approved plans for the construction of the raft. The plaintiff's case was based on the argument that repair was necessary in order to avert a present or imminent danger to the health or safety of the occupant. Gas and drainage pipes had broken as a result of the settlement and there was a risk of further breaks.

The House of Lords held that the council was not liable for the plaintiff's loss, which was economic and not within the accepted categories.

The decision is logical, in the sense that it places local authorities in the same position as other builders. They are not liable in negligence for the cost of remedial measures caused by a defect in the building's construction.

The House considered the complex structure point in *D & F Estates*. They considered that a building or product cannot be regarded as a complex structure if it has been wholly constructed or manufactured by one person, so as to form a single indivisible unit. The idea of a complex structure can be applied to equipment manufactured by different suppliers, e.g. central heating boilers.

A number of points remain unclear after the decision.

(a)   Whether a local authority is liable for breach of statutory duty and to what extent.

(b)   Whether the local authority will be liable for personal injury or property damage suffered by occupiers of houses which have been inspected and the Building Regulations not complied with.

The decision has since been applied in *Department of the Environment* v *Thomas Bates & Son Ltd* [1990] 2 All ER 943.

In the example, neither B nor the local authority would be liable in negligence for the cost of repair to P2's house. The cost of remedying the defect is economic loss and neither party owes a duty of care to P2 in that respect.

QUESTION

Peabody Park is owned and maintained by the Peabody Trust. Admission to the public is granted on payment of 50 pence. This done by placing a 50 pence piece in a ticket dispensing machine. Each ticket bears the words: 'For conditions of entry see notice in Park office.' The conditions referred to include the clause: 'The Trust shall not be liable for damage to visitors or their property whether caused by negligence or otherwise.'

Bertram paid his 50 pence and entered the park. He was badly injured when a rowing boat, which he took on the lake sank, because it had not been properly maintained by the Trust.

Clarence entered the park at the request of the Trust to repair the gas cooker in the cafeteria. He suffered personal injuries when the cooker exploded.

Dick, an eight year old boy, entered the park through a hole in the fence, after the park had closed. He was attracted by some bright red berries on a bush. The berries were poisonous and a notice to this effect was attached to the bush. Dick suffered personal injuries after eating the berries.

Advise Bertram, Clarence and Dick as to their legal position.

Suggested approach

This question is on occupier's liability for defective premises. Although an area of negligence, liability is governed by statute, the Occupiers' Liability Acts 1957 and 1984.

Liability in such case falls on the occupier of the premises. This term is not defined by either Act and was considered by the House of Lords in *Wheat* v *Lacon* (1966). In order to be an occupier a person had to have sufficient control over the premises. In this case the Peabody Trust will be the occupier.

In order to determine which Act is applicable it is necessary to determine the status of the plaintiff. If the plaintiff is a visitor, then the 1957 Act will apply. If the plaintiff is a trespasser, the 1984 Act. Bertram and Clarence would be classed as visitors as they come lawfully onto the land. Dick is a trespasser, as the occupier was unaware of his presence and if he had known of his presence, would have objected to it.

As Bertram is a visitor, the Trust will owe him the common duty of care under s. 2(2) of the 1957 Act. This is a duty to take reasonable care for the visitor's safety for the purposes for which he was permitted to be there. Bertram is also a contractual entrant. If the contract is silent as to the duty owed to the visitor, then the common duty of care in the Act will apply.

Prior to the Act the courts had drawn a distinction between the occupancy duty, which was concerned with dangers due to the state of the premises, and the activity duty, which was concerned with the occupier's activities on his premises. Is a rowing boat within the occupancy or the activity duty? There is no clear case as to whether the Act applies to the activity duty. However, s. 1(3)(a) states that the Act applies to fixed and moveable structures, this could include a rowing boat. Bertram might be well advised to bring his action in the alternative, under the Act and in common law negligence.

What effect would the notice on the ticket have? As Bertram is a contractual entrant, any terms of the contract would have to be brought to his attention at or before, the time when the contract is made. This would be when the money was placed in the ticket machine. It would appear that the Trust have failed to include the notice in the machine as a term of the contract (*Thornton* v *Shoe Lane Parking*). If they have, what is the effect of the term? It attempts to exclude liability. Would the Unfair Contract Terms Act 1977 apply? This would depend on an interpretation of s. 1(3). Are the premises being used for business purposes? If they are then the Act will apply. Under s. 2(1) liability for death or personal injuries caused by negligence cannot be excluded. The notice does not appear to operate as a warning and neither could it raise the defence of *volenti non fit injuria* (Unfair Contract Terms Act 1977, s. 2(3)).

As Bertram is owed a duty of care, the Trust would appear to be in breach of duty by failing to maintain the boat, and Bertram has suffered damage as a result. Bertram would appear to have an action.

Clarence is also a visitor to the premises and is owed the common duty of care. Section 2(3)(a) of the 1957 Act provides that where a person enters in the exercise of his calling, the occupier may expect that that person will appreciate and guard against risks which are ordinarily incident to that calling (*Roles* v *Nathan* and *General Cleaning Contractors* v *Christmas*). However, the fact that a person has a specific skill will not absolve an occupier who has not exercised a sufficient degree of care (*Ogwo* v *Taylor*). Liability in this case would depend on why the cooker exploded. If Clarence had lit a cigarette and that caused the explosion, then the Trust would be under no liability. But if Clarence had exercised reasonable care, the court would have to decide whether the Trust were at fault.

Dick is a trespasser and any duty owed would be under the 1984 Act. The fact that the relationship of occupier-trespasser is established does not establish a duty of care. It is necessary to apply s. 1(3) of the Act. If the plaintiff satisfies these three requirements then a duty will be owed. (NB in an examination a student would be expected to set out and apply these requirements.) If a duty is owed, the court would have to determine whether there had been a breach. The standard of care is the usual negligence one of reasonable care (s. 1(4)).

Would the notice displayed next to the berries suffice as a warning within s. 1(5)? This would appear to depend upon the age of the trespasser. If a duty had been held to be owed to Dick then the occupier had cause to appreciate the presence of the child and the premises would have to be reasonably safe for a child trespasser and an obstacle to entry erected. Although the case is similar on the facts to *Glasgow Corpn* v *Taylor*, the approach on the statute might be different from the old common law approach. What may be important is how Dick got into the park and whether reasonable steps were taken to prevent this.

Further reading

Occupier's liability
Buckley, R (1984) Conv 413
Jones, M (1984) 47 MLR 713
Mesher, J [1979] Conv 58
North, P M Occupiers' Liability (1971)

Builder's liability
Cooke, R (1991) 107 LQR 46
Spencer, J [1974] CLJ 307; [1975] CLJ 48
Wallace, I D (1991) 107 LQR 228

11 | Defective products

INTRODUCTION

After a product is manufactured and put into circulation liability is governed primarily by the chain of contracts between the manufacturer and the ultimate user.

Manufacturer———Wholesaler———Retailer———Purchaser – – – – Donnee

Example

Alice bought a hot water bottle from a retailer which did not give off any heat. The product is defective in the sense that is not of the standard that Alice expected. Alice would have an action for breach of contract against the retailer and could utilise the Sale of Goods Act 1979, ss. 14(2) and 14(3). The product is not of merchantable quality and it is not fit for the purpose for which it was sold.

The retailer in turn would have an action for breach of contract against the wholesaler and the wholesaler against the manufacturer. The loss would then be carried by the person responsible for the defect.

This theory has two problems which arise when the chain of contracts breaks down.

First, if the retailer became insolvent, then Alice would have no contractual remedy. Similarly, any insolvency along the chain would destroy the particular contract action. Further up the chain there may be an exclusion clause which would prevent any contract action. The manufacturer may have sold to the wholesaler on the basis that he would not be responsible for any claims for defective quality.

Second, if Alice gave the hot water bottle to Bert as a present, then Bert would be a donnee and have no contract with anyone. This was the position of the plaintiff in Donoghue v Stevenson.

So far we have looked at the defectiveness of the product. What would be the position if the product was dangerous rather then merely defective. If Alice or Bert filled it with hot water and it leaked causing injury, would either of them have an action? The modern position is that they may have an action for negligence, or under the Consumer Protection Act 1987.

Looking at the claims in terms of types of damage. A claim that the product is not as good as the purchaser expected is a claim for economic loss, which traditionally should be brought in contract. A claim that the product is dangerous and has caused personal injuries or damage to other property (i.e. other than the product itself) is a claim for physical damage and can be brought in either contract, tort or under statute.

Prior to 1932 the courts refused to allow the chain of contracts to be disturbed by tort actions. The view was that people ordered their affairs on the basis of their contractual liability and to allow a third party to sue in tort would upset this arrangement. This was the privity fallacy (see 'Duty of Care', p. 28). Developments before 1932 were limited to where the product was dangerous in itself or where the danger was actually known to the transferor. In *Donoghue* v *Stevenson* in 1932 the House of Lords shaped a general theory of manufacturer's liability in tort for products. This is known as the narrow rule.

The tortious principle gives protection to the ultimate consumer of a product where the product has caused physical damage. The action lies against the manufacturer of the product where he has been negligent. Generally speaking, there is no tort action where the product is merely defective and has not caused any physical damage.

In the example, no claim in tort would lie if the hot water bottle did not give off enough heat. A claim would lie for scalded feet. Either Alice or Bert could bring such a claim if they suffered damage.

The common law was perceived to have certain defects and there was pressure from the EEC to harmonise consumer safety law across the Community. This resulted in the passing of the Consumer Protection Act 1987 which introduces a strict liability regime for defective products.

A consumer who suffers physical damage from a defective product now has a choice between the common law and the statutory actions.

THE NARROW RULE IN *DONOGHUE* v *STEVENSON*

Introduction

Lord Atkin laid down the narrow rule in *Donoghue* v *Stevenson* [1932] AC 562:

> A manufacturer of products, which he sells in such a form as to show that he intends them to reach the ultimate consumer in the form in which they left him with no reasonable possibility of intermediate examination, and with the knowledge that the absence of reasonable care in the preparation or putting up of the products will result in

an injury to the consumer's life or property, owes a duty to the consumer to take reasonable care.

This quotation sets out all the points required for an action. The relevant points will be looked at in turn.

Who owes the duty?

The duty is owed by manufacturers. This expression has been widely interpreted by the courts as meaning anyone responsible for putting into circulation a product which is not reasonably safe. It has therefore been applied to manufacturers in the conventional sense: retailers, wholesalers, repairers of products (such as garages), assemblers and those who hire and lease goods. It might appear strange to classify a retailer as a manufacturer but this will only happen where he is under a duty to inspect the goods and fails to do so.

It would also appear that the rule applies to realty and could be applied to the builder of a house and possibly a local authority building inspector.

A duty to whom?

The duty is owed to consumers. The consumer is anyone whom the manufacturer should foresee would be affected by the product. This will include purchasers, donnees, borrowers, employees of a purchaser and bystanders who happen to be injured.

Stennett v Hancock [1939] 2 All ER 578

The plaintiff pedestrian was struck on the leg by a part of the wheel of the defendant's lorry, which came off as it was being driven along the road. The defendants had repaired the wheel shortly before the accident and were held to be manufacturers. As the repair had been carried out negligently and the plaintiff was a consumer, the action succeeded.

Products

The original rule applied to food and drink but has now been extended to cover all manufactured products. It has been held to cover motor vehicles, lifts, clothes, cleaning fluids and buildings. The rule extends to the packaging in which the goods are supplied.

Breach of duty

The plaintiff must prove that the manufacturer failed to take reasonable care in the preparation or putting up of the product.

In practice this will mean identifying a breakdown in the production process, failure to give adequate instructions for use or a defective design. Problems with the production process may be demonstrated by showing an impurity which should have been removed before the product was put into circulation.

Grant *v* Australia Knitting Mills Ltd [1936] AC 85

The plaintiff contracted dermatitis because of excessive sulphites in underwear manufactured by the defendants. The sulphites had been negligently left in the underwear by the defendants during the manufacturing process, although they could not have been detected by any reasonable examination. The defendants were held liable in negligence. It was important that the underwear was intended to be worn as supplied and no instructions to wash before using were given.

Alternatively the plaintiff may complain that the product was in itself inadequately constructed. If a car manufacturer becomes aware of a significant number of a particular fault on one of its models, then a failure to recall the cars for a check may amount to negligence (*Walton* v *British Leyland* (1978)).

Design defects may pose more serious problems. If the manufacturer is producing at the limits of scientific knowledge, then he may not be able to foresee injury being caused by his product. This is particularly acute with the development of new drugs, as adverse side effects may not be foreseeable.

The product must be supplied with instructions for use and adequate warning of any known danger. If a warning has been given, then on causation grounds this may mean some other person is liable. Typical examples of instructions and warnings can be found on household paints. The consumer will be informed to keep the product away from his eyes but if it does get in the eyes, to wash them out and seek medical advice.

Proof of negligence

The burden of proof is on the plaintiff to establish that the product was defective, that the injury was caused by that defect, and that the injury was caused by the manufacturer's lack of reasonable care.

This may appear to place a heavy burden on the plaintiff but it has been held that he does not have to identify the exact person responsible for the defect (*Grant* v *Australian Knitting Mills*). Negligence may be inferred from the fact that the product left the manufacturer in a defective state. This leaves the manufacturer with the problem of proving that his employees were not negligent and that he was using a safe system. This appears to be very close to the doctrine of *res ipsa loquitur*.

Causation

Causation in defective product cases works on the basis of showing that the goods were intended to reach the consumer in the form in which they left the manufacturer (alternative cause) and that there was no reasonable possibility of intermediate examination.

(a)   Alternative cause

The manufacturer is only liable for damage caused by his own negligence. If another person in the chain of distribution or natural wear and tear has caused the defect, then the manufacturer will be not liable.

It is important that the product reaches the plaintiff in the same form that it left the manufacturer. This is not to be taken literally. The product does not have to remain in the packaging and the mere possibility of someone having tampered with the goods is not sufficient to exonerate the defendant. If the product has been assembled, checked or altered, then this may provide an alternative explanation for the defect.

Evans v Triplex Glass Co Ltd [1936] 1 All ER 283

The plaintiff bought a car fitted with a windscreen made by the defendants. One year later the windscreen shattered and injured passengers in the car. It was held that the plaintiff had to show it was more probable than not that the injury was due to faulty manufacture. He was unable to do this as it was possible that the cause of the defect was faulty fitting.

(b)   Intermediate examination

Where it is reasonable to expect someone to inspect the goods before they are used, the manufacturer may not be regarded as the cause of the damage. If the goods were examined and the defect was negligently not identified, this makes the examiner a cause of the damage. It is not sufficient that someone had an opportunity to examine the goods, it must be shown that the manufacturer could reasonably expect that person to make an examination. For example, it would not be reasonable for a manufacturer to expect that a person would wash underwear before using it.

Griffiths v Arch Engineering Co [1968] 3 All ER 217

The first defendants lent a grinding tool owned by the second defendants to the plaintiff. An employee of the second defendant had fitted an incorrect part to the tool and the plaintiff was injured. The first defendants were liable because they had an opportunity to examine the tool. The second defendants were liable because they could not rely on such an examination taking place.

Where the manufacturer has issued a warning that tests should be carried out before use, it is reasonable to expect an examination.

Kubach v Hollands [1937] 3 All ER 907

The manufacturers sold chemicals to the second defendants with a warning that they should be tested before use. The second defendants sold the chemicals to a teacher without the warning. The plaintiff child was injured when the chemical exploded during a school experiment. Her action against the school (the first defendants) failed but she recovered from the second defendants. Their claim for an indemnity from the manufacturers failed as they had been given an adequate warning and ignored it.

Damage

The narrow rule states that the manufacturer's negligence must result in damage to the consumer's life or property. A claim under the rule will therefore be for physical damage, consisting of personal injuries or damage to the consumer's property. It would also appear that any consequential economic loss may be recovered.

The plaintiff cannot recover damages if his claim is that the product is not worth as much as he expected. This is classed as economic loss and subject to *Junior Books* v *Veitchi*, is only recoverable in a contract action.

Muirhead *v* Industrial Tank Specialities Ltd [1985] 3 All ER 705

The plaintiff's lobsters died after the failure of a pump to oxygenate the water where they were kept. The pump manufacturer was held liable for the value of the lobsters (property damage) but not for the costs of buying and attempting to repair the pumps. Neither was there any liability for loss of profit on the sale of the lobsters.

Problems with the common law

The common law on defective products was subjected to a number of criticisms. The plaintiff may have great difficulty in proving causation as in *Evans* v *Triplex Glass*.

Proof of fault also presents difficulties, especially in cases where the state of technical knowledge was not sufficient to enable the manufacturer to avoid injury, or where the cost to the manufacturer of taking precautions outweighed the risk.

The law on recovery of economic loss presents problems where the consumer was a donnee, or where insolvency prevents a contract action.

Finally it is usually difficult to establish a negligence action against a supplier of goods, although a contract action may often be available.

The European Economic Community produced a Directive on product liability in 1985 (Directive 85/374/EEC) and member states were given three years to introduce national laws which complied with the directive.

In 1987 the Consumer Protection Act was passed with the intention of bringing English law into line with the provisions of the Directive.

CONSUMER PROTECTION ACT 1987

Introduction

Liability for defective products is covered by Part I of the Act. Its purpose is to introduce a strict liability regime on producers of defective products. The intention is that the producer should insure the product against its potential for causing harm.

The basic principle of the Act is in s. 2(1): 'Where any damage is caused wholly or partly by a defect in a product, every person to whom subsection (2) . . . applies shall be liable for the damage.'

The Directive allowed a margin of discretion in introducing national laws but where problems arise over interpretation of the Act reference may be had to the Directive.

Who can be sued

Section 2(2) provides a list of those who can be sued under the Act

(a) Producers

A producer is defined by s. 1(2) as:

(i)   the manufacturer
(ii)   the person who wins or abstracts products
(iii) the person who carries out an industrial or other process which adds an essential characteristic to a product which has not been won, abstracted or manufactured. An example of this would be the freezing of vegetables.

A problem arises with a product finished by one producer but defective because of parts supplied by another. The supplier of the finished product will normally be liable for the supply, provided the finished product is covered by the Act. Where the finished product is exempt from the Act, then the manufacturer is not liable where the defectiveness arises solely from the component part (s. 1(3)). An important exception to this principle exists in the case of buildings. The builder is not liable in respect of supply of the building but is liable for defective components used to construct the building (s. 46(3)).

(b) Suppliers and importers

In order to make the plaintiff's task easier, the Act makes provision for him to sue own-branders, suppliers and importers in certain circumstances.

(i)   *Own-branders.* A person who puts his own name on a product, thereby holding himself out as a producer, will be treated as a producer. This would apply to supermarket chains who sell goods under their own name which are manufactured by someone else (s. 2(2)(b)).
(ii)   *Importers.* A person who, in the course of a business , imports a product into the European Community from outside, is deemed to be a producer (s. 2(2)(c)).
(iii) *Suppliers.* If it is not possible to identify the producer or importer of a product, the Act provides for liability on the part of another supplier (s. 2(3)). This is likely to be the person who supplies the consumer.

It is necessary that a person supplied a defective product for there to be liability and this supply must be in the course of a business. The supply does not need to be to the ultimate consumer.

For a supplier (as opposed to a manufacturer) to be liable, four requirements have to be satisfied.

(a) The consumer must have asked the supplier to identify the producer (s. 2(3)(a)).
(b) The request by the consumer must have occurred within a reasonable time of the occurrence of the damage (s. 2(3)(b)).
(c) It must have become impracticable for the consumer to identify the actual producer (s. 2(3)(b)).
(d) The supplier must have failed within a reasonable time of the request, to comply with it or to identify the person who supplied him with the product (s. 2(3)(c)).

Example

James purchases a tin of baked beans from Megastores. The beans contain an impurity which causes James to become violently ill. The beans were sold as Megabeans but were manufactured for Megastores by Beaneasy. Megastore will be liable under the Act to James as suppliers/own-branders unless they comply with the four conditions. Compliance with the conditions means that Megastore are not liable, even if Beaneasy are insolvent and James has no effective remedy against them.

Products

Products are defined in s. 1(2): 'any goods or electricity and . . . includes a product which is comprised in another product, whether by virtue of being a component part or raw material or otherwise'.

Further definition is provided by s. 45(1) to include substances, growing crops, things comprised in land by virtue of being attached to it, ships, aircraft and vehicles.

Certain things are specifically exempted:

(a) A building supplied by way of a creation or disposal of an interest in land is exempt (s. 46(4)).
(b) Nuclear power is also exempt (s. 6(8)).
(c) Agricultural produce which has not undergone an industrial process is exempt (s. 2(4)). This would cover processes such as packaging, canning and possibly freezing. The Act requires that the process change the essential characteristics of the product. Whether freezing does so is questionable. Where a process has been undertaken, then the producer is liable for pre-existing defects in the product, as well as those he introduces himself.

Defectiveness

Section 3(1) provides: 'there is a defect in a product . . . if the safety of the product is not such as persons generally are entitled to expect'.

In considering what is meant by 'safety', s. 3(2) provides that all the circumstances shall be taken into account including:

> (a) the manner in which, and purposes for which, the product has been marketed, its get-up, the use of any mark in relation to the product and any instructions for, or warnings with respect to, doing or refraining from doing anything in relation to the product;
> (b) what might reasonably be expected to be done with or in relation to the product; and
> (c) the time which the product was supplied by its producer to another.

The gist of the section is that the product must be safe but the Act has no application if it is useless.

Marketing and get-up etc.

The court will have to consider a number of factors. What was the market that the product was aimed at and what sort of advertising was used? If the product is a child's toy then the target market will clearly be important. The instructions supplied with the product will need to be taken into account.

A more controversial point is the court taking into account the purposes for which the product has been marketed. Does this enable the court to take into account the comparative social utility of the product and apply a cost-benefit analysis? In the case of drugs, would the court be able to say that the risk was worthwhile given the benefits that the drug would bring?

It is clear from the section that the producer can negative his liability by providing a suitable warning of any danger, and the warning enables the consumer to avoid the danger.

Reasonable expectations as to use

Where the defect arises from a production defect which renders the product unsafe, then liability will attach under the Act.

If the defect is in design then greater difficulties are created. The court may have to balance the risk against the benefits in deciding whether the decision to market the product was justified.

The conduct of the consumer may also be relevant where he has put the product to a use for which it was not intended. A producer of microwave ovens would not be liable where the consumer used the oven to dry a poodle and the dog died. The question of warnings may be relevant here. A failure to warn that a product is not suitable for a particular purpose may give rise to liability: e.g. that fireworks are not suitable for indoor use. If the use of the product is clearly out of line with reasonable expectations (e.g. the poodle) then failure to give a warning will not be fatal.

Time of supply

Safety is to be judged in terms of the time when the product was supplied. Developments in safety after that time will not make the producer liable if his product has not conformed to them. If furniture was supplied by a producer in 1988 with a certain type of filling and in 1992 a series of fires involving that filling gave rise to new safety features, the producer would be judged by safety standards in 1988 not 1992. This, of course, is subject to the question of whether the producer should have recalled the furniture if the risk was great, or issued warnings to retailers to pass on to consumers.

Causation

The plaintiff must prove that the producer has put the product into circulation, that the product was defective and that the defect has caused damage within the meaning of the Act.

Actions under the Act differ from those at common law in that the consumer does not have to prove fault, but causation still needs to be established and the burden of proof is on the consumer.

The defect need not be the sole cause of the damage. It is sufficient that it was partly responsible for the damage. Where the damage results partly from a defect in the finished product and partly from a defective component, this will be sufficient to make the producer liable. In some cases it may be the consumer's conduct that is regarded as the sole cause of the damage: e.g. the poodle in the microwave oven.

Damage

Losses which can be claimed for under the Act are death, personal injuries and any loss of or damage to property (s. 5(1)).

Certain limitations are placed on property damage.

(a)   No award may be made where the amount is less than £275.
(b)   The property must have been intended for private use, occupation or consumption. There is no liability under the Act for damage to business property.
(c)   The claim may not include damages for damage to the defective product itself.

Defences

The defences are contained in s. 4.

(a)   If the product complies with a mandatory Community or statutory obligation, this is a defence (s. 4(1)(a)).
(b)   If the producer can prove that the defect came about after the time of supply

by him, this will provide a defence (s. 4(1)(d)). To establish this defence the producer must prove that the defect was not present at the time of supply by him.

(c)   Where the defendant can show that: 'the state of scientific and technical knowledge at the relevant time was not such that a producer of products of the same description as the product in question might be expected to have discovered the defect if it had existed in his products while they were under his control' (s. 4(1)(e)).

Member states were allowed a discretion as to whether to include a state of the art defence and its inclusion is controversial as states which do have the defence could become testing grounds for new products.

If the defence is used by a drug manufacturer where a new drug has caused damage to users, then provided he can show that laboratory tests showed no defects, he would be justified in marketing the drug while testing is still under way.

It would appear that the effect of the section will be to apply a fault based regime to new products. The producer will only be liable where he knew or ought reasonably to have known of the defect. The burden of proof will however rest on the defendant.

(d)   Contributory negligence.
The Law Reform (Contributory Negligence) Act 1945 applies (s. 6(4)). The court therefore has the power to apportion damages where the plaintiff has been partly to blame for the harm suffered.

Limitation

The limitation period for actions under the Act runs for three years from the date on which the damage was caused by the defective product.

Alternatively for three years from the date on which the damage could have reasonably been discovered (Limitation Act 1980, s. 11A(4)).

There is a long stop provision which prevents any action against the producer more than ten years from the date on which the product was first put into circulation (s. 11A(3)).

QUESTION

Pyro buys from Dynamight Ltd a box of fireworks manufactured by Sparky Ltd. Pyro asks whether any of the fireworks can be used indoors. Harriet, the shop assistant says, 'I don't suppose the sparklers would cause any harm inside.'

On Bonfire night, Pyro puts on a firework display. He reads the instructions on a firework called a roman candle. These state, incorrectly, that the firework can be held in the hand. As a result of this Pyro and his daughter Nancy, who is standing beside him, are both badly injured.

At the same time Harry, Pyro's son, takes a lighted sparkler into the house. A spark from this firework starts a fire in Pyro's kitchen which causes considerable damage.

Dynamight Ltd have now gone into liquidation.

Advise Pyro and Nancy.

Suggested approach

The primary remedy of the purchaser of a defective product lies in contract against the retailer. Pyro has a contract with Dynamight Ltd and terms of merchantable quality and fitness for the purpose would be implied into the contract under the Sale of Goods Act 1979, ss. 14(2) and 14(3). However, any contract action against Dynamight would be pointless as the judgment could probably not be enforced.

Does Pyro have an action against Sparky Ltd? There are two possibilities. An action under the Consumer Protection Act 1987 or under the 'narrow rule' in *Donoghue* v *Stevenson* in negligence.

The purpose of the Consumer Protection Act was to introduce a strict liability regime on producers of defective products. The basic principle of the Act is in s. 2(2). Where any damage is caused wholly or partly by a defect in a product, any person to whom subsection (2) applies shall be liable.

The action is brought against producers of defective products. A producer is defined by s. 2(2) as the manufacturer. Sparky Ltd are the manufacturers of the product and therefore the defendants.

The producer will be liable for any defect in the product which causes damage. A defect is defined by s. 3(1). There is a defect if the safety of the product is not such as persons generally are entitled to expect. Section 3(2) states that all the circumstances are to be taken into account. These include the purposes for which the product has been manufactured and any instructions or warnings with respect to doing or refraining from doing anything in relation to the product. What might reasonably be expected to be done with the product?

Pyro has suffered two items of damage. As regards his personal injuries there is no warning that the firework cannot be held in the hand. This could amount to a defect. If so, Pyro has an action under the Act as personal injuries are covered by the Act (s. 5(1)) and none of the defences would appear to be relevant, unless Pyro is held to be contributorily negligent, when his damages would be reduced.

The damage to the kitchen is more difficult. Again the case would turn on whether the sparklers were defective. Should a warning have been included that they were not suitable for indoor use? Probably it should have been, as this is a use which the producer should expect the product to be put to. A failure to give the warning may amount to a defect. Provided Pyro's loss exceeds £275, Pyro would have a claim.

If Pyro has a claim under the Act for his personal injuries, then Nancy will also be successful. The Act does not define consumer, but Nancy definitely falls into this category.

Both Pyro and Nancy may have a claim in negligence for their injuries under the narrow rule in *Donoghue* v *Stevenson*. Pyro may also have a claim for his property damage. Sparky is a manufacturer within the rule and Pyro and Nancy are consumers. A consumer is anyone that the manufacturer should foresee would be affected by the product. The fireworks are products within the rule. The difference between an action under the Act and a negligence action, is that in the latter the plaintiff must show that the defendant was negligent, i.e. that he failed to take reasonable care in the preparation and putting up of the product. This covers instructions for use and warnings. The defendant may escape liability if there is an alternative cause for the defect, or the damage could have been avoided by intermediate examination. Would the retailer's failure to warn of the dangers amount to reasonable examination?

Further reading

Law Commission No 82, Cmnd 6831 (1977)
Merkin, R, *Guide to the Consumer Protection Act 1987* (1987)
Newdick [1988] CLJ 455; (1987) 103 LQR 288
Pearson Report Vol 1 Ch 22
Stapleton, J (1986) 6 Oxford J Legal Stud 392

12 | Breach of statutory duty

Where a statute imposes a duty on a person, breach of that duty may give rise to an action for damages by a person injured as a result. This is known as the tort of breach of statutory duty.

The tort is sometimes referred to as statutory negligence but it is preferable to treat the action as separate from negligence as the standard of care owed may differ.

The action has played a strong part in industrial safety but attempts to introduce it into other areas have been less successful.

Example

Alan employs Brian as a machine operator. Statutory regulations applying to the industry state that all machines must be fitted with a guard. The guard on Alan's machine was removed for cleaning and inadvertently not replaced before the machine was used. Brian put his hand into the machine and lost a finger.

Brian would have an action for breach of statutory duty against Alan. He could also sue Alan for negligence. The difference in the actions would be that in the former, the absence of the guard establishes breach of duty, whereas in negligence, Brian would have to prove that Alan had failed to exercise reasonable care.

It is normal for actions in such cases to be pleaded in the alternative. The action for breach of statutory duty is advantageous to the plaintiff when the statutory duty is strict or absolute. However, statutory duties have a limited sphere of operation. If a piece of metal had flown out of the machine and blinded Brian, the court could hold that the purpose of the statute was to keep the employee out, not the machine in. The action would then fail. In a negligence action, the damage has to be a foreseeable risk. The negligence action could therefore succeed where the statutory action failed.

In an action for breach of statutory duty the plaintiff must prove the following points.

(a)   That the statutory duty in question gives rise to an action for damages.
(b)   That the duty was owed to the plaintiff.
(c)   That the duty was broken.
(d)   That the damage was caused by the breach of duty.

The defendant can raise the defences of *volenti non fit injuria* or contributory negligence to the action.

DOES THE STATUTE GIVE RISE TO AN ACTION FOR DAMAGES?

Introduction

Not all breaches of statutory duty will give rise to an action for damages by a person injured as a result. The court must first determine whether the particular statute gave rise to the right to sue for damages.

This is said to depend on the intention of Parliament. The intention is to be discovered by interpretation of the statute. Sometimes the statute will give guidance on this question. The wording, 'nothing in the Act shall be construed as conferring a right of action in any civil proceedings', is conclusive that no action exists (Health and Safety at Work Act 1974, s. 47(1)(a)).

Alternatively the statute may create an action by specific wording, either as a substitute for a common law action (Nuclear Installations Act 1965), or in addition. (Mineral Workings (Offshore Installations)Act 1971, s. 11).

In many cases the statute will be silent on the question and the search for Parliamentary intention will be illusory as Parliament never considered the question.

Tests

The leading modern statement on the test used was given by Lord Diplock.

Lonrho Ltd v Shell Petroleum Co [1982] AC 173

Lord Diplock laid down a presumptions approach to the question:

> One starts with the presumption . . . that where an Act creates an obligation, and enforces the performance in a specified manner . . . that performance cannot be enforced in any other manner. . . . (T)here are two classes of exception to this general rule. The first is where on the

true construction of the Act it is apparent that the obligation or prohibition was imposed for the benefit or protection of a particular class of individuals, as in the case of the Factories Acts and similar legislation. . . . The second exception is where the statute creates a public right . . . and a particular member of the public suffers . . . particular, direct and substantial damage other and different from that which was common to all the rest of the public.

His Lordship added that where the presumptions created a result which was contrary to the intention of Parliament then the presumptions had to give way.

Groves v Lord Wimborne [1898] 2 QB 402

The defendants were subject to a fine of £100 for breach of statutory duty in failing to fence factory machinery. Part of the fine was payable to the plaintiff at the discretion of the Secretary of State. The plaintiff was held to have an action for breach of statutory duty when he was injured as the result of no fencing.

The decision is justified on the grounds that there was no guarantee that the plaintiff would receive any of the fine and that Parliament could not have intended a workman to be deprived of the chance to seek compensation for his injuries. In terms of presumptions, the Act did enforce performance in a specified manner (a fine) but this gives way to the first exception, the obligation was imposed for the benefit of a class of people, factory employees.

Atkinson v Newcastle Waterworks Co (1877) 2 Ex D 441

The defendants supplied water to Newcastle. They were required by statute to keep their pipes at a certain pressure level. Failure to do this could result in a £10 fine. The plaintiff's premises caught fire and as there was insufficient pressure in the pipes, the premises were burned down. In an action for breach of statutory duty it was held that the penalty imposed by the statute was an exclusive one. No action for damages lay. The fact that no part of the fine was payable to an individual damaged was regarded as evidence that Parliament did not intend the statute to give rise to an action.

This case could be regarded as an example of the first presumption applying and neither of the exceptions being relevant. The manner of enforcement was laid down by the statute.

Thornton v Kirklees Metropolitan Borough Council [1979] QB 626

A statute created an obligation on the defendant council to provide housing for homeless persons. No remedy was provided by the statute for enforcement. The plaintiff was held to have an action for breach of statutory duty where the council failed to provide housing.

Although this case provides an example of an action succeeding where no method of enforcement is provided by the statute, it appears unlikely that it will be followed in this area. In *Cocks* v *Thanet District Council* [1983] 2 AC 286 it was held that challenges to administrative decisions made by local authorities must be made by application for judicial review, rather than by actions for breach of statutory duty.

Phillips v Britannia Hygienic Laundry Co Ltd [1923] 2 KB 832

The defendant's vehicle was in breach of the Construction and Use Regulations for motor vehicles. The vehicle was involved in an accident in which the plaintiff's van was damaged. The plaintiff claimed for breach of statutory duty. The enforcement method for the regulations was a criminal penalty. It was held that the regulations did not give rise to an action for damages.

A suggested reason for this decision is that to grant an action would have subverted the common law negligence action which lay in these circumstances. An action for breach of statutory duty would have given a strict liability action in many cases of road traffic accidents. This would have subverted the fault based negligence action.

If the action would reinforce the common law action it may be allowed.

Monk v Warbey [1935] 1 KB 75

The defendant gave permission to an uninsured driver to use his vehicle. This was in breach of the Road Traffic Act. The driver's negligence caused an accident in which the plaintiff was injured. It was not worth the plaintiff suing the driver as he was uninsured and had no money. The court allowed an action for breach of statutory duty against the defendant. In this case the action did not subvert the common law but supplemented it.

A case on these facts would now be covered by the Motor Insurance Bureau Scheme, whereby motor insurers provide a fund to meet claims against uninsured drivers.

Benefit of a class

This was a controversial issue before the *Lonrho* case. Atkin LJ criticised the idea in *Phillips* v *Britannia*: 'it would be strange if a less important duty which is owed to a section of the public may be enforced by an action, while a more important duty which is owed to the public at large cannot be so enforced'.

The *Lonrho* case establishes this as an exception but leaves the court with the problem of determining what is meant by an ascertainable class.

In industrial safety cases there is a well established jurisprudence and unless the statute specifically excludes liability the court will hold that an industrial safety statute gives rise to an action. Employees are an ascertainable class.

In other areas, the test has been less successful. The Court of Appeal held that residential occupiers were not a class for the purpose of the offence of harassment created by the Rent Act 1956 (*McCall* v *Abelesz* [1976] QB 585). The House of Lords held that a provision in the Betting and Lotteries Act 1934 that required track owners to provide available space for bookmakers on the track, was passed for the benefit of the race-going public rather than bookmakers (*Cutler* v *Wandsworth Stadium* [1949] AC 398).

Public right and special damage

The second exception in Lord Diplock's statement has close analogies with public nuisance. (See, 'Nuisance'.)

There must be a public right, the breach of which will constitute a public nuisance and a member of the public must suffer special damage. In the *Lonrho* case, there was a breach of the sanctions order which prevented the supply of oil to Southern Rhodesia. This was held not to create a public right to be enjoyed by all Her Majesty's citizens. It was an instrument of state policy which prevented members of the public from doing what had previously been lawful.

The distinction between a statute creating a public right and a statute prohibiting what had previously been lawful is not a satisfactory one as it does not appear to be based on any particular principle. At present some criminal legislation will give rise to an action on proof of special damage and some will not. How the distinction is to be made is unclear.

Conclusion

The present position outside of industrial safety legislation is clearly unsatisfactory in terms of certainty. It is far from clear, even using the Diplock test, which statutes will give rise to civil liability.

The test of benefit of a class leaves the courts considerable discretion as to how to define the class.

Other tests have been suggested. The Law Commission suggested that if the statute provided no remedy for its enforcement, there should be a presumption of an action (Law Commission No 21 (1969) para 38 and Appendix A(4)). This was not adopted and is unlikely to be, as it conflicts with the court's ability to take into account policy factors and whether the civil action furthers the aims of the legislation. The same criticism though could be directed at the presumptions approach. The court's decision as to what constitutes a class conceals the policy issues in the decision.

In the USA and Canada the action for breach of statutory duty is regarded as a species of negligence called statutory negligence. This has two versions. The first is negligence *per se*. This is that a breach of a statutory requirement constitutes negligence where the statute was passed to prevent a mischief in respect of which the defendant was already under a duty at common law. The standard of care is set by the statute. The second approach is that breach of the statute provides only prima facie evidence of negligence. The statutory negligence approach has not been adopted in England and this is probably a good thing. It would restrict actions to existing tort law and would reproduce the problems which have been encountered with liability for omissions.

Perhaps the most honest judicial statement in this area came from Lord Denning:

> The truth is that in many cases the legislature has left the point open. . . . The dividing line between the pro-cases and the contra-cases is so blurred and ill defined that you might as well toss a coin to decide it. (*Ex Parte Island Records* [1978] Ch 122).

WAS THE DUTY OWED TO THE PLAINTIFF?

The plaintiff must show that the duty was owed to him. Industrial safety legislation will normally confer a right on persons employed. It follows therefore, that a fireman fighting a fire at a factory which is not his place of employment, will not be able to sue for breach of such a statutory duty (*Hartley* v *Mayoh & Co* [1954] 1 QB 383).

The plaintiff must also show that the type of injury that he suffered was the type the legislation sought to prevent.

Gorris v Scott (1874) 9 LR Exch 125

The defendant shipowner was under a statutory duty to provide pens for cattle on board his ship. The purpose of the statute was to lessen the risk of cattle catching a contagious disease while in transit. The defendant was held not liable for breach of statutory duty when the plaintiff's sheep were swept overboard when not in pens. The purpose of the statute was not to protect the animals from the perils of the seas.

BREACH OF DUTY

This is a question of statutory interpretation. There is no single standard of care. The court must look at the words used in the statute, which may impose an absolute, strict or fault based standard.

It is possible that the statute may create absolute liability on the defendant, although the court will be wary of creating a strict liability criminal offence in the absence of clear language.

John Summers and Sons Ltd v Frost [1955] AC 740

The Factories Act 1961, s. 14(1) requires every dangerous part of any machinery to be securely fenced. The plaintiff's hand came into contact with a moving grinding wheel which was not fenced. The defendants argued that if the machine was securely fenced it would be unusable. This was rejected by the court, which refused to read the words, so far as reasonably practical, into the statute.

Some statutes are so specific that there can be no qualification.

Chipchase v British Titan Products Co Ltd [1956] 1 QB 545

The statutory regulations provided that any working platform from which a person is likely to fall more than 6ft 6in, had to be at least 34 inches in width. The defendants were not liable for breach of statutory duty when the plaintiff fell from a 9in wide platform 6ft above the ground.

A form of strict liability may be created by wording that allows for the practicability of precautions. This means that the employer must prove the impracticability of precautions. This may not be easy to prove, as if the precaution is possible it must be taken, even if the risks involved in taking it outweigh the benefits.

Alternatively, the statute may provide for the reasonable practicability of precautions. This wording allows the court to balance the time and expense involved in taking the precaution against the risk of injury. This is similar to a negligence test, but in the statutory action the burden of proof is on the employer.

CAUSATION

It is necessary for the plaintiff to prove that the defendant's breach of statutory duty was a cause of his injuries. Generally speaking, there is no difference between actions for breach of statutory duty and actions for common law negligence. The plaintiff must prove that but for the breach of statutory duty he would not have suffered the injury.

McWilliams v Sir William Arrol & Co Ltd [1962] 1 WLR 295

The defendant employer was in breach of statutory duty in removing safety belts from a building site. The plaintiff scaffolder was injured when he fell and was not wearing a safety belt. The action failed, as the defendant proved that even if the safety belt had been provided, the plaintiff would not have worn it.

The action for breach of statutory duty raises one specialised issue of causation. The statute may impose a duty on an employer to provide safety equipment and ensure that it is used. If the equipment is provided but the employee does not use it, this may have the effect of placing both the plaintiff and the defendant in breach of statutory duty.

Ginty v Belmont Building Supplies Ltd [1959] 1 All ER 414

The plaintiff was an experienced workman employed by the defendant roofing contractors. Statutory regulations binding on both parties required crawling boards to be used on fragile roofs. The defendants provided the boards but the plaintiff did not use them. The plaintiff fell through a roof and was injured. The plaintiff's claim failed as the defendant had done everything possible to ensure that the statutory duty was complied with. The sole reason for the breach was the plaintiff's omission to use the equipment.

This decision was somewhat controversial and a gloss was placed on it in *Boyle* v *Kodak* [1969] 1 WLR 661. If any causal responsibility rests with the employer, he will be liable. Proving the breach of statutory duty establishes a prima facie case. The defendant can escape liability if he proves that the only act or default which caused the breach was that of the plaintiff. But if any blame can be attached to the defendant he will be liable. This could occur if the plaintiff was asked to do a job beyond his competence, the equipment was not easily accessible, or pressure was brought to bear on the plaintiff not to use the equipment.

DEFENCES

Volenti non fit injuria is not usually available as a defence in the industrial safety cases. The exception is where an employee is in breach of his statutory duty and this has the effect of making the employer vicariously liable. If the defence of *volenti* would have been available against the employee, it will be available against the employer (*ICI Ltd* v *Shatwell* [1965] AC 656. See 'Defences to negligence', pp. 90–1.)

Contributory negligence is a defence and the Law Reform (Contributory Negligence) Act 1945 will apply. The courts are usually slow to attribute contributory negligence to an employee where the employer is in breach of statutory duty. (See 'Defences to negligence', pp. 98–9.)

A person who is subject to a statutory duty cannot discharge that duty by entrusting responsibility for its performance to someone else.

BREACH OF STATUTORY DUTY AND NEGLIGENCE

The two actions should be treated separately. In a breach of statutory duty action the duty is imposed by the statute. In negligence actions the courts must determine whether a duty is owed. In negligence actions the standard of care is reasonable care in all the circumstances of the case. In breach of statutory duty, the standard of performance is fixed by the statute and may be strict.

It is normally easier for the plaintiff to succeed in an action for breach of statutory duty but not always.

Rux v Slough Metals Ltd [1974] 1 All ER 262

The employer was under a statutory duty to provide safety goggles, which he did. The plaintiff employee did not wear them and was injured. The action for breach of statutory duty failed, but the negligence action succeeded. The evidence showed that the plaintiff would have worn the goggles if he had been firmly instructed to do so and supervised.

13 | Employer's liability

During the nineteenth century the response of the courts to claims by employees injured at work tended to be hostile. Liability tended to be seen in terms of contractual duties. As the employer dictated the contract of employment there was usually little or no liability.

To counter claims in tort the courts erected the unholy trinity of defences of common employment, *volenti non fit injuria* and contributory negligence.

A claim for negligence by an employee injured by the negligence of a fellow employee, would be met by the defence of common employment. If the risk had been created by the employer, a defence of *volenti* could usually be mounted by the employer, if the employee was aware of the danger and continued to work. Any contributory negligence on the part of the employee would be fatal to his claim.

From the end of the nineteenth century a change in approach is noticeable. The decision in *Smith* v *Baker* (1891) made it difficult for employers to rely on a *volenti* defence. (See 'Defences to negligence', p. 90.) An action for breach of statutory duty on the part of the employee was created by *Groves* v *Lord Wimborne* (1898). (See 'Breach of statutory duty', p. 143.) In 1945 contributory negligence ceased to be a complete defence and became grounds for apportioning liability. (See 'Defences to negligence', p. 95.) The defence of common employment was finally abolished in 1948 by the Law Reform (Personal Injuries) Act 1948. By this time it had lost most of its effect because of the introduction of a personal non-delegable duty on the employer in *Wilsons and Clyde Coal* v *English* (1938). Where the employer was in breach of this duty he could not rely on the defence of common employment. This resulted in a strict demarcation between the employer's personal duty and his vicarious liability.

It should be observed that the most significant contribution to compensation for injured workmen has been through insurance rather than the tort system. The

Pearson Commission found that only 10–15% of industrial injuries are compensated through the tort damages system (Vol 1 Table 5).

Insurance compensation started with the Workmen's Compensation Act 1897. The Act enabled workmen to recover compensation without the necessity of proving fault on the part of the employer. The employer became an insurer for injuries received out of and in the course of employment. This scheme was replaced in 1946 by a state scheme for victims of industrial accidents and prescribed industrial diseases. It is not possible to consider this scheme in a tort book and students should consult a specialist work for detail.

At present an employer's tortious liability for the safety of his employees may take one of three forms:

(a)   The employer may be vicariously liable for the negligence of an employee which leads to the plaintiff employee being injured. The employer's liability here is strict, in the sense that there need be no fault on his part. (See 'Parties to an action', p. 251.)

(b)   The employer may be in breach of statutory duty and the employee suffer injury as a result. (See 'Breach of statutory duty', pp. 141–8.)

(c)   The employer may be in breach of his personal duty of care owed to the employee. This is a particular example of negligence liability but is owed only to employees and not to independent contractors.

The system is backed up by the Employers' Liability (Compulsory Insurance) Act 1969 which makes it compulsory for employers to have insurance for personal injury to their employees. Any employee who can establish a claim in tort is therefore guaranteed to have the judgment met and not be defeated by an insolvent employer.

THE EMPLOYER'S PERSONAL DUTY OF CARE

The duty is to take reasonable care for the safety of employees in the course of their employment. The duty is personal as it cannot be delegated and is discharged by the exercise of due skill and care.

This duty does not extend to protecting the economic welfare of the employee by taking out insurance or warning them of the need for insurance cover. In *Reid* v *Rush and Tompkins* [1989] 3 All ER 228 the plaintiff was injured in a road accident while working in Ethiopia. He could not obtain compensation from the person who had caused the accident and sued his employer for failing to provide insurance or advising him of the need to take out insurance. The court held that the employer owed no such duty in tort. If such a duty was to be owed it would have to be based on an express or implied term in the contract of employment.

The classic exposition of the duty was given by Lord Wright in *Wilsons and Clyde Coal Co Ltd* v *English* [1938] AC 57. The employer must provide a competent staff, adequate material, a proper system and effective supervision.

It is probably not accurate to regard the employer's duty as a series of separate obligations but rather as a single duty to take reasonable care for the safety of employees. For the sake of exposition the duty will be analysed here in four parts. However, when the courts are considering new situations, they will not be constrained by trying to fit them into existing categories.

Competent staff

The employer may be liable when he uses an employee with insufficient experience or training for a particular job and a fellow employee is injured as a result.

The employer may also be liable for a practical joker whom he knows about and fails to take steps to deal with (*Hudson* v *Ridge Manufacturing Co Ltd* [1957] 2 QB 348).

The abolition of the doctrine of common employment has rendered this area of comparatively little importance, as in most cases the employer will be vicariously liable for the torts of his employees. However, where the employee was acting outside the course of his employment, then the employer would not be vicariously liable, but could be personally liable.

Adequate material

The duty is to provide the necessary plant and equipment and take reasonable care to maintain it in proper condition.

At common law the employer did not guarantee the safety of the equipment and could not be held liable for latent defects in the equipment which could not be discovered with reasonable care. This placed the employee at a disadvantage. Where he was injured as a result of equipment having such a defect, he had the onerous task of suing the manufacturer of the equipment under the defective products rule.

The Employer's Liability (Defective Equipment) Act 1969, s. 1(1) now provides:

> Where . . . an employee suffers personal injury in the course of his employment in consequence of a defect in equipment provided by his employer for the purposes of the employer's business and the defect is attributable wholly or partly to the fault of a third party (whether identified or not) the injury shall be deemed to be also attributable to negligence on the part of the employer.

This section has the effect of imposing a form of strict liabilty on the employer for defective equipment. This relieves the employee of the need to identify and sue the manufacturer of the defective equipment. The employer will have a contract with the person who sold him the equipment and will probably be able to recoup his losses through a contract action.

Equipment is defined by s. 1(3) as including any plant and machinery, vehicle, aircraft and clothing. It has been held that a ship is equipment. It comes within the definition machinery or plant (*Coltman* v *Bibby Tankers Ltd* [1988] AC 276).

Safe place of work

Where the employee is working on the employer's premises, the employer must act in the same manner as a reasonably prudent employer. Reasonable care must be taken for the employee's safety (*Latimer* v *AEC* [1953] AC 643. See 'Breach of duty', p. 67). There is no guarantee that the premises are safe.

Safe system of work

The employer must devise a suitable system, instruct his employees what to do and supply any implements they may require. In doing this he must take care to see that the system is complied with and bear in mind that employees are often careless for their own safety.

General Cleaning Contractors *v* Christmas [1953] AC 180

The plaintiff window cleaner was instructed by his employers in the sill method of cleaning windows. He was to hold onto the window sash while cleaning. A window fell on his fingers and he fell to the ground. It was held that the employers were in breach of their personal duty of care, as they should have told the plaintiff to test the sashes to see if they were loose and provided him with wedges. They had failed to provide a safe system.

McDermid *v* Nash Dredging and Reclamation Co Ltd [1987] AC 906

The defendants employed the 18-year-old plaintiff as a deckhand, a job in which the plaintiff had no experience. While the plaintiff was working under the control of an associated company he was injured. The House of Lords stated that the employer had to devise a safe system and operate it. On the facts, a safe system had been devised but when the operation of the system was delegated to the other company it was not operated properly.

Certain factors were relevant in determining whether reasonable care had been taken. These were: the skill and experience of the employee; the nature of the work on which he was employed; the place where the employee was employed; the degree of control exercised over him by the tortfeasor; the relationship between the tortfeasor (associated company) and the employee; and the relationship between the employer and the tortfeasor.

It was held that as the employer's duty was a personal one it could not be discharged by delegation. Performance of the duty was not discharged by delegation.

DEFENCES

The defences of *volenti non fit injuria* and contributory negligence are available to the employer. *Volenti* will rarely succeed and the courts are generally slow to find contributory negligence. (See 'Defences to negligence' for details.)

QUESTION

Arthur, Bert and Charlie are employed by Chartist plc as welders. The Welding Regulations 1970 impose a statutory duty on employers and employees that: 'safety goggles must as far as is practicable be worn at all times when welding operations are being carried out'.

Arthur developed a skin complaint, unrelated to his employment, which made the wearing of goggles painful. He stopped wearing the goggles and was struck and blinded in one eye by a piece of metal.

Bert was told by Arthur, who was known in the firm as a practical joker, that wearing goggles could result in loss of libido. Bert took this seriously, stopped wearing his goggles and suffered partial blindness caused by the glare from the welding torch.

Charlie was wearing his goggles when a piece of molten metal struck them, shattering the protective glass and causing him eye injuries.

Advise Arthur, Bert and Charlie as to any rights of action they might have in tort against Chartist plc and as to any defences with which they might be met.

NB The Welding Regulations 1970 are fictitious.

Suggested approach

An employer can incur tortious liability in respect of his employees in one of three ways. The employer may be in breach of statutory duty, in breach of his personal duty of care, or vicariously liable for the tort of one of the other employees.

Arthur may have an action for breach of statutory duty. He must establish that the statute in question gave rise to an action for damages. This is said to depend on the intention of Parliament but the test is fictitious as Parliament frequently gives no thought to the question. The most generally accepted test is that put forward by Lord Diplock in *Lonrho* v *Shell Petroleum*, based on presumptions. If the statute provides a means of enforcement then it can only be enforced in this manner, unless the obligation is imposed for the benefit of a class and the plaintiff is a member of that class.

This is used with industrial safety statutes such as the Welding Regulations to give employees injured by a breach of statutory duty an action in damages. Arthur is a member of the class (employees) for whose benefit the statute was passed. It is necessary to prove that there was a breach of the statutory duty. This depends on interpretation of the statute. The duty imposed may be strict or fault based. This duty is neither absolute nor negligence based. It is a form of strict liability.

The word practicable means that the employer must prove the impracticability of precautions. The word has been interpreted as meaning that the precaution must be taken even if the risk involved in taking it outweighs the benefit (*Boyton* v *Willment Bros Ltd* (1971)). It would appear that Chartist are in breach of statutory duty. It is also necessary for the plaintiff to prove causation. The normal causation rule of 'but for' applies unless the sole reason the employer is in breach was the plaintiff's omission to use the safety equipment (*Ginty* v *Belmont Building Supplies* (1959)).

As Arthur is in breach of his duty by omitting to wear the goggles, it may be that the court will find that causation is not established. If it is, then Chartist may attempt to raise *volenti non fit injuria* or contributory negligence as defences. *Volenti* would not appear to be applicable but the court might hold that Arthur has been contributorily negligent in respect of his injury and reduce damages accordingly.

Arthur may also have an action in negligence under the employer's personal duty of care. This is a duty to provide competent staff, adequate material, a safe place of work and a safe system of work (*Wilsons and Clyde Coal* v *English* (1938)). On the facts of the problem he is more likely to succeed in the action for breach of statutory duty as that duty on the employer is stricter.

Bert may have an action for breach of statutory duty but may fail for the same reason as Arthur. The damage was caused by Bert not wearing the glasses. Applying the Ginty test the cause of the damage was Bert's breach of statutory duty.

Bert's best chance of success is the personal duty of care, under the head of competent staff. An employer has been held liable where he failed to take steps to deal with a practical joker whom he knew about (*Hudson* v *Ridge Manufacturing* (1957)). Alternatively, the employer could be vicariously liable if Arthur was negligent in respect of his statement to Bert. Arthur would probably be outside the course of his employment though. Again the question could be raised as to whether Bert was *volenti* or contributorily negligent.

Charlie's case raises the question of the employer's personal duty of care and the duty to provide adequate equipment. At common law the employer did not guarantee the safety of the equipment and could not be held liable for a latent defect in it. The Employer's Liability (Defective Equipment) Act 1969, imposes a form of strict liability on the employer. Charlie could sue the employer for his injury and the employer would then have to recover from the manufacturer/supplier of the goggles. No defence is available in this action on these facts.

Further reading

Lang, B (1984) 47 MLR 48

Munkman, JH *Employer's Liability at Common Law* (10th edn 1985)

14 | Medical negligence and related issues

INTRODUCTION

Actions in tort against members of the medical profession increased considerably during the 1980s. This has had the effect of increasing the premiums paid by doctors for medical insurance. This increase has raised fears that the United Kingdom may be about to experience a medical malpractice crisis on the lines of the USA. This crisis, caused by successful damages actions against doctors, is said to result in defensive medicine. This is medicine practised not for the benefit of the patient but to protect the doctor from litigation. A commonly cited example of defensive medicine is the rise in the number of caesarean section births, as opposed to natural births.

This fear may be exaggerated as there are significant differences in the USA and UK legal and health systems. In the USA a lawyer is allowed to work on a contingent fee system. If the client recovers nothing, the lawyer receives no fee, but in a successful case the lawyer receives a percentage of the damages recovered. In the UK, the client must either be eligible for legal aid, or fund the action himself and risk not recovering costs. The existence of a National Health Service paid for out of taxpayers' money in the UK is also thought to affect the claims level.

There is no single reason for the rise in numbers of claims. It may be that the public have more compensation awareness. This means that they are aware of the right to damages for negligently inflicted injury. This is coupled with a change in the doctor–patient relationship. Evidence shows that family doctors are less likely to be sued than hospital doctors, as the former are more likely to have a relationship of trust with their patients than the more anonymous hospital doctors.

From the point of view of the doctor, even an unsuccessful action can have negative effects on career, and the action will be time consuming.

The plaintiff in such an action will be faced with a difficult task in establishing matters such as breach of duty and causation, but the action may be the only way in which he can obtain any compensation for the injury. Research shows that many injured patients simply want to find out what went wrong. Ironically, the system means that they are unlikely to be told, in case they use the information as evidence in an action.

In legal terms actions against doctors are likely to be brought in either battery (trespass to the person) or negligence. The battery action protects personal integrity and guards against treatment without consent. The negligence action acts as a form of compensation for a negligently injured patient and as a deterrent to doctors. A doctor's duty of care can be divided into three areas: advice, diagnosis and treatment.

THE BATTERY ACTION

Consent is central to the idea of medical treatment and to the doctor–patient relationship. There is a general principle that a person cannot complain of that which he has consented to.

A battery is the infliction of unlawful force on another person. (See 'Trespass to the person', p. 213.) A doctor who treats without consent may be guilty of a battery on the patient. The patient may give express consent, for example, by signing a consent form for a surgical operation, or there may be an implied consent, for example by holding out an arm for an injection.

The patient's consent must be real. Once the patient has been informed in broad terms of the nature of the intended procedure and gives consent, then that consent is real.

Chatterton v Gerson [1981] QB 432

The plaintiff suffered a trapped nerve after a hernia operation. She consulted the defendant specialist who performed an operation to free the trapped nerve. As a result of the operation, the plaintiff lost all feeling in her leg. She sued the plaintiff in battery, on the ground that she had not truly consented to the operation, as its effect had not been properly explained to her. The claim failed. A battery action could only succeed where her consent was not real. As the defendant had explained the nature of the operation in general terms, her consent was real for the purposes of battery.

NB Any alleged failure by the doctor to disclose risks about the treatment, which might have enabled the patient to give an informed consent, does not invalidate the consent. Any such action must be brought in negligence.

Consent problems may arise with certain kinds of patients.

The unconscious

Where a patient is unconscious and therefore incapable of giving a consent, the doctor will be entitled to give treatment on the basis of necessity.

F v West Berkshire Health Authority [1989] 2 All ER 545

The test for whether treatment is necessary is whether it is in the best interests of the patient. What is in the best interests of the patient will be judged by the standards of a responsible body of medical opinion. The decision would appear to give the medical profession considerable latitude in deciding what is necessary.

Lord Goff stated that where the unconsciousness was temporary, the doctor may not proceed contrary to the stated interests of the patient, provided the patient was rationally capable of forming such a wish. Neither should the doctor do more than is reasonably necessary in the interests of the patient.

Lord Brandon stated that an operation or treatment would be in the patient's best interests if it was carried out to save the patient's life, ensure improvement, or prevent physical or mental deterioration.

One problem in this area is that of the patient who for religious reasons objects to a blood transfusion. If the patient is conscious and capable, then the doctor must observe his wishes or be liable in battery. If the patient is unconscious and the doctor is unaware of the objection, then provided the best interests of the patient test is satisfied, no liability attaches. If the doctor is aware of the objection, then it would appear from Lord Goff's judgment that the doctor may be liable if he goes ahead with the transfusion.

Minors

In order to give a valid consent, it is necessary that the patient had the capacity to do so. At what age will a child be capable of giving a valid consent? There are two possibilities: status or understanding. If a status test is used, then a particular age is fixed at which consent may be given. This has the advantage for the medical profession of certainty, but does not allow for children maturing at different ages.

The consent of a minor aged 16 years or more is effective and there is no need for parental consent (Family Law Reform Act, s. 8(1)).

In the case of children under 16 years, the court have adopted a test of understanding (Gillick v West Norfolk & Wisbech Area Health Authority [1986] AC 112). The case was concerned with whether a child under the age of 16 years could be given contraceptive advice without the consent of her parents. The House of Lords ruled that she could, provided she had sufficient understanding. The problem with this test is what is meant by understanding. In *Gillick*, a high test of understanding was set, but it is not clear whether this applies to all forms of medical treatment.

Where the child is incapable of giving a valid consent, it is standard practice to seek parental consent where this is possible. If such consent is withheld, then the doctor could seek to have the child made a ward of court. The court can then give consent to the proposed treatment or withholding of treatment, if it thinks this is in the best interests of the child.

Mental disorder

The fact that a person is suffering from a mental disorder within the Mental Health Act 1983 does not preclude a legally effective consent (ss. 57 and 58) The question in each case is whether the person was capable of understanding.

Where a person was not capable of understanding, the doctor must apply the best interests of the patient test. In *F* v *West Berkshire Health Authority* [1989] 2 All ER 545, Lord Goff stated:

> where the state of affairs is permanent or semi-permanent, as . . . in the case of a mentally disordered person . . . there is no point in waiting to obtain the patient's consent . . . the doctor must act in the best interests of his patient, just as if he had received his patient's consent so to do . . . the lawfulness of the doctor's action is to be found in the principle of necessity . . . the doctor must act in accordance with a responsible and competent body of relevant professional opinion . . . it may be good practice to consult relatives and others who are concerned with the care of the patient.

THE NEGLIGENCE ACTION

Introduction

If negligence is alleged against a general practitioner the plaintiff can sue the doctor directly, as general practitioners are solely responsible for the treatment of patients.

If the patient has been referred to a hospital or has sought emergency treatment at a hospital, then he may proceed either against the negligent individual, the relevant Health Authority, or both.

The individual will be primarily liable and the health authority vicariously liable for its employees' negligence. The vicarious liability of hospitals for all their full-time staff was finally established in *Cassidy* v *Ministry of Health* [1951] 2 KB 343.

There is some doubt as to whether a health authority is primarily liable, i.e. that it owes a non-delegable duty to its patients. There is no direct authority in English law, but the Court of Appeal has remarked, *obiter*: 'can see no reason why, in principle, the health authority should not be [directly] liable if its organisation is at fault' (*Wilsher* v *Essex Area Health Authority* [1987] QB 730). This could occur where a mistake is made by a junior doctor who has been required to work long hours because of his contract of employment and made the mistake through exhaustion.

Until 1990, an agreement between the Ministry of Health and the medical defence societies (who provide indemnity insurance for doctors) allowed for the costs of any action to be shared between the two parties. From January 1990, the entire cost of a negligence action will be borne by the National Health Service.

In structure, the negligence action against a doctor is no different to any other negligence case. The plaintiff must prove that a duty of care was owed to him, that this was broken and that reasonably foreseeable damage was caused as a result.

The duty of care

Duty of care presents few problems in this area. The question of whether a duty of care exists is not in dispute. The only problem is what the duty is, i.e. what did the doctor undertake to do, and when the duty came into existence.

One problem area is the primary liability of Health Authorities (see above, p. 158.) One point is clear on this. If the authority can show that a lack of sufficiently qualified staff is due to overall financial problems, then an action would be unlikely to succeed. The issue has, to date, arisen in the context of public law cases alleging misuse of statutory powers.

R v Secretary of State for Social Services ex p Hincks (1979)

Patients sought a declaration that the Secretary of State and health authorities were in breach of duty as they had had to wait an unreasonable time, because of a decision not to build a new block for a hospital on grounds of cost. The application failed, as the decision could only be challenged if the decision was thoroughly unreasonable.

Similar decisions were reached in the cases involving hole in the heart babies who had to wait for treatment because of a shortage of trained specialist nursing staff. It is thought that these cases were brought more for publicity, to force the health authority to act, than in the hope of legal success. Courts will only interfere with a spending decision of a public authority in the most unusual circumstances.

Breach of duty

As this is a negligence action, liability is based on proof of fault. The plaintiff must prove that the defendant fell below the relevant standard of care. The doctor does not guarantee a cure, he only undertakes to use reasonable care.

The standard of care expected of a doctor was laid down in the following case.

Bolam v Friern Hospital Management Committee [1957] 2 All ER 118

The allegation was that a doctor had been negligent in administering electro-convulsive therapy to a patient without a relaxant drug or restraining convulsive movements. The plaintiff suffered a fractured jaw. McNair J stated:

> The test is the standard of the ordinary skilled man exercising and professing to have that special skill. A man need not possess the highest expert skill at the risk of being found negligent. It is a well established law that it is sufficient if he exercises the ordinary skill of an ordinary man exercising that particular art.

On the facts, the defendant was found not liable, as he had conformed with a practice which was approved by a responsible body of medical opinion.

The courts therefore allow the medical profession to set their own standard. A doctor accused of negligence by a patient can defend himself by showing that what he did was accepted practice, provided that practice was approved by responsible opinion in the medical profession.

The Bolam test has come under criticism (not least because it allows the profession to set its own standard) but has survived intact.

Whitehouse v Jordan [1981] 1 All ER 267

Negigence was alleged on the part of a senior registrar in charge of a child birth. It was claimed that he had pulled too long and too hard in a trial of forceps delivery and this had caused the plaintiff's head to become wedged or stuck, resulting in asphyxia and brain damage. At the trial the mother gave evidence that when the forceps were applied she was lifted off the bed. The questions for decision were: (a) in what manner did the defendant use the forceps? (b) was that manner consistent with the degree of skill which a member of his profession is obliged by law to exercise? On (a) the evidence was held not to establish the allegation. On (b) the House of Lords re-stated the Bolam test and rejected any test based on errors of clinical judgment.

In the Court of Appeal Lord Denning had attempted to qualify Bolam by saying that an error of clinical judgment was not necessarily negligence.

Maynard v West Midland Regional Health Authority [1985] 1 All ER 635

Two consultants believed that the plaintiff was suffering from pulmonary tuberculosis but also considered the possibility that she might have Hodgkin's disease. She was in fact suffering from tuberculosis. Tests were carried out but it was decided to operate before the results of the tests were known. The plaintiff claimed damage to the vocal chords as a result of the operation. It was held by the House of Lords that the defendants were not negligent as they had conformed to a practice approved by one responsible body of medical opinion. Where there are conflicting practices (as there were in this case), negligence is not established by proving that the defendant has not followed one practice.

The Bolam test applies to advice, diagnosis and treatment. (But see 'Informed consent', p. 161, on advice.)

The degree of skill will vary according to the post held by the doctor, rather than the experience of the individual. A consultant will be expected to show the degree of skill normally exhibited by a consultant in that field. A novice is expected to show the degree of skill exhibited by a junior doctor, even if it is the first day on the job. The inexperienced should be able to call on the advice of their superiors. Where there is a failure in supervision, then the superior could be negligent. If the system does not provide for supervision, then the health authority could be primarily liable because it is well established that doctors need to do their training on the job.

The duty of care is imposed by law but the standard is a matter of medical practice. Where there is only one accepted practice, then following this practice will not amount to negligence. In exceptional cases the courts may take the view that established practice is unsatisfactory and find negligence. However, there only appears to be one reported case since Bolam where this has occurred (Hucks v Cole (1968) 112 Sol Jo 483).

Where there is more than one accepted practice, then following a practice approved by a responsible body of medical opinion will exonerate the doctor.

Proof of negligence

The burden of proof is on the plaintiff to prove negligence and this may be difficult as he may not know what happened.

The courts may allow the plaintiff to rely on the doctrine of *res ipsa loquitur*. (See 'Breach of duty', p. 161.) The precise nature of the negligence must be unknown and no explanation of the way in which the injury was inflicted offered by the defendant. The injury must be of the kind that does not normally happen unless there is negligence. If the injury sustained was an inherent risk of the procedure, then the doctrine will be inapplicable.

In general, the courts are reluctant to allow the doctrine to be used in medical negligence cases unless there is a clear inference of negligence from the known facts.

Cassidy v Ministry of Health [1951] 2 KB 343

The plaintiff went into hospital with two stiff fingers and came out with four stiff fingers. The court held that this should not have happened if due care had been used and the doctrine was applied. As the defendants were unable to rebut the inference of negligence they were liable.

The doctrine has also been used in cases where swabs have been left in patients after operations (*Mahon* v *Osborne* [1939] 2 KB 14).

Informed consent

In the USA, a doctor will not avoid litigation by simply informing the patient of the nature of the treatment in broad terms. He will be under a duty to warn of dangers in the proposed treatment and to give the information which the patient has the right to expect. The duty is one of reasonable disclosure of the choices available. This duty to disclose is not limited by medical practice, it is set by law. The view is that a consent is not valid unless the patient has enough information to make an informed choice. Any information material to the patient's decision should therefore be revealed. The doctor may exercise therapeutic privilege if he thinks that revealing a particular risk would be adverse to the patient's health (*Canterbury* v *Spence* (1972) 464 F 2d 772).

Is there such a doctrine in England? This will depend on whether the Bolam test applies to the giving of information as well as diagnosis and treatment. The key decision in England is the following.

Sidaway v Board of Governors of the Bethlem Royal Hospital [1985] AC 871

The plaintiff had pain in her neck, shoulder and arms. A neuro-surgeon examined her and recommended an operation. What the plaintiff was told is not clear, as the surgeon had died by the time of the trial. The operation carried with it a 1% risk of damage to the spinal cord and a 1–2% risk of damage to the nerve roots. The surgeon had apparently told the plaintiff about the risk of damage to the nerve roots but not of that to the spinal cord. The operation was carried out without negligence by the surgeon but the plaintiff was severely disabled as a result of damage to her spinal cord.

The House of Lords held that the surgeon had followed approved practice of neuro-surgeons in not disclosing the risk of damage to the spinal cord and was not negligent.

The majority of the House (Lord Scarman dissenting) was prepared to accept a modified version of the *Bolam* test for the giving of information. The major modification was that where the judge thought that disclosure of a particular risk was obviously necessary but it was not medical pactice to disclose, then following standard practice would not avoid liability. The example given was a 10% risk of a stroke. If medical practice was not to disclose the risk, then a court would probably declare practice to be wrong.

Lord Scarman rejected current medical practice as the test for what a patient needs to know and asserted the patient's right to know based on self-determination. He thought the doctor should be liable where the risk is such that a prudent person, in the patient's position, would have regarded it as significant. A doctor would have a defence of therapeutic privilege, if disclosure would have posed a serious threat of psychological detriment to the patient.

The position where the patient specifically asks questions is not clear. In *Sidaway*, Lord Bridge said there was a duty to answer as truthfully and fully as the questioner requires. However, in *Blyth* v *Bloomsbury Health Authority* (1987), the Court of Appeal said there was no duty to pass on all the information available to the hospital. The reply would be satisfactory if it conformed to standard practice.

Finally, it should be noted, that even if the plaintiff manages to overcome the hurdle of proving a duty existed to give him the information, he must still establish causation. This requires him to prove that if the information had been given, his decision as to treatment would have been different.

Causation

The plaintiff must prove that his damage would not have occurred, but for the defendant's breach of duty. (See 'Causation and remoteness', p. 73.)

In practice, medical negligence cases present problems in causation, as medical science may not be able to identify the precise cause of the plaintiff's damage.

Wilsher v Essex Area Health Authority [1988]1 All ER 871

The plaintiff was born three months prematurely. He suffered from retrolental fibroplasia (RLF). This is an incurable condition of the retina which caused almost total blindness. He sued the defendants on the ground that his RLF was caused by an excess of oxygen in his bloodstream, due to lack of proper skill and care in the management of his oxygen supply. The first allegation was that a misplaced catheter gave misleading readings of oxygen pressure. The trial judge found this amounted to negligence. The second allegation was that medical staff allowed the oxygen level to remain above the accepted safety level. The trial judge relied on the causation test in *McGhee* v *NCB* (1973).

The House of Lords allowed the defendant's appeal with the result that the case had to go back for a retrial eleven years after the plaintiff had suffered damage. The problem was in the conflict of medical evidence as to the cause of RLF. It can be caused by a high level of oxygen in premature babies, but it can occur without artificial administration of oxygen. The trial judge had found that the plaintiff's exposure to high levels of oxygen had materially increased the risk of suffering RLF and the defendants had to show on the balance of probabilities that the exposure did not cause the RLF. The House of Lords held that the onus of proving causation lies on the plaintiff. Where the plaintiff is unable to establish what the cause of his injuries was, then the action will fail.

See also *Hotson* v *East Berkshire Area Health Authority* [1987] 3 WLR 232. (See 'Causation and remoteness', p. 163.)

Part IV
TORTS BASED
ON LAND

15 | Trespass to land

Trespass to land is an *unjustifiable interference with the possession of land*. It is important to note that, for historical reasons, the tort is committed against possession and not ownership of land.

As this is a form of trespass the injury must be *direct* rather than consequential. The latter form of interference may give rise to liability in nuisance.

Esso Petroleum Co Ltd *v* Southport Corporation [1956] AC 218

The captain of an oil tanker ran the ship aground and in order to save the ship and the crew large quantities of oil were discharged. The oil was carried by the tide onto the shore. The court held that necessity was a defence to the claim in trespass and nuisance. Two judges in the House of Lords thought that the damage was consequential, not direct, and therefore not capable of constituting a trespass.

The tort is actionable *per se* and the plaintiff need not show any damage to the land as a result of the defendant's act. The remedy sought will in any case often be an injunction to prevent any repetition of the trespass.

As most trespasses are self-evidently intentional because the defendant intends to be there, the question of the state of mind of the defendant is not often of importance. Two points may be noted at this stage. First, if the plaintiff did not intend to be on the land, i.e. if he was thrown there, no trespass is committed (*Basely v Clarkson* (1681) 3 Lev. 37). Second, the fact that the defendant thought that the land was his own will not be a defence (*Smith v Stone* (1647) Sty 65).

It has been clear for a long time that where land adjoining the highway is unintentionally entered, i.e. as a result of a car accident, that the plaintiff must prove negligence (*River Wear Commissioners* v *Adamson* (1877) 2 App Cas 743).

League against Cruel Sports v Scott [1986] QB 240

It was held that where a hunt entered land after permission to enter had been refused, then the master would be liable if he intended the hounds to enter; or, if the entry was caused by his failure to exercise proper control over them, when there was a real risk of entry. If this decision is correct it means that the tort may be committed negligently.

FORMS OF TRESPASS TO LAND

The tort may be committed by entry on land, remaining on land, or by placing objects on land.

Trespass by wrongful entry

This is the commonest form of trespass and consists of a personal entry on the plaintiff's land by the defendant. The slightest crossing of the boundary will be sufficient, such as putting a hand through a window.

Entick v Carrington (1765) 19 State Trials 1029

Plaintiff alleged that officers of the king broke into his house and searched and took documents. The defendants said that they were authorised by a warrant granted by the Secretary of State. The court held that the Secretary of State had no jurisdiction to grant a warrant and the defendants were guilty of trespass.

This form of trespass may also be committed by abuse of right of entry. A person who uses the highway for any purpose other than that of passage becomes a trespasser against the owners of the subsoil.

Hickman v Maisey [1900] 1 QB 752

Where the highway across land in the possession of the plaintiff was used by a racing tout for the purpose of taking notes on the form of a racehorse, a trespass was committed.

Trespass by remaining on land

A person commits trespass if he remains on land when his right of entry has ceased. To refuse or to omit to leave is as much a trespass as to originally enter without any right.

A person who holds over at the end of a lease is not a trespasser until demand is made, as only the person in possession can be trespassed against (*Hey* v *Moorhouse* (1839) 6 Bing NC 52).

Trespass by placing objects on land

It is a trespass to place any chattel on the plaintiff's land. This form of trespass is known as continuing trespass, as the trespass continues as long as the offending article remains on the land. Successive actions will lie from day to day until the article is removed.

Holmes v Wilson (1839) 10 A & E 503

The defendants erected buttresses to support a sinking road. To do this they had to trespass on the plaintiff's land. The plaintiff sued and recovered damages. The defendants failed to remove the buttresses and the plaintiff sued again. The defence was that the action was time barred. This was rejected as it was a case of continuing trespass which continued as long as the buttresses were on the land.

Trespass *ab initio*

Where the defendant's entry is by authority of law as opposed to the plaintiff's authority and the defendant subsequently abuses that right, then he becomes a trespasser *ab initio* (from the moment of entry) (*Six Carpenters Case* (1610) 8 Co Rep 146A). The rule only applies where the subsequent abuse is a positive wrongful act as opposed to an omission.

The modern application of this doctrine lies in the use of police search warrants. The usefulness has been removed by modern cases, which have held that partial abuse of an authority does not render everything done under it unlawful (*Elias* v *Pasmore* [1934] 2 KB 164).

Chic Fashions (West Wales) Ltd v Jones [1968] 2 QB 299

Police searching the plaintiff's premises for stolen goods seized goods which they mistakenly thought to be stolen. The seizure was held to be lawful as police entering premises with a warrant had authority to remove anything which they believed to have been stolen. The Court of Appeal doubted the validity of trespass *ab initio*, as it meant that lawful acts could be made unlawful by subsequent events and the lawfulness of an act should be judged at the time it took place.

Despite this criticism the doctrine was applied without criticism in the later case of *Cinnamond* v *British Airports Authority* [1980] 2 All ER 368 to mini-cab drivers who were unlawfully touting for business.

Trespass above and beneath the surface

The person who owns the land also owns the sky above and the subsoil beneath. Trespass can therefore be committed by a person who digs a tunnel under land or who abuses the airspace.

Kelsen v Imperial Tobacco Co [1957] 2 QB 334

The defendants erected an advertising sign which projected into the plaintiff's airspace by eight inches. This was held to be trespass to land.

This principle could clearly cause severe difficulties to aircraft. The Civil Aviation Act 1982, s. 76(1) and s. 76(2) therefore makes special provision for civil aircraft. No trespass is committed where the aircraft flies at a reasonable height, having regard to wind, weather and all the circumstances of the case. A form of strict liability is also created for damage caused by articles falling from an aircraft whilst in flight.

The position of aircraft has also been clarified at common law.

Lord Bernstein of Leigh *v* Skyviews and General Ltd [1978] QB 479

The defendants took an aerial photograph of the plaintiff's house and were sued for trespass to land. The court held that trespass to air space was not committed where the flight took place at a height which did not affect the use of the land. The plaintiff was in any case prevented from bringing an action by the statutory provision, which is not limited to a bare right of passage and is not lost by the taking of a photograph.

A distinction has since been drawn between aircraft and a structure which overhangs land. In the latter case a trespass is committed even if the structure (a crane) was at a height which did not affect the plaintiff's use of the land (*Anchor Brewhouse Developments Ltd* v *Berkley House (Docklands Developments) Ltd* (1987) 38 BLR 82).

TITLE OF THE PLAINTIFF

Trespass to land is normally only actionable by the person who is in possession of the land. This includes a person who is entitled to immediate and exclusive possession. A landlord cannot normally bring an action for trespass as the tenant is the person who has possession. The landlord may sue if he can prove that actual harm has been caused to the reversion or in the circumstances illustrated in the next case.

Portland Management Ltd *v* Harte [1977] QB 306

A landlord brought an action against persons who were alleged to be squatters. It was held that where an absolute owner brings an action for trespass he must prove title and an intention to regain possession. The slightest act by the owner indicating an intention will be sufficient. The defendant must then show title or a right to possession consistent with the plaintiff's ownership.

The mere use of land without exclusive possession is not sufficient. A lodger or boarder will generally not be able to sue.

Trespass by relation

A person who has the right to immediate possession of the land and enters in exercise of that right, is then deemed to have been in possession ever since the accrual of the right of entry. That person may sue for any trespass committed since the accrual of the right of entry.

This doctrine enables a lessee to sue for any trespass committed between the granting of the lease and his entering in pursuance of it. A landlord who is entitled to enter on the determination of a lease may, on re-entry, sue for any trespass since the lease determined.

Co-owners

A tenant in common or joint tenant of land cannot sue his co-tenant in trespass, unless the defendant's act amounts to the total exclusion or ouster of the plaintiff or destructive waste of the common property. Each of the co-tenants is entitled to possession of the land.

DEFENCES

Licence

A licence is that consent which, without passing any interest in the property to which it relates, merely prevents the acts for which consent is given from being wrongful. Trespass is therefore not committed when the defendant enters with the authority of a licence. This is unless he exceeds the terms of the licence or the plaintiff has legally revoked the licence.

A bare licence, which is one granted other than for valuable consideration, may be revoked at any time on the giving of reasonable notice. A contractual licence may also be revoked at any time, but this may involve the grantor in an action for breach of contract. This appears to be subject to an exception where the licence was granted for a limited period of time and for a specific purpose. If a person bought a ticket for the cinema then he would probably have an irrevocable licence for the period of the film (*Hurst* v *Picture Theatres Ltd* [1915] 1 KB 1). The person ejected could then mount an action for battery and the defence of reasonable force to eject a trespasser would fail.

A licence coupled with an interest, e.g. a profit, is irrevocable, as although the licence itself is only a right *in personam*, it confers a right *in rem* to do something once an entry has been made.

Justification by law

Acts which would otherwise be trespass are not so when justification is provided by law. For example, the police have powers under the Police and Criminal Evidence Act 1984 to enter premises and to search them.

Necessity

It is a defence to show that it was necessary for the defendant to enter the plaintiff's land.

Cope *v* Sharp [1912] 1 KB 496

Fire broke out on X's land. X's servants attempted to put the fire out and Z's gamekeeper set fire to land between the fire and some of Z's nesting pheasants. The gamekeeper was sued for trespass. He was held not liable as there was a real and imminent danger and he had done what was reasonably necessary.

Rigby *v* Chief Constable of Northamptonshire [1985] 2 All ER 985

Police fired CS gas into a shop in an attempt to force a psychopath out. As a result, the plaintiff's shop was burnt down. The court held that necessity was a defence to trespass provided there was no negligence on the part of the defendant. On the facts of the case, the police were held liable in negligence as they had no fire fighting equipment present when the CS gas was fired. The defence of necessity succeeded in the trespass action as the police had not been negligent in creating the emergency.

REMEDIES

Re-entry

A person who is entitled to possession can enter or re-enter the premises. By the Criminal Law Act 1977 s. 6, it is a crime to use or threaten violence for the purposes of securing entry to any premises occupied by another, except by a displaced residential occupier. At civil law reasonable force may be used to evict a trespasser.

Hemmings *v* Stoke Poges Golf Club [1920] 1 KB 720

The plaintiff, a tenant of the defendant, was served with a notice to quit and refused to leave. The defendants entered the plaintiff's cottage and removed the plaintiff and his furniture using reasonable force. Defendants were found not liable in trespass.

Ejectment

A person who has been dispossessed may bring an action for ejectment where he can establish an immediate right to possession. The plaintiff can only recover on the strength of his own title and not on the weakness of the defendant's. The defendant only needs to assert that he is in possession and the plaintiff must then show that his title is better than the defendant's.

Mesne profits

An action lies for damage which the plaintiff has suffered through being out of possession of land. This includes profits taken by the defendant during his occupation and damages for deterioration and the reasonable costs of getting possession.

Distress damage feasant

Where a chattel is unlawfully on the plaintiff's land and has caused actual damage, the plaintiff may retain the chattel until the damage has been paid for. If a football is kicked through a window then the football can be retained until the window is paid for.

The principle used to have particular importance in relation to damage caused by straying livestock but there is now a specific statutory rule in Animals Act 1971, s. 7.

The remedy is generally only available where the chattel is unattended and must be made while the chattel is trespassing. This is an alternative to an action and no action can be maintained while there is distraint of the chattel.

Injunction

Where a trespass is threatened or where the trespass is of a continuing nature, then the plaintiff may seek an injunction. The plaintiff is prima facie entitled to the injunction but it may be refused where the interference is trivial.

Llandudno UDC v Woods [1889] 2 Ch 705

The council sought an injunction to prevent a clergyman trespassing by holding services on the plaintiff's seashore. The application was rejected on the grounds of triviality.

Damages

Where the trespass is trivial then the damages will be nominal; but where the trespass involves some beneficial use of the land, the plaintiff is entitled to a reasonable remuneration for the use of the land, as if the use had been made under an agreement, such as a lease or a contract.

16 | Nuisance

INTRODUCTION

There are three types of nuisance: public, private and statutory. Although the same conduct by the defendant may give rise to liability in any of these, the attachment of the word nuisance to public nuisance is confusing as it originates in criminal law.

Public nuisance is primarily a criminal offence but may give rise to an action in tort where the plaintiff has suffered special damage. The commonest example is probably interferences with the highway.

Private nuisance is a tort which deals with disputes between adjacent landowners. It involves drawing a balance between the right of one person to use his land in whatever way he wishes and the right of his neighbour not to be interfered with. The origins of the modern tort lie in the nineteenth century and the change in land use that came about with the industrial revolution. There was no detailed planning law at this time and the courts used private nuisance as a method of zoning land for particular purposes. This proved inefficient as the courts had to wait for litigants to commence actions and this role has now been taken over by planning legislation. Private nuisance was left with the task of dealing with disputes between neighbouring landowners and the gist of the subject is an unreasonable interference with a person's use or enjoyment of land. One important point to make at this stage is that nuisance is concerned with the type of harm caused and the interest invaded, rather than the defendant's conduct. Students who have become obsessed with negligence should take note!

STATUTORY NUISANCES

The increasing concern of central government for public health and the environment has led to a mass of legislation concerned with noise, run-down premises, clean air and accumulations. Although statutory nuisances are the most important in terms of the environment, they are not dealt with in any detail in a tort course as they are enforced by public bodies.

From the plaintiff's point of view the most significant point about statutory nuisance is that enforcement is in the hands of the local authorities. This saves a person who is affected from the time and expense of having to bring a private action. The normal method of enforcement is for the local authority to serve an abatement order on the offender. Different procedures are used depending upon the relevant statute. In proceedings under the Clean Air Act 1956, non-compliance with an abatement order means that the local authority has to seek a nuisance order in the magistrates court. But under the Control of Pollution Act 1974, Part III, non-compliance means that a criminal offence has been committed.

A local authority will normally attempt to obtain compliance from the offender without taking proceedings and thereby avoid cost. Where proceedings are successfully brought then no compensation is payable to an affected party. However, an injunction is the remedy commonly sought in private nuisance and an abatement notice serves the same purpose.

PUBLIC NUISANCE

Every public nuisance is a crime. It acquires its tortious characteristic by virtue of the rule that a person who suffers special damage may bring an action in tort.

A-G v PYA Quarries [1957] 2 QB 169

Quarrying operations were conducted in such a way that local residents were affected by dust and vibrations from explosions. The court defined public nuisance as: one which materially affects the reasonable comfort and convenience of life of a class of Her Majesty's subjects. The defendant's activities were held to amount to a public nuisance.

Whether the number of persons affected amounts to a class is a question of fact in each case. Where the nuisance is interference with the highway then the class affected will be highway users.

Acts which will amount to a public nuisance are a mixed bag and difficult to precisely define. Two distinct groups can be identified: these are abuses of the highway and carrying on trades which cause discomfort to others. A third group consists of an unclassifiable group of acts such as making a hoax bomb alarm call, keeping a brothel and holding a badly organised pop festival.

In order to sue in public nuisance the plaintiff must prove that he suffered special damage. For this purpose special damage means damage over and above that suffered by the class of persons affected. The damage must be substantial and direct rather than consequential.

Castle v St Augustines Links (1922) 38 TLR 615

The plaintiff car driver was struck by a golf ball hit from the thirteenth tee of the defendant's golf course as he was driving on the highway. Balls frequently went over the highway. The siting of the tee amounted to a nuisance. The class of persons affected were highway users. The plaintiff had suffered special damage, so the defendants were liable in public nuisance.

NB If the plaintiff had been on his own land the action would have been in private nuisance.

Bolton v Stone [1951] AC 850

The plaintiff was hit by a cricket ball struck over a high fence from a distance of 100 yards. The evidence showed that the ball had only been hit out of the ground six times in the last thirty years. The action in nuisance failed as the likelihood of injury would not have been anticipated by the reasonable man.

In a public nuisance action it appears that damages may be recovered for personal injuries, property damage and economic loss. Economic loss has been recovered where the highway was obstructed and business losses incurred. (See *Fritz* v *Hobson* (1880) 14 Ch D 542; *Benjamin* v *Storr* (1874) LRCP 400.)

One distinction between public and private nuisance is that the plaintiff does not need to have an interest in land to sue in public nuisance. He must, however, have suffered special damage.

Tate & Lyle Industries Ltd v GLC [1983] 2 AC 509

The defendants constructed ferry terminals in the River Thames. These caused silting which obstructed the access of vessels to the plaintiff's jetty. The plaintiffs had to spend money on dredging. No action lay in private nuisance as the jetty was not affected. The plaintiffs had no private rights of property in the river bed which was affected. The public right of navigation for river users had been interfered with and the plaintiffs were able to bring an action in public nuisance for their expenditure.

The highway

Many public nuisance cases are concerned with the highway. The usual action is concerned with obstructing the highway. If the highway is unreasonably obstructed this will amount to a public nuisance. The following case brings out the distinct nature of public nuisance.

Dymond v Pearce [1972] 1 QB 497

The defendant left his lorry parked on the highway with its parking lights on and it was visible from a distance of two hundred yards. The plaintiff motor cyclist ran into the lorry. It was held that the defendant had committed a public nuisance but was not liable for the plaintiff's injuries as these were caused entirely by the plaintiff's negligence.

It is also possible to cause a nuisance by creating a danger close to the highway. Occupiers of premises adjacent to the highway are under a duty to keep them in reasonable repair.

Tarry v Ashton (1876) 1 QBD 314

A lamp on the defendant's premises fell and injured the plaintiff. The defendant had employed a contractor to keep the lamp in good repair and argued that this discharged his duty to highway users. It was held that the duty in such cases was to keep the lamp in good repair and that the duty was non-delegable, the defendant was liable.

Wringe v Cohen [1940] 1 KB 229

The Court of Appeal held that the occupier of premises on the highway was under a duty to keep premises in repair whether he knew of a danger or not. This apparent strict liability is somewhat undermined by two exceptions. The defendant will not be liable where the damage resulted from a secret and unobservable operation of nature or from the unforeseeable act of a trespasser, unless he knew or ought to have known of the danger.

Highway authorities are under a statutory duty to maintain highways (Highways Act 1980, s. 41). A defence is provided where they have taken reasonable care in all the circumstances to ensure that the part of the highway to which the action relates was not dangerous for traffic. What constitutes reasonable care will include among other things, the character of the highway, the appropriate standard of maintenance and what amounts to a reasonable standard of repair (Highways Act 1980, s. 58).

PRIVATE NUISANCE

Introduction

Private nuisance is an unlawful interference with a person's use or enjoyment of land, or some right over, or in connection with it. A nuisance which consists of an interference with a right in land is dealt with in land law under the heading of servitudes. This chapter will look at interferences with use and enjoyment. Some idea of private nuisance can be given by looking at the parties to a nuisance action.

Plaintiffs

Private nuisance is concerned with the regulation of land use between neighbours. To bring an action the plaintiff must have an interest in the land affected. Therefore owners and tenants may sue. Reversioners may sue where there is permanent damage to the reversion.

The emphasis on property rights can be illustrated by the rule that a spouse of an owner or tenant has no right of action if they have no interest in the land.

Malone *v* Lasky [1907] 2 KB 141

The wife of the tenant of premises was injured when a cistern was dislodged by vibrations caused by the defendant. The wife had no claim in private nuisance as she had no proprietary or possessory interest in the land.

The position of non-owner spouses has now been altered by statute in matrimonial law. The Matrimonial Homes Act 1983 grants a statutory right of occupation in the matrimonial home to such a person. It is debatable as to whether this statutory right would be sufficient to ground an action in private nuisance. The preferable view is that where the non-owner spouse has obtained an exclusion order against the owner, then there is a sufficient interest to bring proceedings.

There is a general principle in tort law that a person cannot recover for personal injuries in the absence of fault on the part of the defendant. As it is not clear whether nuisance is a fault based or strict liability tort, this raises the question of whether damages for personal injuries are recoverable in nuisance. What is clear is that the plaintiff may recover for personal injuries and discomfort which are incidental to the use and enjoyment of land.

Halsey *v* Esso Petroleum Co Ltd [1961] 1 WLR 683

The defendants operated a refinery in a partly residential area. The plaintiff was able to recover damages for loss of sleep caused by tankers at night and from the nauseating smell which emerged from the refinery.

NB The case provides a good example for students of the links between public and private nuisance and the action in *Rylands* v *Fletcher*.

Defendants

The law on defendants in private nuisance actions is complex and will be divided into three categories of defendant.

(a) Creators

The creator of a nuisance may always be sued even though he is no longer in occupation of the land from which the nuisance originates.

(b) Occupiers

In most nuisance cases it will be the occupier of the land from which the nuisance originates who is sued. The occupier is liable for nuisances created by himself; by his servants (on the basis of vicarious liability); but not for nuisances created by an independent contractor, unless the occupier is under a non-delegable duty or the contractor is working on the highway and creates a danger to highway users.

Bower v Peate (1876) 1 QBD 321

The parties owned adjoining houses. The defendant employed a contractor to work on his house. During the course of the work the support of the plaintiff's house was undermined. The defendant was held liable as he was under a non-delegable duty.

Historically, an occupier was not liable for nuisances created by trespassers or acts of nature. This was in line with the view that ownership of land was a source of rights rather than duties. Recent case law has changed this view.

Sedleigh Denfield v O'Callaghan [1940] AC 880

A trespasser installed piping in a ditch on the respondent's land. Three years later the pipe became blocked and the appellant's land was flooded. One of the respondent's servants had cleaned out the ditch twice a year. As the appellants were presumed to know of the danger and had done nothing to abate it they were liable in nuisance. Liability in these circumstances would arise where the occupier, with knowledge of the existence of the nuisance, adopted it for his own purposes or continued it by failing to take steps to avoid it.

Goldman v Hargrave [1967] AC 645

A redgum tree on the appellant's land was struck by lightning and caught fire. The appellant had the tree cut down and left the fire to burn out. A strong wind got up and the fire spread and damaged the respondent's property. The Privy Council held that where an occupier becomes aware of the existence of a nuisance he is under a duty to take positive action. The standard of care imposed on the occupier is subjective rather than the normal objective standard. In determining the occupier's liability the court must take into account the cost of abatement and balance it against the occupier's resources. In this context resources means financial and physical resources. The appellants were held liable for failing to abate the nuisance.

Leakey v National Trust for Places of Historic Interest or Natural Beauty [1980] QB 485

The defendants occupied a hill which was known to crack and slip as a result of weathering. Debris fell on the plaintiffs' land and the plaintiffs asked the defendants to remove it. The defendants denied their responsibility but were found liable in nuisance. The Court of Appeal held that the principle in *Goldman* applied in English law and extended to nuisances caused by the state of the land itself. The court also held that the action had been correctly brought in nuisance.

Care must be taken to distinguish this action from *Rylands* v *Fletcher*. In the fault based nuisance action, the occupier is potentially liable for dangers in the land itself as in *Leakey*. In *Rylands* it is necessary for the occupier to collect and keep something on the land such as coal spoil.

The modern law can be stated as being that an occupier is liable for nuisances caused by a trespasser or act of nature, where the occupier is or should be aware of the presence of the nuisance on his premises and has failed to take reasonable steps to abate the nuisance. The standard of reasonableness is a subjective one.

(c) Landlords

The law on whether a landlord is liable for a nuisance is complex. The basic principle is that the landlord will not be liable as he has parted with control of the land. There are a number of exceptions to this principle.

Where a nuisance existed at the time of the letting the landlord will be liable if he knew or ought to have known of the nuisance before letting. He will also be liable if he can be said to have authorised the nuisance.

Harris v James (1876) 45 LJQB 545

A field was let by S to J for J to work it as a lime quarry and to set up lime kilns. The plaintiff complained of smoke from the kilns and nuisance caused by blasting in the quarrying. J was liable as occupier and S for authorising the commission of a nuisance.

Tetley v Chitty [1986] 1 All ER 653

The defendant council allowed a go-cart club to use their land. An action in nuisance was brought by nearby residents on the grounds of noise. The council's defence that they were not liable as they had neither created the nuisance nor permitted one to occur was rejected. The noise was an ordinary and necessary consequence of the go-carts and the defendants had therefore expressly or impliedly consented to the nuisance.

If the landlord has taken a covenant in the lease from the tenant, that the tenant will not cause a nuisance and the nuisance is not an inevitable consequence of the letting, (as in *Tetley* v *Chitty*) the landord is not liable. So where a local authority let a house to a problem family who had covenanted not to cause a nuisance, the local authority was not liable for the families' behaviour (*Smith* v *Scott* [1973] Ch 314).

The landlord may also be liable for nuisances arising after the demise, where he has reserved the right to enter and repair in the lease or has the implied right to do so. The landlord will be liable whether he knew of the defect or not (*Wringe* v *Cohen*), unless the defect was due to the act of a trespasser or an act of nature (*Leakey* v *National Trust*).

In the case of residential tenancies for less than seven years, there is a statutory obligation on the landlord to repair the structure and exterior, which he cannot contract out of (Landlord and Tenant Act 1985, ss. 11–14).

There is also a form of statutory liability on landlords. The Defective Premises Act 1972, s. 4 imposes a duty on landlords of premises after their demise. The section applies where the landlord is under an obligation to the tenant for maintenance or repair of the premises. Where the landlord knows or ought to know of the relevant defect, he owes a duty to all persons who might reasonably be expected to be affected by the defects in the state of the premises.

Therefore if L leases premises to T; reserves a right to enter and carry out repairs; the premises develop a defect which L knows about; damage is caused to N, an adjacent property owner; N may have a statutory action by virtue of s.4; or may be able to bring himself within one of the common law exceptional rules on landlords, so as to be able to sue in private nuisance.

Interference with use and enjoyment

Private nuisance is a balancing act between the defendant's right to use his land as he wishes and the plaintiff's right to enjoy his land without interference. The plaintiff must establish that the defendant has caused a substantial interference with his use or enjoyment of his land. No account is taken of trivialities. The interference may take a number of forms but some of the commonest are smells, vibrations, noise, dust and other emissions.

Whether the interference amounts to a nuisance is a question for the court. Normally this will be determined by applying a reasonableness test, but where the interference causes *material damage* to the plaintiff's land, the defendant will be liable unless the plaintiff is over sensitive or one of the defences to nuisance applies.

St Helens Smelting Co *v* Tipping (1865) 11 HL Cas 642

The plaintiff bought an estate near to the defendant's copper smelting works. Fumes from the works damaged the plaintiff's trees and crops. The court drew a distinction between nuisances causing material damage to the land and those which caused sensible personal discomfort. In the latter case the question of locality was relevant. As the plaintiff's land had suffered material damage, the fact that the locality was a manufacturing area was irrelevant and an injunction was granted.

The problem with this decision is that it is difficult to determine what is meant by material damage. Any substantial interference with residential land may lower its value, but unless the land itself is damaged the locality factor may defeat the plaintiff's claim.

The reasonableness test

Where the interference causes sensible personal discomfort the court will apply a reasonableness test to determine whether it amounts to a nuisance. A number of factors may be taken into account either in isolation or conjunction to determine whether the defendant's conduct was reasonable.

Locality

Sturges *v* Bridgman (1879) 11 ChD 852

A confectioner had for more than twenty years used industrial pestles and mortars. This caused no interference until the plaintiff doctor built an extension consulting room in his garden, adjacent to the confectioner's premises. At this stage the noise and vibration were alleged to be a nuisance. The doctor's action succeeded. The court took into account the fact that the area consisted largely of doctors' consulting rooms and stated; that which would be a nuisance in Belgrave Square would not necessarily be so in Bermondsey.

The effect of this rule is to make it difficult for those who live in industrial areas to succeed. But for a successful case see the following.

Rushmer *v* Polsue and Alfieri Ltd [1906] 1 Ch 234

The plaintiff milkman lived in a printing area of London. He found it difficult to sleep at night and sought an injunction for nuisance by noise. The injunction was granted although the plaintiff was the only resident, as the noise went beyond the boundaries of what was acceptable.

Duration

The longer the interference continues the more likely it is to be a unreasonable. The question frequently arises in connection with building works. The courts have laid down a principle that provided these are carried on with reasonable skill and care and interference is minimised, then no nuisance is committed (*Andreae* v *Selfridge & Co Ltd* [1938] Ch 1).

The duration principle raises difficulties with one-off nuisances where there is an isolated or single escape. These occur where there is a state of affairs on the defendant's land which causes damage on one occasion to the plaintiff.

Spicer *v* Smee [1946] 1 All ER 480

Defective electrical wiring was installed in the defendant's premises. This caused a fire which destroyed the plaintiff's adjacent house. The defendant was held liable in nuisance. The nuisance was the state of affairs on the defendant's land which foreseeably exposed his neighbour's property to danger.

The cases on isolated escape illustrate a connection between nuisance and negligence. In *Bolton* v *Stone* [1951] AC 850, (see 'Breach of duty', p. 65), the isolated escape of a cricket ball from the ground was held not to be a nuisance. Whether there is a state of affairs on the land sufficient to give rise to liability in nuisance will depend on the frequency with which balls escape. This is also a factor in determining negligence.

Sensitivity

If the damage is due more to the sensitivity of the plaintiff's property than to the defendant's conduct then no nuisance is committed.

Robinson *v* Kilvert (1889) 41 ChD 88

The plaintiff occupied the ground floor of the defendant's premises and used it to store brown paper. Heat created by the defendant's manufacturing process damaged the paper. It was held that the damage was due more to the sensitivity of the paper than to the defendant's activities and there was no nuisance.

Bridlington Relay Co v Yorkshire Electricity Board [1965] Ch 436

The defendant's overhead power cables interfered with the transmissions from the plaintiff's television booster mast. The plaintiff's action failed as their activity was held to be sensitive and television reception as a leisure activity of little value to its users was not protected by nuisance.

NB It is likely that an English court would now follow Commonwealth decisions on the latter point and find that television reception was protected. The sensitivity point is still valid.

As in nervous shock cases the courts will grant protection in sensitivity cases if it can be shown that the breach of duty would have affected non-sensitive interests.

McKinnon Industries Ltd *v* Walker [1951] 3 DLR 577

The defendant's factory emitted sulphur dioxide which damaged the plaintiff's commercially grown orchids. As the interference would have damaged non-sensitive plants, the plaintiff was able to recover the full extent of the loss, including the damage to the sensitive orchids.

Public utility

Can the defendant advance the argument that although his activity may be causing damage to the defendant, it is in the public interest that he be allowed to continue? The traditional view is that public interest is irrelevant to the question of private rights and will be ignored. This is dramatically illustrated by a case where Ireland's only cement factory was closed down for causing a nuisance at a time when building was an urgent public necessity (*Bellew* v *Cement Co Ltd* [1948] IR 61).

The modern view would appear to turn on what remedy is being sought. In deciding whether or not to grant an injunction the court may take into account public utility.

Miller *v* Jackson [1977] QB 966

Cricket balls frequently entered the plaintiff's garden from the adjacent cricket club despite the attempts of the club to prevent this. The Court of Appeal held by 2-1 that a nuisance had been committed but refused by 2-1 to grant an injunction on the grounds of public utility. The court felt that the utility of the club to the community outweighed the plaintiff's interest.

NB See also 'Remedies for nuisance', pp. 185–6, for the grounds for granting an injunction. One method of taking into account public utility is for Parliament to grant statutory authority to the defendant for his activity. On this see 'Defences to nuisance', pp. 187–8.

Malice

The bad motive or malice of the defendant may make what would otherwise have been reasonable conduct, unreasonable and a nuisance.

Christie *v* Davey [1893] 1 Ch 316

The plaintiff and defendant lived in adjoining houses. The plaintiff gave music lessons in the house. This annoyed the defendant who responded by banging trays on the wall and shouting while the lessons were in progress. The plaintiff was held entitled to an injunction. The defendant's malice made his conduct unreasonable and a nuisance.

Hollywood Silver Fox Farm v Emmett [1936] 2 KB 468

The plaintiff bred silver foxes. The defendant, after an argument, ordered guns to be fired on his own land but close to the plaintiff's land. His intention was that the noise would prevent the foxes from breeding. An injunction was granted to restrain the defendant. What would otherwise have been a reasonable act was a nuisance because of his malice.

NB On malice generally see 'General principles', p. 9.

NUISANCE AND FAULT

Is it necessary for the plaintiff to prove that the defendant was negligent in order to succeed in a nuisance action? If this was the case then the tort of nuisance would become redundant, as all actions would be brought in negligence.

There is a distinction between nuisance and negligence. In negligence the court will look at the way the defendant did something, whereas in nuisance the court is looking at a protected interest of the plaintiff and balancing it against what the defendant did.

Example

Take a factory which is built with the latest state of the art pollution control machinery. Despite this, the factory still emits foul smells which nearby residents allege amount to a nuisance and/or negligence. In the negligence action the court will have to ask whether the defendant took all reasonable care. If he used the best available equipment and maintained it properly, then the negligence action will fail. In the nuisance action the court will have to balance the interests of the two parties using the tests set out above. The question is whether the defendant acted reasonably, not whether he used all reasonable care. The court could find that the defendant's activity was unreasonable and grant an injunction in nuisance.

The law in this area was confused by dicta of Lord Reid in *Wagon Mound (No 2)* (1966) 1 AC 617.

> Negligence is not an essential element in nuisance. Nuisance is a term used to cover a wide variety of tortious acts or omissions and in many negligence in the narrow sense is not essential . . . And although negligence may not be necessary, fault of some kind is almost always necessary and fault generally involves foreseeability.

Negligence in the narrow sense means breach of duty in negligence, i.e. that the defendant failed to act with reasonable care. This is not essential to a nuisance action except in certain areas. Where the nuisance was due to the act of a trespasser or act of nature, then negligence of this kind is necessary, albeit with a subjective rather than an objective test. Where the damage was due to an isolated escape then the plaintiff probably needs to establish facts which would establish negligence in order to succeed in nuisance. The problem is what Lord Reid meant by fault of some kind. As the case was concerned with remoteness of damage and established the test for remoteness of damage in nuisance as being reasonable foreseeability of damage, fault in this sense may mean that the defendant will not be liable unless he could have foreseen the kind of damage which occurred.

REMEDIES

Injunction

The injunction is the primary remedy in nuisance actions and its objective is to force the defendant to cease his activities. The injunction may be perpetual and terminate the activity or limit it to certain times. It is possible for the court to suspend the injunction and give the defendant the opportunity to eliminate the source of the complaint.

Injunctions are equitable remedies and as such are not available as of right. The question of when the court should exercise its discretion to refuse an injunction was considered in the following case.

Shelfer v City of London Electric Lighting Co [1895] 1 Ch 287

Vibration and noise were caused by the defendant's activities. The defendant claimed that the plaintiff should be limited to damages as the award of an injunction would deprive many Londoners of electricity. The court held that the discretion not to award the injunction should only be exercised in exceptional circumstances:

(a)   where the injury to the plaintiff's legal right is small; and
(b)   is capable of being estimated in money terms; and
(c)   is one which can be adequately compensated by a small money payment; and
(d)   it would be oppressive to the defendant to grant an injunction.

There is no mention of refusing the injunction in the public interest. But in *Miller* v *Jackson* (see above, p. 183) the Court of Appeal did refuse the injunction in the public interest of the playing of cricket. That there is no trend in this direction is shown by:

Kennaway v Thompson [1981] QB 88

The plaintiff lived by Lake Windermere which was used by the defendants for power boat racing. The noise from the boats amounted to a nuisance and an injunction was granted to restrain the number of events and the noise level of boats. The social utility argument of the defendants was rejected as not compatible with the *Shelfer* principle.

Damages

In public nuisance actions the plaintiff must prove special damage in order to succeed. Damage must usually be proved in a private nuisance action but may be presumed.

The remoteness of damage test in nuisance is the same as that in negligence; the defendant must have been able to reasonably foresee the kind of damage which occurred (*Wagon Mound (No 2)* [1967] AC 617).

Where the nuisance causes damage to the land, the measure of damages will usually be the depreciation in value of the land. Where the nuisance consists of interference with use and enjoyment, then proof of depreciation will assist the plaintiff's case but is not essential.

Bone *v* Seale [1975] 1 All ER 787

The defendant's pig farm was adjacent to the plaintiff's land. The plaintiff sought an injunction and damages in nuisance in respect of smells caused by pig manure and the boiling of pig swill. The court held that there was no damage to the plaintiff's property or his health and awarded damages of £1,000 based on the amount that would have been awarded in a personal injuries action for loss of sense of smell.

Damages may be awarded for damage to the land itself and for damage to the plaintiff's chattels on the land. Recovery of damages for personal injuries is more obscure. It is clear that the plaintiff can recover for injury associated with his enjoyment of the land, such as loss of sleep or discomfort caused by smells.

If the action is in public nuisance, then the plaintiff can recover damages for economic loss. There is little authority on economic loss in private nuisance, but as the plaintiff must have had a property interest damaged before he can sue, the same problems are not present as in negligence.

Abatement

This remedy is a form of self-help and consists of the plaintiff taking steps to stop the nuisance e.g. by cutting off the branches of overhanging trees or unblocking drains.

Where the exercise of the remedy requires the plaintiff to enter another person's land then notice must be given, otherwise the abator will become a trespasser.

It is fair to say that the law does not usually favour this remedy and in most cases it is not advisable.

DEFENCES

There are a number of issues which might be thought to be defences but which are generally not. These will be dealt with first, followed by the established defences to nuisance.

Coming to the nuisance

This is not a defence. The defendant cannot argue that the plaintiff was aware of the nuisance when he moved to the area.

Sturges v Bridgman (1879) 11 ChD 852

(For facts see above under 'Locality', p. 181.) The confectioner argued that when the doctor built his extended consulting room he was aware of the noise and had therefore come to the nuisance. The court rejected this argument as this was not a recognised defence in nuisance.

Miller v Jackson [1977] QB 966

(For facts see 'Public utility', p. 183.) Lord Denning argued that as the plaintiffs had bought a house next to a cricket field they could not be heard to complain about interference by cricket balls. This was rejected by the rest of the Court of Appeal so far as establishing a nuisance was concerned, but it was a factor in the decision of the majority not to grant an injunction.

Usefulness

This is simply the question of public utility as a defence, rather than a factor going towards reasonableness. The fact that the defendant's activity is a useful one is not a defence.

Nuisance due to many

Where the nuisance is caused by a number of persons, it is not a defence for the defendant to prove that his contribution alone would not have amounted to a nuisance.

Prescription

In actions for private nuisance it will be a defence to show that the nuisance has been actionable for a period of twenty years and the plaintiff was aware of this during the relevant period.

Sturges v Bridgman (1879) 11 ChD 852

(For facts see 'Locality', p. 181.) The defence of prescription failed, as the noise from the confectioner's activities only became a nuisance when the doctor had his extended consulting room built. Only from this time did the twenty years start to run.

Statutory authority

In the light of what has been said about nuisance, a person would be justified in looking quizzically at certain parts of the industrial landscape of England and Wales. The answer lies in the defence of statutory authority. During the nineteenth century it became common for industrial operators to obtain the passing of a private Act of Parliament to give them authority to commit a nuisance, provided that there was no negligence on their part. This was done by the railway companies, as the operation of steam trains would cause a nuisance by smoke, noise and vibration.

Where a statute orders something to be done, there will be no liability in nuisance for doing this and for any inevitable consequences. An inevitable consequence is one which cannot be avoided by the use of due skill and care.

In the absence of negligence, most cases will involve the interpretation of the statute and the court may take into account the national interest.

Metropolitan Asylum District *v* Hill (1881) 6 App Cas 193

A local authority was given statutory power to build a smallpox hospital. They were restrained from erecting it in a place which would have been a source of danger to the local community. In this case the power could have been carried out without committing a nuisance, by siting it in a less populated area.

Allen *v* Gulf Oil Refining Co [1981] 1 AC 1001

The defendants were given statutory power to compulsorily purchase land and build an oil refinery and associated works. The plaintiff complained of nuisance caused by smell, noise and vibration. On a preliminary point the House of Lords held that statutory authority was available as a defence. The plaintiff had argued that the statute empowered the construction of the refinery but not its use. The court took into account the preamble to the statute and the public demand for oil and that Parliament would not have authorised the construction of the refinery but not its use.

The problem created by statutory authority, taking away private rights in the public interest, could be avoided if Lord Denning's suggestion in the Court of Appeal had been taken up. He suggested that although the injunction could not be granted the plaintiff should be entitled to damages. The House of Lords did not agree.

Contributory negligence

There is little authority on whether contributory negligence is available as a defence to nuisance. There is dicta in *Trevett* v *Lee*. [1955] QB 966 to the effect that it operates as a defence in public nuisance cases.

QUESTION

An unidentified person entered the premises of the Cosmetic Photography Co and dropped a burning cigar into a a pile of leaves, which began to smoulder.

The managing director of the firm noticed the smoke but took no steps to extinguish the fire, even though there were inflammable chemicals nearby. He now states that he took no action as the wind was blowing the smoke away from the chemicals.

The wind direction changed, the fire spread to the chemicals and there was an explosion.

A pedestrian on a nearby road was injured. A customer's car in the firm's yard was destroyed. Prize ferrets on a nearby farm stopped breeding as a result of the noise of the explosion.

Advise the Cosmetic Photography Co as to their potential liability in tort.

Suggested approach

In any question of this nature it is necessary to see where each plaintiff suffered their damage in order to assess which tort they may be able to use. The question clearly points to nuisance but there may be actions in negligence or *Rylands* v *Fletcher* as well.

What would the company's liability in nuisance be? They have not created the nuisance so any liability would stem from their occupation of land on which the nuisance occurred. Is an occupier liable for nuisances created by trespassers? To determine this it is necessary to consider the law developed in the trilogy of cases of *Sedleigh Denfield* v *O'Callaghan; Goldman* v *Hargrave; Leakey* v *National Trust*.

The principle that emerges from the cases is that an occupier is liable if he knew or should have known of such a nuisance and failed to take reasonable steps to abate the nuisance. The firm are clearly aware of the potential nuisance. What amounts to reasonable steps? The test is similar to that for negligence with the exception that it is subjective rather than objective. The court will look at the cost/effort required to abate and will balance this against the occupier's financial/physical resources.

On this basis there would appear to have been a breach of duty. Given that a state of affairs existed on the defendant's land which amounted to a potential nuisance, for what damage is the occupier liable? The test for remoteness of damage in nuisance is whether the kind of damage was reasonably foreseeable (*Wagon Mound (No.2)*). However, in order to sue in private nuisance, a person must have an interest in the land affected (*Malone* v *Lasky*). In order to sue in public nuisance it is necessary to show that the plaintiff suffered special damage (*Castle* v *St Augustine's Links*).

The pedestrian on the road does not have an interest in land and therefore has no action in private nuisance. Could he sue in public nuisance? The nuisance must affect a class of HM subjects (*A-G* v *PYA Quarries*). The class would be highway users. The plaintiff must have suffered special damage. The pedestrian satisfies this criterion as he was injured by the explosion. Personal injuries can be compensated by a public nuisance action. The pedestrian could also sue the firm in negligence if he could establish that they owed him a duty of care.

Would an action lie under *Rylands* v *Fletcher*? The problem points in such an action would be whether there had been a non-natural user of land and whether personal injuries can be compensated by the tort. Where industrial material is stored on land and there is an escape causing damage, the courts may use the test in *Mason* v *Levy Auto Parts*. Look at the nature of the area, the quantity of the goods and the way in which they are stored. As this virtually amounts to a negligence test it is unlikely that the plaintiff would succeed in *Rylands* if he were to fail in negligence. The question of personal injuries in *Rylands* is confused. On the one hand there is *obiter dicta* from the House of Lords that such damage is not recoverable (*Read* v *Lyons*). On the other hand there are first instance cases which state that such damage is recoverable (see e.g. *Perry* v *Kendricks Transport*). The correct view may be that if the plaintiff has an interest in land then such damages are recoverable. This approach would rule out the pedestrian.

An action in respect of damage to the car could not be brought in private nuisance (no interest in land) or in *Rylands* (no escape). A public nuisance action is doubtful and the best course of action would be to sue in negligence under the Occupiers' Liability Act 1957. The plaintiff is a visitor to the premises and is owed the common duty of care under s. 2(2). The failure to extinguish the fire may amount to a breach of the duty and reasonably foreseeable damage has been caused.

The owner of the prize ferrets may have an action in private nuisance as he has an interest in the land affected. The difficulty here would be with sensitivity. If normal animals would have been affected by the noise then an action will lie for the full extent of the damage, even to sensitive property (*Robinson* v *Kilvert; McKinnon Industries* v *Walker*). A *Rylands* action could be prevented on the grounds of non-natural user or on a defence of act of a third party.

Further reading

Buckley, RA *The Law of Nuisance* (1981)
Buxton, RJ (1966) 29 MLR 676
Dias, RWM [1967] CLJ 61
Kodilinye, G (1986) 6 Leg. Stud 182
McLaren, JPS (1983) 3 OJLS 155
Newark, FH (1949) 65 LQR 480
Ogus, AI and Richardson, GM [1977] CLJ 284
Tromans, S [1982] CLJ 87

17 | *Rylands* v *Fletcher* and liability for fire

INTRODUCTION

The rule in *Rylands* v *Fletcher* arose as a result of the Industrial Revolution in the nineteenth century. As land was put to industrial use, damage was frequently inflicted on neighbouring landowners. The rule represented a judicial attempt to impose strict liability on industrialists who did this. This was on the basis that if a person exploited land for profit and imposed costs on a neighbour as a result, then those costs should be met by the profit taker, without the need for the loss maker to prove fault.

The rule has had a rather unhappy history and has been treated with hostility by some of the judiciary who were obsessed by the fault principle. A further obstacle to its development was the fact that it was misunderstood by some judges and applied to inappropriate circumstances such as falling flagpoles and escaping caravaners. This wider application increased judicial hostility as it was perceived as strict liability undermining the fault based tort system.

The gist of the tort is that it governs liability for escapes from land, used for a non-natural purpose, which cause damage. It overlaps with nuisance and liability may lie in the alternative. There are distinctions between the torts and these will be pointed out as we go through the elements of *Rylands*.

Rylands *v* Fletcher (1865) 3 H&C 774; (1868) LR 3 HL 330 (House of Lords)

The defendant had employed contractors to build a reservoir on his land to supply water for his factory. The contractors negligently failed to block a disused mine shaft and when the reservoir was filled the plaintiff's adjoining mine was flooded. At first instance, Blackburn J laid down the following rule:

A person who, for his own purposes, brings on his land, and collects and keeps there anything likely to do mischief if it escapes, must keep it at his peril, and, if he does not do so, he is prima facie answerable for all the damage which is the natural consequence of its escape.

The House of Lords approved the decision subject to the addition of the requirement that the defendant's user of his land should be non-natural.

No existing action would have been possible. There was no trespass as the damage was not direct and immediate. At this time no nuisance action would lie for an isolated escape and an employer was not liable for the negligence of his independent contractor. Although Blackburn J concealed the creation of a new legal principle by appealing to a strand of strict liability in English law, there is no doubt that new law was created.

THE PLAINTIFF'S CASE

Things likely to do mischief if they escape

The thing which is brought onto the land must be likely to do damage if it escapes. The rule is not confined to things which are intrinsically dangerous. Some tangible thing must be accumulated. This makes the rule narrower than nuisance liability where there need be no accumulation. Examples of things within the rule include: water, electricity, fire, chemicals, explosives, gas, slag heaps, chair-o-planes, caravan dwellers and things which give off noxious gases and fumes.

Accumulation

The thing must have been accumulated or brought onto the defendant's land. The rule therefore only applies to things which are artificially brought or kept on the defendant's land and does not apply to things which are naturally on the land. In such cases the plaintiff must look to nuisance or negligence. (See e.g. *Goldman* v *Hargrave; Leakey* v *National Trust*.)

In the case of water, the defendant will not be liable for escape where the water was naturally on the land and the defendant was not responsible for its presence there (*Smith* v *Kenrick* (1849) 137 ER 205).

In the case of trees which are naturally there or self-grown, these would appear to be outside the rule.

Where the defendant accumulates a slag heap and there is an escape then there will be liability under the rule. But where the land itself cracks and weathers, causing an escape, liability will lie in nuisance rather than *Rylands* (see *Leakey* v *National Trust*).

Non-natural user

At first instance Blackburn J said that the rule applied only to a thing which was not naturally there. In the House of Lords, Lord Cairns said that the rule applied when the accumulation was a non-natural use of the land.

At first it was uncertain whether natural meant non-artificial or ordinary and usual. It has since been given the latter and narrower meaning.

Rickards *v* Lothian [1913] AC 263

A tap in part of a building which was leased to the defendant was turned on by an unknown person and overflowed. This caused damage to the plaintiff's stock on the floor below. There was held to be no liability under the rule, as the defendant was making an ordinary and proper use of the building. Lord Moulton defined non-natural use as: 'some special use bringing with it increased danger to others and must not merely be the ordinary use of the land or such use as is proper for the general benefit of mankind'.

This is not an objective test as was shown when the use of land as a munitions factory in wartime was held to be a natural use (*Read* v *Lyons*), when in peacetime it had had been held to be non-natural (*Rainham Chemical Works Ltd* v *Belvedere Fish Guano Co Ltd*).

The courts have used the idea of non-natural user to remove the strict liability aspect of the rule. There is a tendency to interpret it almost as a negligence test.

Mason *v* Levy Auto Parts of England Ltd [1967] 2 QB 530

The defendant stored quantities of combustible materials on his land. These caught fire under mysterious circumstances and burnt the plaintiff's ornamental hedge. In determining whether there had been a non-natural user, regard had to be had to: (a) the quantities of materials stored; (b) the way in which they were stored; and (c) the character of the neighbourhood. The court recognised that satisfaction of these requirements would also justify a finding of negligence.

British Celanese *v* AH Hunt [1969] 1 WLR 959

The defendants manufactured electrical components on an industrial estate. The plaintiffs alleged that metal foil strips had escaped and caused a power failure at their electricity sub-station. On the *Rylands* action it was held that the defendants were not liable as there was no non-natural user of the defendants' land. The defendants were held liable in negligence and nuisance. This suggests, in contrast to *Mason*, that there is a difference between negligence and *Rylands*. However, Lawton J took a different approach to non-natural use. The use of land in the vicinity had to be looked at and as it was an industrial estate the land was being used for the purpose for which it was designed. There were no special risks attached to the storage of foil and the use was beneficial to the community.

In terms of the original rule *British Celanese* is probably correct. Equating *Rylands* with negligence is the wrong approach. *Rylands* is to deal with extraordinary or special risks where the use of reasonable care should not excuse the defendant. The concept of non-natural user should enable the court to distinguish between hazardous operations and those which are part and parcel of everyday life.

Escape

There must be an escape from the land of which the defendant is in occupation or control.

Read v J Lyons & Co Ltd [1947] AC 156

The plaintiff was employed in the defendant's munitions factory and was injured when a shell exploded in the factory. It was held that the *Rylands* principle was not applicable as there had been no escape of the thing causing injury from the defendant's land. In the absence of negligence the plaintiff could not succeed.

This rule creates an unfortunate distinction between those outside the premises and those inside. This is illustrated by the Abbeystead pumping station disaster. The North West Water Authority invited a group of local residents to tour the pumping station. A build up of methane gas caused an explosion while they were on the premises. The victims had to prove negligence but had they been outside might have been able to rely on the strict liability rule.

The harm which is caused need not be immediately caused by the thing which is accumulated. If explosives are stored on land and used to blast rocks which are blown onto adjacent land and cause damage, then an action may lie.

It is necessary that the escape takes place from land of which the defendant is in control.

Smith v Scott [1973] Ch 314

A local authority let a house to a homeless family who covenanted not to commit a nuisance. The plaintiff lived next door and found the anti-social behaviour of the family intolerable. It was held that the rule in *Rylands* could not be applied to a landlord as he no longer had the control over the tenant which the rule required.

NB It was also held that there is no duty of care owed by a landowner to his neighbour in respect of persons to whom he lets his property. The action in nuisance also failed as the landlord had expressly forbidden the commission of a nuisance.

The normal action will be where there is an escape from land under the defendant control to the plaintiff's adjacent land. The courts have also had to consider cases where an escape occurred on the highway. This can arise where two companies use the highway for utility purposes. Where water escapes and damages adjacent electricity cables, then liability may lie. There may also be liability where a dangerous thing is brought onto the highway.

Rigby v Chief Constable of Northampton [1985] 2 All ER 985

Police fired CS gas into a shop in an attempt to flush out a dangerous psychopath. There were no fire fighting appliances standing by. The shop was set on fire by the gas. It was held that the rule applied to the escape of things from the highway. But it probably does not apply to the intentional or voluntary release of a dangerous thing. If it does apply to a voluntary release then the defence of necessity will apply.

NB The court also held that the defence of necessity was available in a trespass action provided that there was no negligence on the part of the defendant.

Damage

The tort is not actionable *per se*, so damage must be proved.

The rule on remoteness is not clear. Blackburn J stated that the defendant would be liable for all the damage which was the natural consequence of the escape. The *Wagon Mound (No 1)* principle does not govern *Rylands*, but the decision in *Wagon Mound (No 2)* leaves the remoteness rule unclear. There are two possibilities: either the test is directness, in the sense that all the damage which is the natural consequence of the escape is recoverable; or the reasonable foreseeability test applies, in that the kind of damage that could reasonably have been foreseen is recoverable. It is submitted that a test based on foreseeability is inappropriate to strict liability torts and a directness test is appropriate.

British Celanese Ltd *v* AH Hunt Ltd [1969] 1 WLR 959

Defendants made electrical parts. Metal foil on their site blew onto an overhead cable, which caused a power failure, stopping production at the plaintiff's factory. There was held to be no liability under *Rylands* as there was no special risk. The court took the view that the damage had to be the natural consequence of the escape.

NB The defendants were held liable in negligence and nuisance for materials which solidified in the plaintiff's machines.

Damages are recoverable where there is damage to the land or to chattels on the land.

The position with regard to damages for personal injuries is not clear. The difficulty stems from *obiter* in *Read* v *Lyons*, where it was stated that negligence must be proved in order for damages for personal injuries to be recovered. If *Rylands* is regarded as a tort of strict liability, then such damages would appear not to be recoverable. There are cases before *Read* v *Lyons* where damages for personal injuries were recoverable, but these could technically be regarded as incorrect. But in some subsequent cases such damages have been stated to be recoverable (*Perry* v *Kendricks Transport Ltd* [1956] 1 WLR 85; *Rigby* v *Chief Constable of Northampton*). The correct view would appear to be that if the plaintiff has an interest in the land affected, he may recover for personal injuries, but not a plaintiff without such an interest.

It is equally unclear whether damages for economic loss may be recovered.

Weller *v* Foot and Mouth Disease Research Institute [1966] 1 QB 569

A virus escaped from the defendant's premises and caused a ban on the movement of livestock. The plaintiff cattle auctioneers sued for loss of income. It was held that they had no action under *Rylands* as they had no interest in any land to which the virus escaped.

Whether developments in negligence have affected this position is unknown. But given the courts tendency to equate *Rylands* and nuisance with property interests it is unlikely.

DEFENCES

Liability in *Rylands* is said to be strict. This means that the absence of negligence on the part of the defendant is not a defence. However, as liability is strict and not absolute, there are certain defences to the action.

Consent of the plaintiff

If the plaintiff expressly or impliedly consents to the presence of the thing on the defendant's property, then the defendant is not liable for damage caused by the escape unless he has been negligent.

Peters *v* Prince of Wales Theatre (Birmingham) Ltd [1943] 1 KB 73

The plaintiff had leased a shop from the owners of an adjoining theatre. The plaintiff's shop was flooded when pipes for a sprinkler system in the theatre burst during cold weather. There was held to be implied consent on the part of the plaintiff to the existence of the sprinkler system, which existed at the time he took his lease.

Where the consent of the plaintiff is relevant, it is an illustration of the general defence of *volenti non fit injuria*.

Common benefit

The defence of consent of the plaintiff overlaps with a defence called common benefit. The basis of the defence is that no action will lie when the source of the danger is maintained for the benefit of both parties to the action: e.g. a box for water collection which leaks.

Could this defence be maintained by utility companies?

Dunne *v* North Western Gas Board [1964] 2 QB 806

A gas mains exploded without any negligence on the part of the defendants. The court considered common benefit and the judge doubted whether the defendants, as a nationalised industry, could be said to accumulate the gas for their own purposes.

NB Would the same approach be taken with a privatised monopoly?

Act of a stranger

Where the escape is caused by the act of a stranger over whom the defendant has no control, this will be a defence.

Perry v Kendricks Transport Ltd [1956] 1 WLR 85

The defendants parked their coach on their car park. The petrol tank had been drained. The child plaintiff was crossing waste land adjacent to the car park, when he was injured by an explosion caused by a small boy throwing a lighted match into the petrol tank. An unknown person had removed the cap from the petrol tank. The defendants were held not liable, as the explosion was caused by the act of a stranger over whom they had no control.

The basis of the defence is the absence of control by the defendant over the act of a stranger on his land. If the act was foreseeable and could have been guarded against, then there can be liability.

Hale v Jennings Bros [1938] 1 All ER 579

The mountings on a chair-o-plane at a fair ground were tampered with by an unknown person. The chair-o-plane became detached and landed on a tombola stall, causing injury to the occupant. The defendant was held to have had sufficient control to prevent this from happening.

Once the defendant has successfully shown that the escape was caused by the act of a stranger, then the action effectively becomes one of negligence. The plaintiff must show that the defendant should have foreseen this risk and guarded against it. This tends to undermine the original purpose of the rule, which was intended to place liability for exceptional risks on the person creating the risk. This defence has the effect of making liability dependent on a negligent failure to control the risk. *NB* Does an escaping chair-o-plane come within exceptional risk!

Act of God

This is a defence which is remembered by students but which has little application. It is available when the escape is caused by natural forces, in circumstances which no human foresight can provide against and of which human prudence is not bound to recognise the possibility.

Nichols v Marsland (1876) 2 Ex D 1

The defendant had three artificial lakes made on his land by damming a natural stream. A heavy thunderstorm accompanied by unprecedented rain caused the banks of the lakes to burst and water to destroy four bridges on the plaintiff's land. It was held that the flooding was caused by an Act of God for which the defendant was not liable.

This decision has since been criticised (*Greenock Corpn* v *Caledonian Railway* [1917] AC 556) and its application is extremely limited. It may apply in the case of earthquakes, lightning or tornadoes. In principle, it should not be a defence, as it is the defendant who has created the risk. The effect of Act of God is to shift attention to whether he ought to have foreseen the event. Again this brings negligence principles into strict liability.

Default of the plaintiff

Where the escape is due to the default of the plaintiff he will have no action.

Eastern and SA Telegraph Co Ltd v Cape Town Tramways Co Ltd [1902] AC 381

The defendants stored electricity to run their tramways. Electricity escaped and interfered with the plaintiff's cable, which was used for sending messages. The plaintiffs were unable to recover, as the damage was caused by the sensitivity of their equipment.

Where the plaintiff's default amounts to contributory negligence he will have his damages reduced in proportion to his responsibility for the damage suffered.

Statutory authority

Whether a statute confers a defence under *Rylands* is a question of construction of the statute.

Green v Chelsea Waterworks Co (1894) 70 LT 547

The defendant's water main burst and flooded the plaintiff's premises. The defendants were obliged by statute to maintain a water supply. The court held that bursts were inevitable from time to time and in the absence of negligence there was no liability.

Charing Cross Electricity Co v Hydraulic Co [1914] 3 KB 772

On similar facts to the above case the defendants were held not to have a defence of statutory authority, as they only had a power to supply water and were not under a duty to do so.

NB A statute may expressly impose strict liability for the escape of dangerous things: e.g. Reservoirs Act 1975. Not even express statutory authority to construct the reservoir will exonerate the defendant.

THE FUTURE OF *RYLANDS* v *FLETCHER*

Whether the original purpose of the rule was to impose strict liability for extra-hazardous activities, or simply to extend nuisance, the courts seem to view *Rylands* now as simply an extension of nuisance. There are differences between the torts; in *Rylands* the plaintiff need have no interest in land to sue; in nuisance the plaintiff need not show an accumulation or non-natural user.

The dominance of the fault principle in the twentieth century has succeeded in eradicating virtually any claims the tort may have had to being strict liability and distinct from nuisance or negligence. This is apparent in non-natural user and the defences of act of a stranger, common benefit, Act of God and statutory authority. In most cases, an action in negligence would succeed on the same facts as a successful *Rylands* action. For this reason and the problem posed by the requirement of escape and the confusion surrounding personal injuries, there are very few successful actions.

The vexed question of strict liability has been examined by the Law Commission (Law Commission No 23 (1970)) who made proposals based on dangerous things and dangerous activities. However, they made no recommendation for change until the entire fault principle had been examined. The Pearson Report (1978) is the nearest that England has come to such an examination. The report, almost as an afterthought, put forward a scheme limited to death and personal injuries (Vol 1 Ch 31) but this was not well thought through and like so much else of Pearson nothing has come of it.

LIABILITY FOR FIRE

Most of the cases which now come before the courts fall under the Fires Prevention (Metropolis) Act 1774, s. 86. Despite its title the operation of the Act is not confined to London.

No one will be liable for a fire which begins on his premises, unless he has been negligent in respect of it. But if the fire arises by accident, then the occupier may be liable if he is negligent in allowing it to spread.

Musgrove *v* Pandelis [1919] 2 KB 43

A fire accidentally started in the carburettor of the defendant's car. The defendant's employee negligently failed to turn off the petrol tap and the fire spread. The defendant was held liable not for the original fire but for the spreading of the fire.

As the Act confers immunity for the original fire where it accidentally begins, then if the fire was produced by negligence or nuisance it is actionable. If the circumstances of the fire come within the rule in *Rylands*, then there will be liability: e.g. if a person brings onto land a highly explosive article which amounts to a non-natural user.

Where liability is for the spread of the fire this may lie in negligence, nuisance or *Rylands*.

Further reading

Rylands
Law Commission Report No 32 (1970)
Newark, FH (1961) 24 MLR 557
Pearson Commission Report Vol 1 Ch 31
Stallybrass, WTS [1929] CLJ 376
Williams, DW [1973] CLJ 310

Fire
Ogus, IA [1969] CLJ 104

Part V
MISCELLANEOUS TORTS

18 | Liability for animals

INTRODUCTION

Liability for damage caused by animals falls under two heads. There are specific statutory rules contained in the Animals Act 1971 and a person may also be liable at common law in a number of torts. It is the former that we will be concerned with here, but brief mention will be given of the common law rules.

Where an action is brought in a tort such as negligence or nuisance, for damage caused by animals, the usual rules of that tort will apply and can be found in the appropriate chapter.

Pitcher v Martin [1937] 3 All ER 918

The defendant was walking his dog on a long lead. The dog broke away and the plaintiff pedestrian became entangled in the lead, fell and was injured. The defendant was held liable in both negligence and nuisance.

Draper v Hodder [1972] 2 QB 556

The infant plaintiff was savaged by a pack of Jack Russell terriers which had rushed out from the defendant's adjacent premises. The dogs had not previously misbehaved so they had no dangerous propensity for the purposes of strict liability. But the owner was held liable in negligence for allowing the dogs to escape. Jack Russells in a pack have a tendency to attack moving persons or objects. The defendant as an experienced breeder should have known this and, given the dogs tendency to dash next door, some damage (although not the extent or precise manner of its infliction) was foreseeable to the plaintiff. The failure to secure the dogs was a breach of duty.

Historically there had been examples of stricter forms of liability for animals, such as the *scienter* rule and liability for cattle trespass. These were replaced by the Animals Act 1971, which also contains provisions about dogs and animals on the highway.

DANGEROUS AND NON-DANGEROUS ANIMALS

The Animals Act 1971 replaced the common law rules which had divided animals into fierce and docile categories for the purpose of establishing liability. The Act divides animals into dangerous and non-dangerous species. Some of the old case law may still be relevant, but the fact that an animal was classed as docile at common law does not mean that it will be a non-dangerous species under the Act. Camels were treated as docile but are now a dangerous species.

A dangerous animal is defined by s. 6(2):

(a) A species not commonly domesticated in the British Isles; and
(b) whose fully grown animals normally have such characteristics that they are likely, unless restrained, to cause severe damage or that any damage that they may cause is likely to be severe.

Dangerous animals

Clearly only a limited number of British animals will fall into this category, e.g. wild stags, foxes and wild cats.

No distinction is made between individual animals within a species.

Behrens *v* Bertram Mills Circus [1957] 2 QB 1

The plaintiffs were injured by the defendant's Indian elephant. Although the elephant in question was was 'no more dangerous than a cow', it was held to be *ferae naturae* (dangerous).

If the animal is not commonly domesticated in the British Isles then it must meet one of two criteria before it is classified as dangerous: it must be likely to cause severe damage, e.g. snakes or tigers; or any damage which they do cause, even if this is unlikely, is likely to be severe, e.g. elephants on account of their bulk.

Liability for dangerous animals is governed by s. 2(1):

where any damage is caused by an animal which belongs to a dangerous species, any person who is a keeper of the animal is liable for the damage, except as otherwise provided by this Act.

Liability under this section is therefore strict, unless the defendant can bring himself within one of the defences in s. 5.

Keeper is defined by s. 6(3):

a person is a keeper of an animal if –
(a) he owns the animal or has it in his possession; or
(b) he is the head of a household of which a member under the age of sixteen owns the animal or has it in his possession.

The second part of the definition deals with the problem of an animal which is in theory owned by a child.

Non-dangerous animals

Liability for non-dangerous animals is governed by s. 2(2):

Where damage is caused by an animal which does not belong to a dangerous species, a keeper of the animal is liable for the damage . . . if

(a) the damage is of a kind which the animal, unless restrained, was likely to cause or which, if caused by the animal, was likely to be severe; and

(b) the likelihood of the damage or of its being severe was due to characteristics of the animal which are not normally so found in animals of the same species or are not normally found except at particular times or in particular circumstances; and

(c) those characteristics were known to that keeper or were at any time known to a person who at that time had charge of the animal as that keeper's servant or, where that keeper is the head of a household, were known to another keeper of the animal who is a member of that household and under the age of sixteen.

Cummings v Grainger [1977] 1 All ER 104

The plaintiff was bitten by the defendant's Alsatian which was used as a guard dog in a scrap yard occupied by the defendant. The dog was allowed to run around loose in the yard. The plaintiff had entered the yard with a friend who had a licence to be there. A notice on the gates stated 'Beware of the Dog'.

On the question of whether s. 2(2) was satisfied:

Lord Denning: Section 2(2)(a): this animal was a dog of the Alsatian breed. If it did bite anyone, the damage was likely to be severe. Section 2(2)(b): this animal was a guard dog kept so as to scare intruders and frighten them off. On the owner's own evidence, it used to bark and run round in circles. . . . Those characteristics – barking and running around to guard its territory – are not normally found in Alsatian dogs except in the circumstances where used as guard dogs. Those circumstances are particular circumstances within s.2(2)(b). It was due to those circumstances that the damage was likely to be severe if an intruder did enter on its territory. Section 2(2)(c): those characteristics were known to the keeper.

NB The plaintiff's case failed on the grounds of defences under s. 5. (See below.)

Wallace v Newton [1982] 1 WLR 375

The plaintiff was the defendant's groom and had charge of a horse which was known to be nervous. The horse was being loaded on a trailer when it became aggressive, jumped forward and caused the plaintiff to injure her arm. It was held that in order to succeed the plaintiff did not have to prove that the horse had a vicious tendency to attack people, merely that it exhibited a tendency not found in horses generally.

Defences

Defences to actions brought under s. 2. are provided by s. 5:

Section 5(1): A person is not liable under sections 2 to 4 of this Act for any damage which is due wholly to the fault of the person suffering it.

Section 5(2): A person is not liable under section 2 of this Act for any damage suffered by a person who has voluntarily accepted the risk thereof.

Section 5(3): A person is not liable under section 2 of this Act for any damage caused by an animal kept on any premises or structure to a person trespassing there, if it is proved either –

(a) that the animal not was kept there for the protection of persons or property; or

(b) (if the animal was kept there for the protection of persons or property) that keeping it there for that purpose was not unreasonable.

The operation of these defences can be seen in the following case.

Cummings *v* Grainger [1977] 1 All ER 104

(For facts see above, p. 205.)

> *Lord Denning*: It follows that the keeper of the dog is strictly liable unless he can bring himself within one of the exceptions in s. 5. Obviously s. 5(1) does not avail. The bite was not *wholly* due to the fault of the [plaintiff] but only *partly* so. Section 5(3) may, however, avail the keeper. It shows that if someone trespasses on property and is bitten or injured by a guard dog, the keeper of the guard dog is exempt from liability if it is proved that keeping it there for that purpose was not unreasonable. [Lord Denning went on to hold that it was not unreasonable to keep a guard dog because of the nature of the area (East End of London) and the fact that the yard contained scrap metal.]
>
> *Ormrod LJ*: [After agreeing with Lord Denning on s. 5(3).] The other defence which is open to him is under s. 5(2). . . . They are, to my mind, fairly simple English words . . . I do not think it is open to any doubt . . . she accepted the risk. No doubt she knew about the dog, she said that she was frightened of the dog. For whatever reason she went in . . . I would myself come to the conclusion that she accepted the risk, and it is no answer to say that she had Mr Hobson with her.

NB. Since this decision the Guard Dogs Act 1975 has made it a criminal offence to use or permit the use of a guard dog on premises without the guard dog being at all times under the control of a handler. Although the Act provides for no civil penalty, it may be that contravention of the Act would mean that use of a guard dog was unreasonable for the purposes of s. 5(3).

TRESPASSING LIVESTOCK

Strict liability for trespassing livestock is of ancient origin and was one of the strands of precedent drawn on in creating the rule in *Rylands* v *Fletcher*. The present law is in the Act.

Livestock is defined by s. 11 and includes cattle, horses, asses, mules, hinnies, sheep, goats, poultry and deer not in a wild state. The definition does not include dogs and cats.

Livestock trespassing onto land

Liability is governed by s. 4:

(1) Where livestock belonging to any person strays on to land in the ownership or occupation of another and –
(a) damage is done by the livestock to the land or to any property on it which is in the ownership or possession of the other person; or
(b) any expenses are reasonably incurred by that other person in keeping the livestock while it cannot be restored to the person to whom it belongs or while it is being detained in pursuance of section 7 of this Act, or in ascertaining to whom it belongs; the person to whom the livestock belongs is liable for the damage or expenses, except as otherwise provided by this Act.

Two points should be noted on this section. First that liability is strict. The plaintiff does not have to show that the keeper was aware of a tendency by the livestock to stray. Second, that there is no liability under the section for personal injuries or for damage to the property of a third party. In such cases the plaintiff would need to rely on s. 2(2) or the common law.

Defences

The only defences to an action under s. 4 are provided by s. 5:

Section 5(5): A person is not liable under section 4 of this Act where the livestock strayed from a highway and its presence there was a lawful use of the highway.
Section 5(6): . . . the damage shall not be treated as due to the fault of the person suffering it by reason only that he could have prevented it by fencing; but a person is not liable under that section where it is proved that the straying of the livestock on to the land would not have occurred but for a breach by any other person, being a person having an interest in the land, of a duty to fence.

The s. 5(5) defence is of ancient common law origin, based on the idea that a person driving livestock on the highway should only be liable where there was negligence involved.

Matthews v Wicks (1987) *The Times* 25 May

The defendant's sheep were left to graze on common land and were also left free to wander onto the highway. The sheep entered the plaintiff's garden and caused damage. The Court of Appeal held that s. 5(5) had no application as letting the sheep wander on the highway did not constitute a lawful use.

Section 5(6) should be read with s. 5(1). In general, the fact that the plaintiff could have prevented the livestock entering by fencing his land, will not be a defence. This is because there is no general duty in English law to fence out. But where there is a duty to fence out imposed on the plaintiff, who is in breach of the duty, and the defendant's animals stray onto his land, there will be a defence under s. 5(6).

Detention of trespassing livestock

Section 7 of the Act provides a partial remedy in the case of trespassing livestock. This replaces the old common law remedy of distress damage feasant. A person may detain the livestock until the damage is paid for. If the right of detention is exercised, then notice must be given to the police and the owner (if known) within 48 hours. If an offer is made to pay for the damage, then the livestock must be released to the owner. The detainer must feed the livestock during the detention. After 14 days the livestock may be sold at market or auction. After deducting the costs of the sale, keeping the livestock and compensation for any damage caused, any surplus must be returned to the owner.

Animals escaping onto the highway

At common law there was no liability where an animal escaped from land onto the highway and caused damage to highway users. This immunity from liability existed before modern traffic conditions and was abolished by s. 8 of the Act:

> (1) So much of the rules of the common law relating to liability for negligence as excludes or restricts the duty which a person might owe to others to take such care as is reasonable to see that damage is not caused by animals straying on to a highway is hereby abolished.
> (2) Where damage is caused by animals straying from unfenced land to a highway a person who placed them on the land shall not be regarded as having committed a breach of the duty to take care by reason only of placing them there if –
> (a) the land is common land, or is land situated in an area where fencing is not customary, or is a town or village green; and
> (b) he had a right to place the animals on that land.

Liability under the Act is therefore based on negligence and the court will consider all relevant matters on the question of reasonableness, such as the possibility of fencing, the nature of the animal, the amount of traffic on the highway and whether there is a local custom of fencing. There is no general duty imposed on landowners to fence animals in. This is a question of local custom except where s. 8(2) specifically applies.

Davies v Davies [1975] QB 172

The defendant worked on a farm owned by his mother. He owned sheep which he kept on the farm. His mother was entitled to graze cattle and sheep on adjacent common land and the defendant also grazed his sheep there. The plaintiff collided with the sheep on the highway as he was driving past the common land. It was held that s. 8(2) protected persons with a legal right to place animals on the common land and anyone licensed by the owner to place his animals there. The defendant was therefore not liable for the damage to the plaintiff.

SPECIAL LIABILITY FOR DOGS

Two sections of the Act provide special liability in the case of dogs.

Section 3 provides that where a dog causes damage by killing or injuring livestock, then the keeper of the dog is liable for the damage unless he can bring himself within one of the defences provided by the Act. The relevant defences would be fault of the plaintiff (s. 5(1)), assumption of risk (s. 5(2)), and contributory negligence (s. 10 and s. 11). There is also a specific defence in s. 5(4), where the livestock had strayed onto land and the dog belonged to the occupier of the land or its presence on the land was authorised by the occupier.

Section 9 provides that it is lawful for a person to kill or injure a dog which:

(i) is worrying or is about to worry livestock, and there are no other reasonable means of ending or preventing the worrying; or
(ii) the dog has been worrying livestock, has not left the vicinity, is not under the control of any person and there are no practicable means of ascertaining to whom it belongs.

The person harming the dog must also show:

(i) that he was a person entitled to act for the protection of livestock (i.e. he owns either the livestock or the land on which it is, or is authorised by either owner);
(ii) that he gives notice to the police within 48 hours.

A specific defence is provided by s. 5(4) where the dog was entitled to be on the land and the livestock was not.

REMOTENESS OF DAMAGE

The Act is silent on the question of remoteness. The strict liability provisions in the Act on trespassing livestock and the scienter rule, (s. 2) are closely related to the rule in *Rylands* v *Fletcher*. As the House of Lords in *Wagon Mound (No 1)* specifically exempted *Rylands* from the foreseeability test for remoteness, it might be assumed that the remoteness test for the strict liability provisions under the Act was directness.

For s. 2(2) to apply, the keeper of the animal has to be aware of a particular characteristic of the animal to be liable. If damage is of a kind likely to be caused by this characteristic, then the keeper will be liable. But if the damage is not of such a kind, then the keeper will not be liable: e.g. if a dog has a tendency to bite people, the keeper will be liable for bites. But if a child who does not know the dog runs away and falls over, it is unlikely that the keeper would be liable under the section for this kind of damage.

Further reading

North, PM *The Modern Law of Animals* (1972)

19 | Trespass to the person

INTRODUCTION

Trespass to the person encompasses the three torts of battery, assault and false imprisonment. Although not a trespass, the rule in *Wilkinson* v *Downton* will also be dealt with here.

Trespass has certain features which will be examined first.

Actionable per se

All trespasses are actionable *per se*. This means that the plaintiff does not have to prove actual damage as part of his case. The tort protects personal integrity, which is regarded as being so important that it is protected even in the absence of damage. An unwanted contact may amount to trespass to the person even though there is no physical injury to the plaintiff.

Direct and physical

The trespass action is derived from the ancient writ of trespass. One of the requirements of the writ was that the defendant's act had to be direct and physical. Where the infringement is caused by an indirect act there may be a remedy in a tort derived from case, such as nuisance or negligence, but not in trespass. If the defendant throws a log and it hits the plaintiff, this is trespass. If the log lands in the road and the plaintiff later trips over it, this is case (negligence).

Scott *v* Shepherd (1773) 2 W Bl 892

The defendant threw a lighted squib into a crowded market place. It landed on a market stall and was thrown on. It landed on another stall and exploded, injuring the plaintiff. The defendant was held liable for the injuries to the plaintiff as they were a direct result of the defendant's act. The act of throwing the squib on did not break the link between defendant's act and plaintiff's injury, as it was instinctive.

Defendant's state of mind

At one time it was thought that trespass to the person was a tort of strict liability, in the sense that it did not require any fault on the part of the defendant. This view was rejected in *Stanley* v *Powell* [1891] 1 QB 86, where it was held that trespass to the person was not actionable in the absence of intention or negligence. The decision confirmed that trespass is a fault based tort, but left open the question of burden of proof.

Fowler *v* Lanning [1959] 1 QB 426

A shot from the defendant's gun hit the plaintiff. The plaintiff's statement of claim alleged simply that, the defendant shot the plaintiff. The defendant applied to have the action struck out as disclosing no cause of action. Diplock J ruled that the burden of proof in a trespass action was on the plaintiff, who had to show that the defendant acted either intentionally or negligently. The decision was controversial as there was authority in both directions, but it removed one of the supposed major advantages of the trespass action, that the defendant had to prove he was not at fault.

The argument over the state of mind required continued. At first it was a question of whether there was actually such a thing as a negligent trespass, or whether trespass was solely an intentional tort.

Letang *v* Cooper [1965] 1 QB 232

The plaintiff was sunbathing on a hotel car park. The defendant negligently drove his car over her legs and caused injury. The action was brought more than three years after the incident. The defendant said that the action was statute barred by limitation. The plaintiff said that her cause of action was in battery and that the limitation period there was six years. The Court of Appeal held that as the action was for a failure to take reasonable care, it was, for the purposes of the Limitation Act, an action in negligence.

Lord Denning was of the opinion that where the act causing the damage was intentional, the correct cause of action was trespass. Where the act was negligent, the cause of action was in negligence. There was no overlap between trespass and negligence (Danckwerts LJ agreed). This view seems to have been accepted in *Wilson* v *Pringle* [1986] 2 All ER 440 (see below).

Diplock LJ was not prepared to hold that a trespass could not be committed negligently, but proceeded to eliminate any advantages that the plaintiff might have in suing in trespass. He said the burden of proof in terms of fault was on the plaintiff in trespass and actual damage is a necessary ingredient in unintentional trespasses.

Whichever view is accepted, there now appears to be no practical advantage to a plaintiff in bringing an action based on lack of reasonable care in trespass, rather than negligence. The only remaining differences are the remoteness rules and the fact that no duty need be owed in trespass. However, it appears unlikely that a court would allow a plaintiff to proceed in trespass where no duty was owed in negligence.

Trespass to the person has now ceased to be a tort in the mainstream of personal injuries litigation. This function is now performed almost exclusively by negligence. There is some overlap between criminal cases and trespass to the person. Where the defendant's act amounts to a criminal offence, the plaintiff may prefer a criminal prosecution to be brought, rather than face the hazards of litigation. If the defendant is convicted, the plaintiff may be able to obtain compensation through the Criminal Injuries Compensation Scheme. The remaining importance of trespass to the person is in the area of civil liberties. It offers some protection against the over-officious policeman, the practical joker and the office wolf.

BATTERY

A battery is the direct and intentional application of force to another person without that person's consent.

Mental state required for battery

The courts have always been faced with the problem of distinguishing those contacts which are part of everyday life and those which are unacceptable and illegal.

This presents difficulties for the courts. Contact between persons ranges from violent assaults through to accidental bumps in crowded streets. In between are people who play practical jokes, people who indulge in sexual harrassment and doctors who need to treat unconscious patients. How is a court to draw a line?

Collins v Wilcock [1984] 3 All ER 374

Goff LJ stated that the court started with the fundamental principle that every person's body is inviolate. Interference with a person's body will generally be lawful where he consented to it. There is also a broad exception to allow for the exigencies of everyday life such as jostling in the street and social contact at parties. This is a question of physical contact which is generally acceptable in the ordinary conduct of everyday life.

In 1986 the Court of Appeal attempted a test to make the distinction.

Wilson v Pringle [1986] 2 All ER 440

The defendant, as a practical joke, pulled the plaintiff's schoolbag from his shoulder, causing injury. The Court of Appeal held that the act of touching the plaintiff had to be intentional and the touching had to be a hostile touching. The relevant intention was the intention to do the act. There need be no intention to cause damage. A blow struck by a person undergoing an epileptic fit would therefore not be trespass, as there would not be the relevant intent.

Hostility was not to be construed as malice or ill-will and would be a question of fact in each case. The act of touching in itself might display hostility. If not, then the plaintiff must plead the facts which he claims demonstrates that the touching was hostile.

The intention of the Court of Appeal was to remove the necessity for the courts to find implied consent in some cases where they did not wish to hold that a touching was a battery. The requirement of hostility was supposed to remove the need for implied consent because, a touching which is hostile can scarcely be said to be consented to.

The attempt to frame a test of this nature has not been particularly successful. The first problem is what is meant by hostile? The Court of Appeal gave a number of examples of what it is not, but only one example of what it is. A police officer who touches a person with the intention of restraining them, with no legal power to do so, is acting with a hostile intent. (See also *Collins* v *Wilcock* [1984] 3 All ER 374.)

Battery has always operated against the person who pushed unwanted attention on a person as well as against the violent. The unwanted kiss is as actionable as the unwanted punch. If hostile is taken in its literal sense then the practical joker and the molester could be immune in this tort. The dividing line in *Wilson* v *Pringle* was drawn at what was generally acceptable in the ordinary conduct of daily life. However, what is perfectly acceptable to one person may be totally repugnant to another.

The hostility test has not been particularly well received by the House of Lords. One of the areas in which it was thought it could operate was medical cases. Where a doctor had to touch a person in an emergency, instead of saying there was an implied consent, the court would say that there was no hostility on the part of the doctor and therefore no battery. This view has now been rejected by the House of Lords (*F* v *West Berkshire Health Authority* [1989] 2 All ER 545). Lord Goff stated:

> and it has recently been said that the touching must be hostile . . . I respectfully doubt whether that is correct. A prank that gets out of hand, an over-friendly slap on the back, surgical treatment by a surgeon who mistakenly thinks that the patient has consented to it, all these things may transcend the bounds of lawfulness, without being characterised as hostile. . . . In *Wilson* v *Pringle* the Court of Appeal considered that treatment or care of such persons [the mentally disordered] may be regarded as falling within the exception relating to physical contact which is generally acceptable in the ordinary conduct of everyday life. Again, I am, with respect, unable to agree. That exception is concerned with the ordinary events of everyday life, jostling in public places and such like, and treatment, even treatment for minor ailments, does not fall within that category of events. The general rule is that consent is necessary to render such treatment lawful.

The present position is not clear. In medical cases the hostility requirement has been rejected. In order to avoid an action for battery, a doctor must show either that consent was given for the touching, or that the touching was necessary in the best interests of the patient. (See 'Medical Negligence', pp. 156–8.) In other cases it appears that Lord Goff's general exception for everyday contact may take precedence over hostility.

Contact

As battery is derived from the writ of trespass it must be direct and physical. This means that there must be some contact with the plaintiff before a battery is committed. Merely obstructing a person's progress without any contact is not a battery.

ASSAULT

An assault is an act which causes another person to apprehend the infliction of immediate, unlawful, force on his person (*Collins* v *Wilcock*).

The torts of assault and battery normally go together. If a person waves his fist, this is an assault. If the blow is struck, that is a battery. If the plaintiff is unaware of the impending blow, e.g. if he is struck from behind or is unconscious, then only battery is committed.

For assault to be committed the plaintiff must be in reasonable apprehension of an immediate battery. If the defendant does not have the means to carry out the threat, then no assault is committed. Violent gestures by pickets at colleagues who are still working and pass by in buses is not an assault (*Thomas* v *National Union of Mineworkers* [1985] 2 All ER 1). However, where the defendant attempts to land a blow on the plaintiff but is restrained by a third party, the tort of assault is committed (*Stephens* v *Myers* (1830) 4 C & P 349).

Where a loaded gun is pointed at the plaintiff an assault is committed. Is there an assault if the gun is unloaded? In principle the answer should be yes, provided the plaintiff is unaware of the fact the gun is not loaded. There is dicta to the effect that this is not an assault (*Blake* v *Barnard* (1840) 9 C & P 626). But in a criminal case it was stated that it was an assault (*R* v *St George* (1840) 9 C & P 483). Most commentators take the view that the latter case is correct.

There is some difficulty with whether words alone can amount to an assault. The problem dates back to an old case where it was said that no words or singing are equivalent to an assault (*R* v *Meade* (1823) 1 Lew CC 184). Many commentators feel that this is wrong and where words spoken by the defendant induce fear in the plaintiff, this should be actionable. Support for this can be found in a criminal case where it was considered that the words, 'get out knives', would constitute an assault (*R* v *Wilson* [1955] 1 WLR 493).

What is clear is that words may negative what would otherwise have been an assault.

Turberville *v* Savage (1669) 1 Mod Rep 3

The plaintiff and defendant were involved in an argument. The defendant placed his hand on his sword and said, 'if it were not assize time I would not take such language from you'. It was held that the words negatived what would otherwise have been an assault.

DEFENCES TO ASSAULT AND BATTERY

Consent

Following *Wilson* v *Pringle* there is some dispute as to the extent to which consent is a defence to trespass to the person, or whether it is a part of the tort itself. The argument centres around the requirement of hostility. If the contact must be made with hostile intent, then any consent to the contact would negate an inference of hostility. (See 'Battery', pp. 213–14.) The substantive importance lies in the burden of proof. Does the plaintiff have to prove a lack of consent or does the defendant have to establish there was consent? There is no clear answer to this, but the preferable view in the light of developments in the medical cases is that consent is a defence and the burden of proof is on the defendant.

Express consent does not present problems where the plaintiff is legally capable of giving it. A surgeon will be protected from an action in battery by the signing of a consent form by the patient. (See 'Medical Negligence', pp. 156–8.)

Implied consent presents more difficulties. It has been rejected in favour of necessity in medical cases. (See above and 'Medical Negligence', pp. 156–8.) A participant in a sporting event is said to impliedly consent to contacts in accordance with the rules of the game. A punch thrown at an opponent will not be within the rules and there will be a battery committed (*R* v *Billinghurst* [1978] Crim LR 553). In boxing no action will lie for a punch within the rules, as a participant consents to this by getting into the ring. But a foul punch is not consented to and may give rise to a battery action.

Any consent given will be limited to the act for which permission is given. A customer going to the hairdresser consents to having their hair cut and any other treatment they specifically agree to. But a customer who gives consent for a permanent wave does not agree to a tone rinse. The hairdresser will be liable in battery (*Nash* v *Sheen* [1953] CLY 3726).

SELF-DEFENCE

Self-defence is a defence where reasonable force is used in defence of the plaintiff's person, property, or another person. What amounts to self-defence will be a question of fact in each case but the basic principle is that the force used must be reasonable in proportion to the attack.

Lane *v* Holloway [1968] 1 QB 379

The plaintiff and defendant were neighbours. The plaintiff had been drinking and was talking to a friend outside his house. The defendant's wife shouted, 'you bloody lot'. The plaintiff replied, 'shut up you monkey faced tart'. The defendant heard this and said he wanted to see the plaintiff on his own. The plaintiff came out and thinking he was about to be hit, hit the defendant on the shoulder. The defendant hit the plaintiff in the eye, which needed 19 stitches. The defendant's blow was held to be out of proportion to the circumstances and the action succeeded.

The defence of *volenti non fit injuria* also failed, as although a participant in a fight takes the risk of injury, he does not accept the risk of a savage blow out of proportion. Where the violence used is in proportion, then the plaintiff may be defeated by either *volenti non fit injuria* or *ex turpi causa*. (See 'Defences to Negligence'.)

Contributory negligence

Whether the Act applied to trespass to the person was formerly a matter of dispute. The issue was considered by the Court of Appeal.

Barnes v Nayer (1986) *The Times* 19 December

The defendant killed the plaintiff's wife with a machete and was convicted of manslaughter. His defence to a civil action by the plaintiff was that he had been provoked by the deceased. He put forward three defences. The first was *ex turpi causa*. It was held that the defence could apply in an appropriate battery case, but on these facts was not established. The second was *volenti*. Again this was not made out on the facts. The third defence was contributory negligence. It was established that the plaintiff's contributory negligence could constitute fault within the Law Reform (Contributory Negligence) Act 1945, s. 1, but because the defendant's response was out of all proportion to the plaintiff's act, it was not applicable on these facts.

FALSE IMPRISONMENT

False imprisonment is the unlawful imposition of constraint on another's freedom of movement from a particular place.

The tort does not require incarceration as such and can be committed by any unlawful detention. Forcing a person to remain in a field by threatening them with a gun would be false imprisonment. It could also be an assault.

The commonest modern examples of the tort are wrongful arrest by police officers or shop detectives. In such cases it is necessary to consider the powers of arrest of the defendant and whether they have been complied with.

The restraint must be total

Bird v Jones (1845) 7 QB 742

The defendants wrongfully roped off part of the footpath on a bridge. The plaintiff was prevented from crossing the bridge by this route. This was held not to be false imprisonment as the restraint was not total. Lord Denman dissented and was of the opinion that if a person had a right to go somewhere and was prevented from doing so, then that should be false imprisonment.

The decision means that if a person has a reasonable means of escape, the tort will not be committed. But if the means of escape involves any danger, it is not reasonable to expect a person to take it. If the door to a room is locked but there is an open french window at ground level, this would not be false imprisonment. But it would not be reasonable to expect a person to climb from a second floor window.

The House of Lords has considered the position of a person serving a term of imprisonment and whether such a person has an action for false imprisonment if the conditions of his detention are altered.

Hague v Deputy Governor of Parkhurst Prison; Weldon v Home Office [1991] 3 All ER 733

In one case the governor of the prison had ordered the transfer of a prisoner to another prison and his segregation from other prisoners. In the other case a prisoner alleged that he had been placed in a strip cell without lawful authority. The House of Lords held that a person lawfully committed to prison had no residual liberty which could be protected by private law remedies, since while in prison he had no liberty to be in any place other than where the prison regime required him to be. He therefore had no liberty capable of deprivation by the prison regime which could constitute the tort of false imprisonment.

A prisoner who is subjected to intolerable conditions of detention which are seriously prejudicial to his health, has a public law remedy by way of judicial review. He may also sue in negligence if he suffers actual injury to his health.

Knowledge of the detention

Does the plaintiff have to be aware that he has been falsely imprisoned? If he was asleep, unconscious, drunk or insane at the time of the detention, he might not have been aware he was detained. This raises the question of which interest is protected by the tort. Freedom of movement as such, or the mental stress caused by knowledge of detention.

In a nineteenth-century case it was held that a child kept behind at school as his parents had not paid the fees had no action, as he was unaware of the detention (*Herring* v *Boyle* (1834) 1 Cr M & R 377). However, modern authority indicates that knowledge is not a necessary ingredient of the tort.

Meering v Grahame-White Aviation Co Ltd (1920) 122 LT 44

The plaintiff was suspected of theft and was taken to his employer's offices. Two policemen remained close to him while he was questioned. The defendants, in an action for false imprisonment, argued that the plaintiff was unaware of any detention. Atkin LJ stated that knowledge of the detention was irrelevant to whether the tort had been committed. Knowledge might, however, be relevant to the assessment of damages.

This view has now been approved by the House of Lords in *Murray* v *Ministry of Defence* [1988] 2 All ER 521. Where a person was unaware of his detention and had suffered no actual harm, he would receive only nominal damages. The US view that knowledge was necessary was rejected because of the importance of liberty of the individual.

The restraint must be unlawful

A person may be able to impose a lawful restraint on a person. An occupier of premises may be able to stipulate certain restrictions on a visitor, including the method by which he is to leave.

Robinson v Balmain Ferry Co Ltd [1910] AC 295

The plaintiff paid one penny to enter the defendant's wharf, intending to leave by ferry. He missed a ferry and wished to leave the wharf via the turnstile. The defendants refused to let him out unless he paid a penny. This was held not to be false imprisonment. The condition that a penny should be paid was a reasonable one and the plaintiff had contracted to leave the wharf by another way.

This decision does not give a general right to imprison to enforce contractual rights. An innkeeper who locked up the plaintiff when he refused to pay his bill was held liable in false imprisonment (*Sunbolf* v *Alford* (1838) 3 M & W 248).

Herd v Weardale Steel, Coal and Coke Co Ltd [1915] AC 67

A coalminer, in breach of contract, refused to continue with his work and demanded to be taken to the surface. His employers refused for some time. This was held not to be false imprisonment. The miner had consented to remain underground until the end of his shift and was not entitled to be taken to the surface until then.

Although the case was decided on the basis of consent, an alternative explanation is that the defendant had omitted to act, rather than acting positively, and that this is not trespass. Would this mean that a failure to let a person out of a locked room was not false imprisonment?

What these cases establish is that a passenger on a bus cannot insist on getting off except at a scheduled stop.

Lawful arrest

Where the defendant is carrying out a lawful arrest no tort is committed. The correct procedure must be carried out in order to make an arrest. The arrested person must be told the true grounds on which he is being arrested and unless he is physically seized, must be told that he is being arrested. Exceptions are provided where a person makes it impossible to inform by resisting and in the case of citizens' arrests, no reason need be given where it is obvious. If a private citizen makes an arrest, he must hand the arrested person over to the police within a reasonable time (*Lewis* v *Tims* [1952] AC 676).

The question of power of arrest is a complex one and will only be dealt with in outline here.

A police officer arresting with a warrant will be protected from an action for false imprisonment. Any defects in the warrant are not his concern.

The main powers of arrest without a warrant are found in the Police and Criminal Evidence Act 1984, ss. 24 and 25.

An arrest may be made for an arrestable offence. This is an offence where: the sentence is fixed by law (e.g. murder); those for which a person may be sentenced on a first conviction to five years or more in prison; offences specifically designated by the Act as arrestable.

Anyone may arrest a person who is in the act of committing an arrestable offence or anyone whom he has reasonable grounds for suspecting to be committing such an offence.

Where an arrestable offence has been committed, anyone may arrest a person whom he has reasonable grounds for suspecting to be guilty of it. This applies even where the wrong person was arrested, provided there were reasonable grounds for suspecting him.

A police officer is protected where no arrestable offence has been committed but where he had reasonable grounds for suspecting that it had. A private citizen who arrests where no arrestable offence had been committed is guilty of false imprisonment.

A police officer may also arrest where he has reasonable grounds for suspecting a person is about to commit an arrestable offence. Certain powers are also given under the Act for police officers to arrest for non-arrestable offences.

There is also a common law power for any person in whose presence a breach of the peace is being committed, or is about to be committed, to make an arrest.

THE RULE IN *WILKINSON* v *DOWNTON*

Closely associated to trespass is the rule in *Wilkinson* v *Downton* [1897] 2 QB 57. The defendant, as a practical joke, told the plaintiff that her husband had broken both legs in an accident. As a result the plaintiff suffered nervous shock. The court held the defendant liable for the damage. Wright J laid down a principle:

> The defendant has . . . wilfully done an act calculated to cause physical damage to the . . . plaintiff, i.e., to infringe her legal right to personal safety, and has thereby in fact caused physical harm to her. That proposition, without more, appears to me to state a good cause of action, there being no justification alleged for the act.

The action could not have been brought in trespass as there was no contact made or physical force used. At the time there was no liability in negligence for nervous shock, which has since been introduced. This perhaps explains the fact that there is only one other reported decision on the principle. In *Janvier* v *Sweeney* [1919] 2 KB 316 the plaintiff recovered damages after the defendant told her that her husband was a German spy and she suffered nervous shock.

There is no reason to suppose that the principle is confined to nervous shock. If a person dresses up as a ghost and causes a person to fall down stairs with fright, then an action would probably lie.

The potential of the action for introducing a tort based on intention has not been taken up.

QUESTION

Alan was invited to a party by Bob. Christine, one of the guests, dressed up as a ghost and jumped out at Alan, who was of a nervous disposition. Alan passed out, and was carried into a spare bedroom by David, another guest. Some time later Bob saw that the bedroom door was open and without looking inside, locked the door, as the room contained his priceless collection of country and western records. David and Christine later went to see if Alan was all right but found the door locked. They asked Bob for the key but he refused as he was busy tuning his banjo. One hour later he opened the door. Alan was still unconscious but as Bob poured cold water over him, he swung his fist in a reflex action and knocked some of Bob's teeth out.

What torts, if any, have been committed and which defences do you consider to be relevant?

Suggested approach

With a question of this nature it is best to take each incident separately. Start by defining the three relevant torts.

With the ghost incident, two torts may have been committed. There may be an action under the principle in *Wilkinson* v *Downton*. There has been an intentional act without lawful justification but has Alan suffered damage? If he suffered nervous shock then yes. Likewise, if he received physical injuries. There may be an action in assault. The advantage of this tort is that it does not require damage (actionable *per se*). Was Alan placed in immediate fear of a battery?

When David carries Alan is there a battery? If there is a requirement of hostile intent, then no, as the act is performed for Alan's benefit. If hostility is not required for the tort then David will need to find a defence. This could be implied consent or necessity.

Placing Alan in the room does not constitute false imprisonment as there is a means of escape through an unlocked door. When Bob locks the door, does he commit false imprisonment? He is unaware of anyone's presence in the room and cannot have intended to commit the tort. Was he negligent in not checking and can the tort be committed negligently? Recent case law on state of mind in trespass has concentrated on battery, but it appears that the tort can only be committed intentionally. If this is the case in false imprisonment, the tort would appear not to have been committed.

Does Bob commit the tort when he refuses to open the door? This raises the question of whether false imprisonment can be committed by an omission. See *Herd* v *Weardale*.

Does Bob commit a battery when he pours water on Alan? Again consider the question of hostility. If this element is not required then Bob would appear to have committed a battery. He could defend on the grounds of either implied consent or necessity.

Alan's punch would appear not to be a battery as he does not intend to do the act. His action is similar to an epileptic striking a person during a fit.

Further reading

Tan, KF (1981) MLR 166
Trinidade, FA (1982) 2 Oxf JLS 211

20 | Defamation

The torts of libel and slander are collectively known as defamation and protect a person's interest in his reputation. Defamation presents particular problems, as any law which protects reputation will also infringe on freedom of speech. A good law should draw a balance between these competing interests. The English law on defamation has been criticised for favouring protection of reputation at the expense of freedom of speech, and adverse comparisons have been drawn with the law in the USA, where freedom of speech is protected by the constitution. Any protection which is given to freedom of speech in England is provided by the defences to defamation. A preliminary point for students to note is that these are as important as the requirements for the plaintiff's case. A frequent error in defamation answers is to ignore the defences.

A frequent criticism of defamation is that it is only available as a remedy to the wealthy as legal aid is not available.

Defamation actions are tried by jury. This is said to give rise to two problems. The outcome of cases is said to be unpredictable and recently there has been publicity given to the massive damages awards which have been awarded by juries.

A person's reputation does not survive his death and a defamation action will terminate on the death of the plaintiff. This can work to the advantage of the defendant, especially in the case of an old or infirm plaintiff, leading to a reluctance to settle.

LIBEL AND SLANDER

A defamatory meaning can be conveyed by any medium, but it is the choice of medium which determines whether the action lies in slander or libel. If the defamatory meaning is conveyed in a permanent form then the action is libel. If it is in a temporary form, then slander. Modern technology has created difficulties in drawing the distinction but there are some established examples of each tort.

Libel is committed where writing or printing is used. The placing of a wax effigy in the chamber of horrors by mistake has also been stated to be libel (*Monson* v *Tussauds Ltd* [1894] 1 QB 671).

Youssoupoff *v* Metro-Goldwyn-Mayer Pictures Ltd (1934) 50 TLR 581

The defendants made a film which falsely imputed that the plaintiff had been raped or seduced by Rasputin. The defamatory matter was in the pictorial (as opposed to the soundtrack) part of the picture and was held to be libel. It must therefore be regarded as unsettled whether a defamatory soundtrack is libel or slander.

Slander is generally committed by speech or by gestures.

Certain areas are settled by statute. The Defamation Act 1952, s.1 provides that words or visual images broadcast for general reception are libel. This will cover BBC, ITV and other commercial broadcasts but not police radio or CB broadcasts. The Theatre Act 1968 provides that the publication of words in the course of performance of a play shall be treated as libel.

Some areas are still uncertain, such as reading aloud letters, sky writing, gramophone records and deaf and dumb language.

The importance of the distinction

There are two important distinctions between libel and slander.

A libel which tends to provoke a breach of the peace is a crime. Slander is only tortious.

Libel is actionable *per se* (without proof of actual damage). Slander is actionable only on proof of actual damage except in the following circumstances.

(a) *Imputation of a criminal offence.* The offence must be punishable with imprisonment but a specific offence need not be mentioned. 'I know enough to put you in gaol', is therefore a slander actionable *per se*.

(b) *Imputation of a disease.* There is some doubt about the scope of this rule but it is clear that the allegation must be that the plaintiff is presently suffering from a contagious or infectious disease. Venereal disease, leprosy and plague are within the rule.

(c) *Imputation of unchastity or adultery to any woman or girl.* This is a statutory rule. Section 1 of the   Slander of Women Act 1891 states: 'Words spoken and published . . . which impute unchastity or adultery to any woman or girl shall not require special damage to render them actionable'. An imputation of lesbianism is within the section.

(d) *Imputation of unfitness or incompetence.* This exception relates to allegations of unfitness, incompetence or dishonesty in any profession, trade, calling or business held or carried on by the plaintiff.

Section 2 of the Defamation Act 1952:

> In an action for slander in respect of words calculated to disparage the plaintiff in any office, profession, calling, trade or business held or carried on by him at the time of the publication, it shall not be necessary to allege or prove special damage, whether or not the words are spoken of the plaintiff in the way of his office, profession, calling, trade or business.

The effect of the section is that it is no longer necessary for the words to slander the plaintiff in the context of his office provided that they are likely to injure him within it.

THE PLAINTIFF'S CASE

In order to establish an action in defamation the plaintiff must prove three things: that the words were defamatory, that they referred to him, and that they were published by the defendant.

DEFAMATORY MEANING

As it is impossible to produce a list of words which are defamatory, there needs to be a general test which can be applied to the alleged defamatory statement. It is important to remember that the words must be taken in the context in which they were used and that words change their meaning over time. In the past it has been held to be defamatory to call a person a German or a Catholic. Neither of these words would now carry a defamatory meaning. Until recently the word gay had a universally complimentary meaning. To describe a person as a gay fellow today might be to invite proceedings for defamation.

The most generally accepted definition of a defamatory statement is that of Winfield: 'Defamation is the publication of a statement which tends to lower a person in the estimation of right thinking members of society generally; or which tends to make them shun or avoid that person.'

Two things should be noted at this stage.

First defamation is essentially an attack on reputation. If a person says that a businessman runs his business dishonestly or incompetently, this is defamatory. But if it is stated that a business has closed down, this is not defamatory, although financial loss may be caused. (An action may lie in malicious falsehood.) Likewise, it is not defamatory to say that a pop star has joined a closed order of monks, as this will not affect his reputation, although it may affect his bookings.

Secondly, defamation need not impute moral turpitude. This is shown by the *Youssoupoff* case and cases where it has been held to be defamatory to allege insanity.

Function of judge and jury

Defamation actions are tried by judge and jury. The judge's functions are:

(a)   To direct the jury on the legal meaning of defamation.
(b)   If he thinks that no reasonable person would regard the words as defamatory he must withdraw the case from the jury.
(c)   If the words are obviously defamatory, the judge may indicate to the jury that the evidence cannot bear any other interpretation.

Whether the words are in fact defamatory is a question for the jury.

Capital and Counties Bank Ltd *v* Henty (1882) 7 App Cas 741

The defendants had a disagreement with the managers of the plaintiff bank and sent out a circular telling their customers they would not take cheques drawn on the plaintiff bank. The plaintiffs contended that the circular implied insolvency on their part. It was held that the circular taken in conjunction with the circumstances in which it was published did not constitute evidence from which reasonable persons would infer the imputation. There was therefore no case to go to the jury.

If more than one defamatory meaning is alleged then the judge must rule whether the words are capable of bearing each, and if so, which of those meanings.

Lewis *v* Daily Telegraph [1964] AC 234

The defendant newspaper stated the fraud squad were investigating the affairs of a company and named the chairman, one of the plaintiffs. The plaintiffs claimed that the statement meant not only that the company was being investigated for fraud but also that they were guilty of fraud. The House of Lords held that the statement was not capable of bearing that alternative meaning. To have ruled otherwise would have meant that crime investigations could not be reported.

Innuendo

Words may be self evidently defamatory or defamatory in the light of additional facts or circumstances known only to persons to whom the words are published.

Where the words are alleged to have this hidden meaning, this is known as an innuendo. The plaintiff must specifically plead the meaning he attributes to the words used and must prove the existence of facts to support that meaning.

There is a distinction drawn between the false innuendo and the true innuendo. The former is where the plaintiff pleads that the words in their natural and ordinary meaning have a particular meaning which can be discovered without the need for additional evidence. An example of the false innuendo is *Lewis* v *Daily Telegraph* (see above).

Allsop *v* Church of England Newspaper [1972] 2 QB 161

The plaintiff was a well known broadcaster. The defendant newspaper referred to his 'pre-occupation with the bent'. The plaintiff sued on the ordinary meaning of the word 'bent'. It was held that as the word was used as slang in the context of pornography, its meaning was not precise and the plaintiff had to plead all the meanings he claimed to be inherent in the words.

Identifying possible innuendoes is one of the most difficult tasks facing a libel lawyer. The following cases are illustrations.

Tolley *v* Fry & Sons Ltd [1931] AC 333

The plaintiff was a well known amateur golfer. The defendants, without the plaintiff's knowledge, produced an advertisement using the plaintiff, to show that their chocolate was as good as his golfing ability. The plaintiff successfully sued for libel. The innuendo was that he had accepted money for the advert and thereby lost his amateur status.

Cassidy *v* Daily Mirror Newspapers Ltd [1929] 2 KB 331

The defendants published a picture of a couple with a caption, stating that it was Mr C and Miss X, whose engagement had just been announced. Mrs C sued for libel, claiming that people who knew them would interpret the article as meaning she was not married to Mr C. The plaintiff's action succeeded.

Byrne *v* Deane [1937] 1 KB 818

Police raided a golf club and took away an illegal fruit machine. A verse appeared on the club noticeboard: 'but he who gave the game away may he byrne in hell and rue the day'. The plaintiff sued the golf club, alleging that the verse imputed that he had informed the police. The action failed, as the statement would not lower the plaintiff in the eyes of right thinking members of society, who would have informed the police of the commission of a criminal offence.

Linked publications

Can the plaintiff put together a defamation action from two or more publications?

Hayward *v* Thompson [1981] 3 WLR 471

In the first article the defendants stated that the police had the names of two more people associated with the 'Scott' affair and that one was a wealthy benefactor of the Liberal party.

The affair referred to was an alleged murder plot. The second article a week later named the plaintiff and stated that the police wanted to interview him. The plaintiff was a wealthy man who had given large sums of money to the Liberal party. The Court of Appeal upheld the trial judge's ruling that the jury could look at the second article to see to whom the first article referred.

REFERENCE TO THE PLAINTIFF

It is essential that the defendant's statement is shown to refer to the plaintiff. The defendant need not have intended the statement to refer to the plaintiff, provided that people who know the plaintiff understand that he was pointed at by the words used. It is not necessary that everybody should know that the plaintiff was referred to, provided that reasonable people knowing the plaintiff would believe that he was referred to. The reference may be latent rather than express.

There are a number of recurring situations which raise problems in this area.

The fictional name

What is the position where the defendant uses a name for a character who is supposed to be fictional and a real person with the same name claims to have been defamed?

Hulton & Co v Jones [1910] AC 20

The defendants published an article containing defamatory statements of 'Artemus Jones', a churchwarden from Peckham. The article was alleged to be fictitious. A barrister named Artemus Jones from North Wales sued for libel as some of his friends thought that the article referred to him. The defendants were held liable although they had not intended to defame the plaintiff.

NB Section 4 of the Defamation Act 1952 might now provide a defence in these circumstances. (See 'Defences', p. 231.)

Two people with the same name

What is the position where the statement is intended to refer to one person but another person with the same name claims that it refers to him?

Newstead v London Express Newspapers Ltd [1940] 1 KB 377

Harold Newstead, a thirty year old unmarried hairdresser of Camberwell, sued for libel in respect of a statement published by the defendants that Harold Newstead, a thirty year old Camberwell man had been convicted of bigamy. The statement was true of one Harold Newstead, but clearly not of the plaintiff. The defendants were held liable.

This is the reason that court reports always contain the address, age and occupation of the accused.

No person named

Where no person is named in the article but the plaintiff claims that persons who know him think the article refers to him, can he succeed?

Morgan v Odhams Press Ltd [1971] 1 WLR 1239

A newspaper article alleged that a girl had been kidnapped by a dog doping gang and kept at a house in Finchley. No-one was mentioned by name in the article except the girl. At the relevant time the girl had been staying with the plaintiff in Willesden. The plaintiff sued for libel and called six witnesses who thought that the article referred to the plaintiff. The House of Lords held there need be no key or pointer in the words themselves and that the plaintiff could introduce extrinsic evidence to show that he was referred to. On these facts there was sufficient material to leave to the jury. In determining the impression on the mind of the reader, regard should be had to the character of the article and the class of reader likely to read it.

Where the defamatory material appears in one article and the plaintiff is identified in another see *Hayward* v *Thompson* (above).

Class defamation

A statement may be defamatory of a class of people: e.g. 'All doctors are quacks.' The question then arises as to whether any individual doctor may sue.

Knupffer v London Express Newspaper Ltd [1944] AC 116

The defendants published an article which referred to an emigre Russian movement and linked them with Fascism. The movement had a membership of about 2,000 and the UK branch of 24. The plaintiff, a Russian resident in London, sued for libel, alleging that the article referred to him. The House of Lords laid down that the crucial points were:

(a)   Were the words published of the plaintiff, in the sense that he can be said to be personally pointed at.
(b)   Normally, where the statement is directed to a class of persons no individual belonging to that class is entitled to sue.
(c)   The words may be actionable if there is something which points to a particular plaintiff or plaintiffs.
(d)   If the reference is to a small group then each member of the group will be able to sue: e.g. the trustees of a trust. This is if the words may be said to refer to each member.

The plaintiff's action failed as the words were defamatory of a class and there was nothing to point to him as an individual.

The law on class defamation is confusing and involves questions as to how small a group must be before each member may sue. The Court of Appeal has remarked its disapproval of class defamation (*Orme* v *Associated Newspapers Ltd* The Times 4 February 1981), and it may be preferable simply to apply the general rules on reference to the plaintiff.

An attempt was made to address the problems of unintentional reference to the plaintiff in s. 4 of the Defamation Act 1952. This section should be borne in mind by students considering reference to the plaintiff.

PUBLICATION

Publication is the communication of the words to at least one person other than the person defamed. The defendant must be responsible for this publication, either by publishing himself or by asking others to do so.

A person cannot be defamed in his own eyes, so the defendant will only be liable when he is responsible for communicating the defamatory statement to a third party. It is the publication, not the composition of a defamatory statement that is the actionable wrong.

The publication need not consist of a positive act. If a person refrains from removing defamatory material from his premises he may be responsible for publication. An example of this can be seen in *Byrne* v *Deane* (above, p. 226.) where the golf club were the appropriate defendants as they had failed to remove the offending material.

A communication between husband and wife is not a publication as it is covered by privilege. If H says to W that X is a thief, X has no action against H. But if X says to H that W is a thief, then W will have an action against X.

The rules on publication can be illustrated by defamatory statements sent through the post. If X sends a letter to Y which is defamatory of Y, then Y will have no action. The only person who is entitled to open the letter is Y. If Y communicates the contents of the letter to a third party then it is Y who is responsible for the publication, not X. But if the statement is sent on a postcard then Y would have an action as there is a presumption that a postcard has been read during the course of its journey. A similar principle would apply if the defamatory material was on the envelope rather than in the letter.

Negligent publication

Where the defendant intends to publish the words about and concerning the plaintiff there is no great difficulty with the publication requirement. But can the defendant be liable where the publication has occurred as a result of his negligence?

Theaker *v* Richardson [1962] 1 WLR 151

The defendant and plaintiff were members of a local council. The defendant wrote a letter which stated that the plaintiff was: 'a lying, low down brothel keeping whore and thief'. The letter was sealed in an envelope and put through the plaintiff's letter box. The plaintiff's husband opened and read the letter, thinking that it was an election address. The jury found that the defendant anticipated that someone other than the plaintiff might open and read the letter and it was probable that the plaintiff's husband would do so. There had therefore been a publication and the defendant was liable.

Huth *v* Huth [1915] 3 KB 32

The defendant posted a letter in an unsealed envelope to the plaintiffs. The plaintiff's butler opened the envelope and read the letter. This was held not to amount to a publication as the butler's behaviour was not a direct consequence of sending the letter.

If a defamatory letter sent to a businessman is opened and read by his secretary this would amount to a publication. The way to avoid this would be to mark the letter personal or private.

Repetition

Every repetition of defamatory words is a fresh publication and creates a fresh cause of action against each successive publisher. Thus a libel which is printed will bring liability to the author, printer and publisher. In theory this could bring liability to even secondary publishers such as newsagents and booksellers.

In order to mitigate the hardship that this would bring the courts have introduced a defence of innocent dissemination.

Vizetelly *v* Mudie's Select Library Ltd [1900] 2 QB 170

The publishers of a book had asked for its return as it contained defamatory material. The defendants, who operated a circulating library, were held liable for allowing people to to use the book after they had received the warning. The court stated that secondary publishers (distributors) would not be liable if they could show:

(a)   They were innocent of any knowledge of the libel contained in the work in question.
(b)   There was no reason for them to be aware that the work contained libellous material.
(c)   They were not negligent in failing to know that the work was libellous.

Goldsmith *v* Sperrings Ltd [1977] 1 WLR 478

A libel action was brought against *Private Eye* and thirty-seven of its distributors. Some actions against the distributors were settled on the ground that they would no longer sell *Private Eye*. Negotiations with the primary publishers and other distributors continued. The plaintiff had agreed to discontinue all actions and not impede sales if his terms were accepted.

The negotiations failed and actions against the distributors continued. Lord Denning held that this was an abuse of the judicial process. He refused to accept an action lay against the distributors and the effect of the plaintiff's action would be to seriously affect freedom of the press. The majority of the Court of Appeal felt that a plaintiff does have an action against a distributor and such an action should not be stayed at the interlocutory stage unless it can be shown that the primary motive in bringing such an action was to destroy the paper. If his purpose was to vindicate his reputation then the actions should not be stayed. In this case the primary purpose of the action was to vindicate the plaintiff's reputation.

DEFENCES

Defamation should be a balance between protection of reputation and freedom of speech. Such balance as exists in England is given by the defences to defamation. There are four major defences which are dealt with below. A few preliminary matters will be dealt with first.

Unintentional defamation

This defence was provided by Section 4 of the Defamation Act 1952. The intention was to avoid litigation in circumstances where the defamer was unaware of the facts which would make the statement defamatory. Unfortunately the section has so many qualifications and technical requirements that it has had only limited success.

The defence is available if a person *innocently* publishes words alleged to be defamatory and has exercised *all reasonable care* in relation to the publication.

'Innocently' has two meanings:

(a)   If the publisher did not intend to publish the words of and concerning the plaintiff and did not know of circumstances by virtue of which they might be understood to refer to him. This would have application in cases such as *Hulton* v *Jones*. The defence would not be available in cases such as *Newstead* as reasonable care had not been used.

(b)   If the words were not defamatory on the face of them and the publisher did not know of circumstances by virtue of which they might be understood to be defamatory of that person. A possible example of this meaning would be *Cassidy* v *Daily Mirror*.

If either of the above applies but the defendant has not used all reasonable care, then the defence fails.

Ross v Hopkinson (1956) *The Times* 17 October

The defendants used a *nom de plume* for the character of an actress in a book and were sued by the plaintiff, an actress with the same name. Section 4 failed as a defence as the defendants had not used all reasonable care. They could have checked in *Spotlight* to see if the name was currently being used as a stage name.

If the publisher can satisfy the two requirements, he may make an offer of amends accompanied by an affidavit (signed sworn statement) of the facts on which he relies. There must be an offer of a suitable correction and printed apology and reasonable steps to notify people who received copies that the words are alleged to be defamatory.

If the offer is accepted and duly performed then no proceedings for defamation may be taken or continued. If the offer is rejected then it may be used as a defence in any action brought in respect of the defamatory statement. A drawback here is that the defendant may only rely on the facts as stated in the affidavit.

Consent

If the plaintiff has agreed to the publication then no action will lie.

Chapman v Lord Ellesmere [1932] 2 KB 431

A horse trainer's licence was granted subject to a condition that the licence might be withdrawn and that this would be published in the *Racing Calendar*. Such a publication was held not to be actionable as the plaintiff had consented to its publication.

Journalists are frequently advised to show a copy of what is to be published to the subject of the article and to incorporate a statement from the subject explaining his side of the story.

JUSTIFICATION

It is a defence for the defendant to prove that the words alleged to be defamatory were true. Notice that the burden of proof here is on the defendant to prove that the words are true rather than on the plaintiff to show that they were untrue.

The words must be true in substance and fact and if an innuendo has been pleaded the truth of that must also be proved. The success or failure of the defence will turn on the interpretation of the facts.

Wakley v Cooke and Healey (1849) 4 Exch 511

The defendant called the plaintiff a 'libellous journalist'. In evidence the defendant proved that the plaintiff had once been successfully sued for libel. The defence of justification failed as the court took the view that in context the words meant that the plaintiff habitually libelled people. The defendant had failed to justify this meaning.

Section 5 of the Defamation Act 1952:

> In an action for libel or slander in respect of words containing two or more distinct charges against the plaintiff, a defence of justification shall not fail by reason only that

the truth of every charge is not proved if the words not proved to be true do not materially injure the plaintiff's reputation having regard to the truth of the remaining charges.

For example, the plaintiff is described as a murderer, rapist, arsonist, thief and liar. The plaintiff proves the truth of the first four charges but is unable to justify the last. Section 5 will afford a defence.

One drawback with s. 5 is that it is the plaintiff who chooses the ground for the action. In the example above the plaintiff might choose only to sue on the allegation that he knows the defendant is unable to justify. The plaintiff would then not be free to advance evidence on the other charges.

The defence of justification may be a dangerous one. It is the jury that awards damages and they are unlikely to be impressed by a defendant who has persisted in an untruth. There are practical difficulties in mounting the defence as a trial may take place many years after the publication and witnesses may be dead or unable to remember.

FAIR COMMENT

Whereas justification provides a defence on questions of fact, fair comment defends opinions which by their nature cannot be true or false. Sometimes called the critics defence, fair comment defends honest and fair criticism. The defence has certain requirements.

The comment must be on a matter of public interest

London Artists Ltd *v* Littler [1969] 2 All ER 193

Actors gave notice to terminate their employment in a play staged by the defendant. The defendant wrote to each actor alleging a plot and deploring their conduct and informed the press of the contents of the letters. The court stated that public interest could be divided into two groups. The first is matters of public interest, in the sense that the public in general have a legitimate interest in them. The second consists of matters which are expressly or impliedly subjected to public criticism or attention, such as theatre productions.

The first group would cover government, national and local, and the management of public institutions. Where an office holder's private life impinges on his public office then this will be of public interest. The second group would seem to cover questions of artistic merit and matters such as sport and religion.

The comment must be an opinion based on true facts

In *London Artists* v *Littler* the defence of fair comment failed as the defendant was unable to prove that there was a plot and there were therefore no facts on which the comment could be based.

This requirement distinguishes fair comment from justification as a defence. To say that, 'X is a thief and is therefore unsuited to be a bank manager', requires the defendant to justify 'X is a thief' and to prove fair comment for the remainder of the statement.

What is fact and what is opinion is not always easy to determine.

Kemsley v Foot [1952] AC 345

The defendant published an article which referred to one of the Beaverbrook newspapers under the heading, 'Lower than Kemsley'. Kemsley was the owner of another group of newspapers. Was this fact or opinion? The House of Lords decided that as the conduct of the Kemsley Press was the fact on which the comment was made the defence of fair comment was available. It is not necessary that the facts on which the comment is based should be stated in the alleged libel.

Section 6 of the Defamation Act 1952:

> In an action for libel or slander in respect of words consisting partly of allegations of fact and partly expression of opinion, a defence of fair comment shall not fail by reason only that the truth of every allegation of fact is not proved if the expression of opinion is fair comment having regard to such facts alleged or referred to in the words complained of as are proved.

For interpretation of this section students should refer to s. 5 under justification. What is clear is that justification and fair comment are separate defences and should be pleaded in the alternative.

The facts on which the comment is alleged to be based must be facts which were in existence at the time the comment was made. The defendant cannot rely on facts which occurred after the comment.

If the facts are untrue but were stated on a privileged occasion, then fair comment can succeed as a defence. This could occur if the facts were stated in court and subject to absolute privilege.

The comment must be fair

Fairness means that the comment must be an honest expression of the defendant's opinion: 'The question which the jury must consider is this – would any fair man, however prejudiced he may be, however exaggerated or obstinate his views, have said that which this criticism has said' (*Merivale* v *Carson* (1888) 20 QBD 275, 281). It could be said that the defence therefore protects *unfair* comment.

Campbell v Spottiswoode (1863) 3 B & S 769

Plaintiff wrote an article on a scheme for spreading the gospel amongst the Chinese. The defendant published an article suggesting that the plaintiff was a hypocrite who only wanted to increase circulation of his own journal. This meant that the defendant had alleged a bad motive as opposed to merely criticising the work. Not only had the opinion to be an honest expression of the defendant's opinion, there also had to be some foundation for that opinion. Here the defence failed as there was no foundation for the allegations made.

The comment must not be malicious

Since 1906 the defence of fair comment has been able to be defeated by malice. In this sense, malice means spite or an evil motive.

Thomas *v* Bradbury, Agnew & Co Ltd [1906] 2 KB 627

A book reviewer for *Punch* wrote a very critical review of the plaintiff's book. The defendant's malice was ascertained from the review itself and his conduct in the witness box. The defence of fair comment failed because of the defendant's malice.

It is not clear whether one defendant's malice will infect a co-defendant's plea of fair comment: e.g. if a newspaper prints a letter and both the letter writer and the newspaper are sued. Both plead fair comment but the writer's defence fails because of malice. Can the newspaper succeed in its defence?

ABSOLUTE PRIVILEGE

There are certain occasions where freedom of speech outweighs protection of reputation. On these occasions privilege is granted to the statement. Privilege may be absolute or qualified. The distinction is that absolute privilege is not affected by malice whereas a defence of qualified privilege is destroyed by malice.

Parliamentary privilege

No action will lie for defamation in respect of anything said in Parliamentary proceedings, either in debate or committee or in petitions to Parliament (Bill of Rights 1688).

Any statement in a paper published by the authority of either House is privileged (Parliamentary Papers Act 1840).

Church of Scientology of California *v* Johnson-Smith [1972] 1 QB 522

The plaintiffs sued the defendant MP for a libel alleged to have been made on a television interview. The defence was fair comment. Plaintiffs pleaded malice. To establish malice they wanted to use extracts from *Hansard*. It was held that this evidence could not be used because of Parliamentary privilege.

Judicial privilege

Statements which are made in the course of judicial proceedings by judge, juror, counsel, solicitor, parties or witnesses are absolutely privileged. The privilege also applies to documents used. The statement must be connected with the case and does not extend, e.g., to interruptions from the public gallery.

Judicial proceedings covers ordinary courts of law and tribunals acting judicially. Military inquiries, courts martial and disciplinary hearings of the Law Society are covered. The privilege does not extend to the activities of administrative bodies and so would not cover proceedings of the licensing justices.

A fair, accurate and contemporaneous newspaper or broadcast report of public judicial proceedings in the United Kingdom is absolutely privileged (Law of Libel Amendment Act 1888).

To be fair, the report must present a summary of both sides of the case. If only the prosecution case has been heard then the report should say 'continuing' at the end.

To be accurate, the report should contain no material inaccuracies: e.g. it should not identify someone who is a witness as a defendant. The proceedings do not have to be reported verbatim.

To be contemporaneous, the report should be in the first issue of the newspaper after the hearing. Non-contemporaneous reports carry qualified privilege.

Communications between solicitor and client attract privilege although it is not certain whether this is absolute or qualified.

Executive privilege

Statements made by one officer of state to another in the course of duty are absolutely privileged. There is some doubt as to how high ranking the official has to be in order to attract this privilege.

QUALIFIED PRIVILEGE

Qualified privilege is a complex area of law. It differs from absolute privilege in that it can be defeated by malice. Where qualified privilege is invoked it is the communication that is privileged not the occasion.

Privileged reports

Parliamentary proceedings

Fair and accurate reports of Parliamentary proceedings are covered by qualified privilege. The whole debate does not need to be reported and the reporter may select only those bits which are of public interest.

Cook v Alexander [1974] QB 279

The plaintiff had been a teacher at an approved school and his criticisms of the school had led to it being closed by the Home Secretary. The closure order was debated in the House of Lords. The *Daily Telegraph* reported the debate and published a Parliamentary sketch of those parts of the debate which the reporter thought were of public interest. The Court of Appeal held that the sketch was privileged as it was made fairly and honestly.

Reports of judicial proceedings

Fair and accurate reports of public judicial proceedings which are not covered by absolute privilege attract qualified privilege. This covers reports which are not contemporaneous or are not made in a newspaper.

Reports privileged under the Defamation Act 1952

The Schedule to the Defamation Act 1952 provides that a number of reports are covered by qualified privilege. These are divided into Part I and Part II reports.

Part I reports are privileged without explanation or contradiction provided they are fair and accurate and made without malice. These are reports of:

(a)   Public proceedings of Commonwealth Parliaments.
(b)   International organisations of which the UK is a member.
(c)   Public proceedings of international courts.
(d)   Court proceedings in the Commonwealth.
(e)   Public inquiries in the Commonwealth.

Part II provides that certain reports are privileged subject to explanation or contradiction, provided they are fair and accurate and without malice.

(a)   A report of the findings and decisions of the following bodies is privileged. A report of the proceedings is not.
      Bodies concerned with:

      (i)   Art, science, religion or learning.
      (ii)   Trade, business, industry or the professions.
      (iii)   Games, sport or pastimes.

(b)   Reports of public meetings, bona fide and lawfully held for a lawful purpose in the United Kingdom for the furtherance of any matter of public concern are covered by qualified privilege. Admission may be general or restricted. In this case the privilege applies to the proceedings.
(c)   Reports of the following carry qualified privilege:

      (i)   Local authorities (including committees and sub-committees).
      (ii)   Licensing justices.
      (iii)   Tribunals open to the public.
      (iv)   Local inquiry.
      (v)   Inquiries set up by Act of Parliament or a Minister.
      (vi)   General meetings of public companies.
      (vii)   Notices issued by government departments, local authorities or a chief officer of police.

It should be noted that Part II reports are privileged subject to explanation or contradiction: e.g. a reporter attends a meeting of the Licensing Justices. X has applied for a licence to sell alcoholic drinks. The police object to the granting of the licence because of X's known criminal associates. The reporter's paper carries a report of the proceedings. This is privileged under Part II. X writes to the newspaper and asks them to publish his letter which sets out his side of the story. If the paper does not publish the letter then it risks losing the privilege.

Common law privilege

A statement which is made in the performance of a duty will attract qualified privilege provided that the person making the statement has a legal, moral or social duty to make the statement and the person receiving it has an interest in doing so. A simple example of this is a reference given by a present employer to a potential future employer.

Watt *v* Longsdon [1930] 1 KB 130

The defendant, a director of a company, received a letter from the foreign manager of the company. The letter made allegations of drunkenness, dishonesty, and immorality about the plaintiff, also an employee of the company. The defendant showed the letter to other directors and to the plaintiff's wife. It was held that the publication to the directors was covered by qualified privilege but the publication to the plaintiff's wife was not, as the defendant had no duty to make the communication.

Bryanstone Finance Co Ltd *v* de Vries [1975] 2 All ER 609

The defendants issued a writ against the plaintiffs, with whom they had had business dealings. To force a settlement the defendants had documents prepared alleging that the plaintiffs had committed serious misdemeanours against the Bryanstone Co. They threatened to send these documents to the shareholders. A letter was drafted to go out with the documents. The documents were dictated to a typist and then handed to an office boy for copying but never sent out. The plaintiff sued for libel.

The defendant claimed that the publication to the typist was privileged. The Court of Appeal held that such a publication was privileged but were divided as to whether the privilege was an original one or an ancillary one. If the former view is correct then it does not matter whether the intended publication (in this case to the shareholders) was privileged or not.

Malice

A defence of qualified privilege will be defeated by malice. Malice means either: that the defendant did not honestly believe in the truth of what he said; or that a privileged occasion was used for an improper purpose.

Horrocks *v* Lowe [1974] 2 WLR 282

Plaintiff and defendant were elected members of a local authority. The plaintiff made defamatory remarks about the defendant at a council meeting. The defendant pleaded privilege. The plaintiff claimed that the privilege was destroyed by malice. The House of Lords held that as the plaintiff honestly believed that his statement was true there was no malice. Malice would only exist if it could be shown that he had been actuated by spite or ill will.

Angel v H Bushel Ltd [1968] 1 QB 813

The plaintiff dealt in scrap and was introduced to the defendants by a mutual friend. The parties did business together but things went wrong. The defendants wrote to the mutual friend alleging that the plaintiff was 'not conversant with normal business ethics'. The defendants pleaded qualified privilege but it was held that the privilege was destroyed by malice. The letter was unnecessary and written out of anger.

REMEDIES

The normal remedy in a defamation action is damages which are awarded by the jury. This is subject to a power in the Court of Appeal to set aside the award on the ground that it was in all the circumstances unreasonable and excessive (*Sutcliffe* v *Pressdram* (1989)).

The jury may award punitive or exemplary damages in a libel action where the defendant decided to publish a libel calculating that the possible damages would be exceeded by the profit he would make on the book (*Cassell* v *Broome* (1972)).

If the alleged libel comes to the plaintiff's attention before publication he may seek an injunction to prevent publication. An interlocutory injunction will generally not be granted where the defence is that the words are not defamatory, the plaintiff is not referred to, or justification.

REHABILITATION OF OFFENDERS ACT 1974

The Act provides that after a period of time a criminal conviction is spent and should not be referred to. Whether a conviction is spent depends on the sentence passed: e.g. sentences of more than two and a half years in prison are never spent; prison sentences of 6 months to two and a half years are spent after 10 years; prison sentences of less than six months are spent after 7 years.

The Act affects defamation actions in two ways. Where a spent conviction is referred to then the defendant can still plead justification as it is a fact that the conviction existed at one stage. But in these circumstances malice will destroy the defence of justification: i.e. that the defendant's major motive in revealing the spent conviction was to injure the plaintiff's reputation.

Secondly, where a spent conviction is referred to in court and is held inadmissible, the defendant cannot plead privilege.

QUESTION

Peter, a political agent, had an argument with Helen, the constituency MP. Peter dictated a speech onto a dictaphone, intending to make the speech at a constituency meeting. In the speech he said that, 'ignorance, vanity and corruption are all too common in politics today; the virtues of honesty and adherence to the law are rarely adhered to'.

Peter gave the tape to his secretary Janet to type up but by an error Janet sent the tape to Helen. The parcel was opened by Helen's husband, Alfred, who played the tape. Helen is also a barrister. Advise Helen.

Suggested approach

There are three major issues in a defamation answer. Is the statement slander or libel? The three elements in the plaintiff's case. Are there any relevant defences?

Libel is where a defamatory meaning is conveyed in a permanent form. Slander is where a temporary form such as speech is used. The old maxim 'was slander to the ear and libel to the eye'. However modern means of communication have made this uncertain. There is no direct authority on tape recordings or dictaphones so the case could be either slander or libel. The major distinction is that libel is actionable *per se*, without proof of damage. Slander requires proof of damage except in four cases. It would appear that the words used here would come within the exception in s. 2 of the Defamation Act 1952.

Helen must prove that the words used were defamatory, that they referred to her and that they were published by the defendant.

The test for whether words are defamatory should be stated and applied to the facts of the question. The words corruption, ignorance and vanity and corruption would appear to be defamatory on the face of them, as would the words honesty and non-adherence to the law. The latter two may also be defamatory by virtue of innuendo. Helen is a barrister and this fact is known to Alfred.

The words must refer to the plaintiff. Helen is not mentioned by name but this is not necessary. Neither is it necessary for everyone who might hear the words to be able to identify her. The test is that laid down in *Morgan* v *Odhams Press* (1971). Alfred's special knowledge would be relevant here.

If a class of persons is defamed then normally no member of the class may sue unless the class is small enough or there is something which particularly identifies the plaintiff. Politics and law are probably too large as groups.

Section 4 of the Defamation Act 1952 provides a specific defence for innocent defamation. In this case the defendant did not intend to refer to the plaintiff but had been negligent. The latter point would appear to preclude Peter from using the section.

Publication identifies the defendants to the action. Peter has published to Janet and to Alfred. Janet has also published to Alfred. With regard to Janet she would appear to have a defence of innocent dissemination. (State the requirements and apply.) The publication by Peter to Janet will probably attract qualified privilege. *Bryanstone Finance* v *de Vries* (1975). The publication to Alfred will come under negligent publication. Had Helen opened the parcel there would have been no publication. Apply *Huth* v *Huth* and *Theaker* v *Richardson*.

Peter may be able to plead justification or fair comment as defences. If the statement is factual then justification is appropriate. If comment, then fair comment. (Apply the relevant points.) As the parties have had previously bad relations then malice may be relevant. It appears unlikely that qualified privilege is relevant as Peter is not under a duty to communicate the information to Alfred.

Helen could apply for an injunction to restrain delivery of the speech but as reference to the plaintiff is likely to be raised it is unlikely to be granted.

Further reading

Duncan, C and Neill, B *Defamation* (2nd edn 1983)
Gatley, JCC *Libel and Slander* (8th edn 1981)
Kaye, JM (1976) 91 LQR 524
Weir, JA [1972] CLJ 238

21 | Deceit, malicious falsehood and passing off

DECEIT

Introduction

The tort of deceit is committed when the defendant makes a false statement to the plaintiff, knowing it is false, or reckless as to its truth, with the intention that the plaintiff acts on it, the plaintiff does act and suffers damage as a result (*Pasley* v *Freeman* (1789) 3 TR 51).

The tort is related to the action for negligent misstatement. The distinction is that the latter action is based on negligence and covers statements of fact and opinion, whereas deceit is based on fraudulent misrepresentation and covers only statements of fact.

False statement of fact

For deceit to be committed there must be a false representation of fact. The representation must generally be a positive act made by words or conduct. The words may be oral or written. This rule is in support of the point that there is usually no duty of disclosure in English law.

Students of contract law will be familiar with this principle if they have studied misrepresentation. They will also be familiar with the point that if a statement of fact was made which was true at the time but later became false, a failure to correct the misrepresentation is actionable (*With* v *O'Flanagan* [1936] Ch 575). In the case of contracts *uberrimae fidei,* such as an insurance contract, there may also be a duty to disclose any material fact.

The statement must be one of existing fact and not opinion. This distinction may not be easy to make.

Bisset v Wilkinson [1927] AC 177

The vendor of land in New Zealand said that the land would support two thousand sheep. This turned out to be incorrect but the statement was held to be one of opinion and not fact and therefore not a misrepresentation. Two factors appear to have been important in the decision. The land had never been used for sheep before and neither of the parties had any special knowledge of sheep.

It would appear that if the maker of the statement has special knowledge, the statement is more likely to be held to be one of fact. An example of this can be seen in *Esso Petroleum* v *Mardon* [1976] QB 801.

Knowledge of the falsity of the statement

To be liable in deceit the defendant must have knowledge that the statement is false or be reckless as to whether it is true or false.

Derry v Peek (1889) 14 App Cas 337

Directors of a company issued a prospectus stating that they had the right to run trams on steam power. Board of Trade approval was necessary to do this and such approval had not been obtained. The directors believed that such approval would be given as a matter of course but the Board of Trade refused to give its approval. The company was wound up and the plaintiff, who had bought shares in the company relying on the prospectus, brought an action in deceit. The House of Lords held that such an action did not lie. In order to succeed in deceit the plaintiff had to prove fraud. Fraud would arise where a false representation of fact had been made:

(a)   knowingly
(b)   without belief in its truth
(c)   recklessly, careless as to whether it was true or false.

This case had a long lasting effect on English law in the area of statements. Until *Hedley Byrne* v *Heller* (1964), it was authority for the point that no action lay on a careless but honest statement. It is now possible for a plaintiff to sue for damages on a statement in the tort of negligence or under the Misrepresentation Act 1967, s. 2(1). Both of these actions are easier to prove than establishing fraud for the purpose of deceit (see Chapter 5).

Intention that the statement be acted on

The defendant must intend that the statement be acted on. Only those persons or class of persons whom the defendant intended to act on the statement can sue. The easiest way of establishing this is to prove that the defendant made the statement to the plaintiff but this is not necessary to establish liability. It is sufficient that the plaintiff was a member of a class to whom the statement was addressed.

Langridge v Levy (1837) 2 M & W 337

The plaintiff's father purchased a gun from the defendant, whom he told he was going to pass the gun on to his son. The defendant knowingly and falsely said that the gun was sound. The father gave the gun to his son, the plaintiff, who was injured when the gun burst. The defendant was held liable in deceit.

The plaintiff must act on the statement

The plaintiff must prove that he acted on the statement to his detriment. It must be reliance on the statement that caused the plaintiff's loss. The statement need not be the only or indeed the decisive factor in causing the plaintiff to act in the way that he did, provided that it was a material factor.

Damage to the plaintiff

The test for remoteness of damage in deceit is the directness test rather than reasonable foreseeability. The defendant will be liable for all losses flowing directly from the fraudulent inducement (*Doyle* v *Olby* [1969] 2 QB 158).

The measure of damages is the reliance measure. It is unclear whether the plaintiff can recover exemplary damages but aggravated damages may be awarded.

Archer *v* Brown [1984] 2 All ER 267

The plaintiff was induced to enter a partnership with the defendant by the latter's deceit. The plaintiff was held entitled to the amount that he had paid for his shares; interest on a loan taken out to buy the shares; damages for injured feelings; but not to loss of profit which he expected the partnership to make. He was, however, entitled to loss of earnings sustained by entering the partnership.

MALICIOUS FALSEHOOD

Introduction

This tort was originally called slander of title, as it involved a statement which questioned a person's title to land, with the result that the land was unsaleable. In the nineteenth century the tort was extended to slander of goods and passing off. (See below 'for passing off', p. 246.)

At the end of the nineteenth century the Court of Appeal fused an action of general application.

Ratcliffe *v* Evans [1892] 2 QB 524

The defendant newspaper proprietor published an article that implied the plaintiff's firm had gone out of business. The article was false and was published with malice. The plaintiff sued to recover his resulting business losses. The action would lie for a false statement which was maliciously published with the intention of causing damage. The tort was not actionable *per se*, so the statement must have actually caused damage.

How does this tort differ from defamation and deceit?

Defamation is concerned with protecting a person's reputation. Malicious falsehood (sometimes called injurious falsehood) is generally concerned with the plaintiff's economic interests and the tort can be committed without impugning reputation. It is not defamatory to say that a firm has stopped trading or that a pop star has entered a closed order of monks. Neither of these statements would lower the plaintiff in the eyes of right thinking members of society.

Deceit is concerned with false statements made to the plaintiff with the intention that he should act on them. Malicious falsehood is concerned with false statements made to third parties about the plaintiff with the intention that loss will be caused to the plaintiff.

There are three requirements for the tort:

(a)   a false statement of fact
(b)   malice
(c)   damage.

False statement

The defendant must make a false statement of fact to some person other than the plaintiff. As with deceit, it must be a statement of fact rather than a statement of opinion. This causes problems with distinguishing a trade puff and an actionable misrepresentation. A considerable amount of advertising is based on the merits of a product while impliedly denigrating the quality of rival products. Provided that a person sticks to the qualities of his own goods, even if this includes saying that they are superior to other products, the tort is not committed. But if false reasons are given for the lack of quality in another person's goods, then the statement may be actionable.

De Beers Abrasive Products Ltd *v* International General Electric Co of New York [1975] 1 WLR 972

Both parties made diamond abrasives which were used for cutting concrete. The defendants, to boost sales, published a pamphlet with what purported to be a laboratory report comparing the parties' products. This report contained adverse comment on the plaintiff's product. The test to be applied was whether a reasonable man would take the claim being made as a serious claim or not. An indication that the claim was meant to be taken seriously was a claim that a rival's goods had been subjected to a proper scientific test. To say that your goods are better than those of a rival is acceptable. But to denigrate the goods of a rival without grounds was a falsehood.

Malice

The statement must be made with malice. Malice means without just cause or excuse and with some indirect, dishonest or improper motive. The burden of proof is on the plaintiff to establish malice.

If the defendant makes the statement knowing it is false or if he is reckless as to the truth of the statement, then the statement is made with malice. Where the defendant honestly believes that the statement is true but it is false, there is no malice.

Damage

The plaintiff must prove that he suffered damage as a result of the defendant's statement. This is usually done by proving a general loss of business.

Defamation Act 1952, s. 3 provides:

> it shall not be necessary to prove special damage:
> (a) if the words on which the action are founded are calculated to cause pecuniary damage to the plaintiff and are published in writing or some other permanent form; or
> (b) the words are calculated to cause pecuniary damage to the plaintiff in respect of any office, profession, calling, trade or business held or carried on by him at the time of publication.

PASSING OFF

Introduction

This is normally considered as a separate tort from malicious falsehood, but some writers treat it as part of malicious falsehood.

The tort is committed by the defendant passing off his goods as the plaintiff's. The plaintiff's interest which is protected is his financial interest in his property.

The modern version of the tort was set out in the following case:

Even Warnink BV v Townend & Sons (Hull) Ltd [1979] AC 731

The plaintiffs made a drink called advocaat. The defendants began to make a drink called Old English Avocaat. The plaintiffs applied for an injunction to restrain the defendants from using the name advocaat. Lord Diplock identified five essential elements of the tort

(a)   A misrepresentation
(b)   made by a trader in the course of his trade
(c)   to prospective customers of his or ultimate consumers of goods or services supplied by him
(d)   which is calculated to injure the business or goodwill of the trader by whom the action is brought or will probably do so
(e)   which causes actual damage to a business or goodwill of the trader by whom the action is brought or will probably do so.

As the name which was used by the plaintiffs distinguished the plaintiff's product from any others, the plaintiffs were entitled to the injunction.

Methods of committing the tort

Using the plaintiff's name

This may be done by using the plaintiff's actual name where that name has a particular connection with the plaintiff's business. It is not possible to open a French restaurant with the name Maxim's, as the public would think it had a connection with the famous restaurant of that name in Paris (*Maxim's Ltd v Dye* [1977] 1 WLR 1155). What if the defendant had been called Maxim? Would he be entitled to use his own name? Generally, a person is entitled to use his own name unless this would mislead the public as the name is associated with goods made by the plaintiff alone (*Parker Knoll Ltd v Knoll International Ltd* [1962] RPC 265).

Alternatively, the defendant may use a name similar to the name of the plaintiff's goods as in the advocaat example above. Similarly, an injunction was granted to prevent wine being called Spanish Champagne. The name champagne referred to a particular area of France and only producers in that area were entitled to use the name on their product (*J Bollinger v Costa Brava Wine Co Ltd* [1960] Ch 262).

If the name applies to a type of goods, such as vacuum cleaners, the name is not protected.

If the parties are not in the same trade it is difficult to obtain an injunction. A well known children's broadcaster called Uncle Mac, failed to prevent a cereal company calling a breakfast cereal Uncle Mac's Puffed Wheat (*McCullough v May* [1947] 2 All ER 845).

Imitating the appearance of the plaintiff's goods

Not only the name of the goods is protected but also the physical appearance and the way the goods are advertised. If the plaintiff has used an advertising campaign linking his goods to a virile sporting image and can establish that the public exclusively link that image with their product, the defendants can be prevented from using a similar image (*Cadbury-Schweppes Pty Ltd v Pub Squash Co Pty Ltd* [1981] 1 WLR 193).

Claiming that the plaintiff's goods belong to the defendant

This is one of the original forms of the tort and is committed when the defendant claims ownership of goods which in fact belong to the plaintiff.

Remedies

The normal remedy in passing off is an injunction to prevent the defendant from using a name etc. The plaintiff may also claim damages or an account of profits.

Part VI
PARTIES, DEFENCES AND REMEDIES

22 | Vicarious liability

INTRODUCTION

Vicarious liability is where one person is made liable for the tort of another person. It is important to draw a distinction between primary liability and vicarious liability. This can be illustrated by the medical negligence cases. A health authority may be vicariously liable for the torts of its employees and it may also be primarily liable where it fails to provide adequate levels of staffing in one of its hospitals and an accident results.

The commonest example of vicarious liability in tort is that of an employer for the torts of his employee. Two things are necessary for such liability to arise. There must be a particular relationship between the employer and the employee. A distinction is drawn here between employees and independent contractors. The employer is liable for the torts of the former but not the latter. Secondly, the tort committed must be referable to the employment relationship. This is expressed by saying that the tort must be committed in the course of employment.

Example

Andrew was run over and injured by a vehicle driven by Brian. The vehicle was being driven negligently at the time. If the vehicle was a lorry, Brian was employed as a lorry driver by Charles and Brian was in the course of his employment, then Charles will be vicariously liable for Brian's negligence. If Brian was on what is sometimes called a frolic of his own, then Brian will be outside the course of his employment and Charles will not be vicariously liable.

If the vehicle was a taxi which had been stopped by Charles, then Brian, the driver, will be an independent contractor in relation to Charles and Charles will prima facie not be liable for Brian's negligence.

Vicarious liability is an example of strict liability, in the sense that there need be no fault on the part of the employer before he can be made liable. What, therefore, is the justification for imposing vicarious liability?

JUSTIFICATION FOR IMPOSING VICARIOUS LIABILITY

Although the doctrine of vicarious liability is accepted in English law there is no clear and convincing rationale for its imposition. A number of theories have been put forward to explain the deviation from the prevalent fault based theory of liability.

It has been suggested that the employer is in control of the behaviour of his employee. This is no longer convincing as many employees perform skilled tasks which the employer is incapable of understanding. To say that a health authority chief executive controls the work of a consultant is stretching the meaning of the word.

Alternative suggestions have included the fact that the employer may have been careless in selecting the employee. However, liability is not based on this premise and a perfectly competent employee is capable of behaving negligently at some stage in his employment.

The modern approach is entirely pragmatic and is based on social convenience and rough justice. The imposition of liability is based on the employer's greater ability to pay any damages and the fact that this involves loss spreading. The employer is the best insurer against liability and any extra cost to the employer can be passed on to the public in the form of higher prices. This may encourage accident prevention, as a firm which raises its prices too high will go out of business.

The doctrine can be justified on a moral basis as the employee inflicts loss on the plaintiff while pursuing the employer's business interests. As the employer obtains a benefit from the employee's work, he should also bear the costs of accidents arising out of it.

WHO IS AN EMPLOYEE?

An employer is vicariously liable for the torts of an employee committed in the course of his employment but not those of an independent contractor. This has caused severe difficulties for the courts and continues to do so. Where employment does not fall into a traditional pattern, even the parties may be unaware of their employment relationship. This may happen with casual workers for example. Employers may also attempt to avoid their legal liabilities by attempting to classify employees as independent contractors. It is clear that the label attached to the relationship by the employer is not conclusive.

A number of tests have been used to attempt to draw a distinction. Traditionally a distinction was made between a contract of service (employee) and a contract for services (independent contractor). This distinction is no help in telling which is which.

For a time the control test was popular. If the employer retained control over the work and told a person how to do it, that person was an employee. The test reflected a society where ownership of the means of production coincided with the possession of technical knowledge and skill. The typical employer would be the Victorian engineer who knew all aspects of the work done in his firm. As so many employees are now skilled, the employer may be able to tell them what to do but not how to do it. The computer specialist, lawyer or accountant employed by a firm does not fit the control test.

The problems with the control test led the courts to search for alternatives. One suggestion was the business integration test put forward by Lord Denning (*Stevenson, Jordan and Harrison Ltd* v *McDonald and Evans* (1952) 1 TLR 101). A person would be an employee if his work was an integral part of the business. An independent contractor would work for the business but as an accessory rather than an integral part of it. On this basis it would be possible to distinguish between a chauffeur and a taxi driver and a staff reporter and a newspaper contributor. In practice the test proved too vague to apply, as did a variation of whether the person was in business on their own account (*Market Investigations Ltd* v *Minister of Social Security* [1969] 2 QB 173).

The courts have now abandoned the search for any single factor to act as a test and will look at all the circumstances of the particular case.

Ready Mixed Concrete (South East) Ltd *v* Minister of Pensions [1968] 2 QB 497

The following criteria for a contract of service were put forward:

(a) The employee agrees in return for a wage or other remuneration, that he will provide his work and skill for the employer.
(b) The employee agrees expressly or impliedly to be subject to his employer's control.
(c) The other terms of the contract are consistent with there being a contract of employment.

These three factors are not all the courts will look at. If the parties have specified that a person will be self-employed and the terms of the contract reflect self-employed status then the contract will be regarded as a contract for services.

O'Kelly *v* Trusthouse Forte plc [1983] ICR 728

Wine butlers who worked at the Grosvenor House Hotel were described as regular casual workers and only worked when required. They could refuse work if they wanted. They were held not to be employees for the purpose of employment protection legislation but what would the position have been if one of them had negligently injured a guest or his property? The economic reality of the situation surely dictates that they would be employees for the purpose of vicarious liability. As the objective of vicarious liability is to enable the plaintiff to satisfy a judgment, the risk-bearing capacity of the parties and the solvency of the employees would point towards this solution.

Lending an employee

What is the position where an employer A lends his employee B to another employer C and B commits a tort within the course of his employment? Who will be vicariously liable, A or C?

Mersey Docks and Harbour Board v Coggins & Griffith (Liverpool) Ltd [1947] AC 1

A employed B as a mobile crane driver and hired B and the crane to C. The contract between A and C provided that B should be the employee of C. However, B continued to be paid by A who also had the power to dismiss. A person was injured as a result of B's negligent handling of the crane. The House of Lords laid down principles to determine whether A or C was vicariously liable for B's negligence:

(a)   A term in the contract between A and C is not decisive.
(b)   The burden of proof is on the permanent employer A to show that C was B's employer for the purposes of vicarious liability.
(c)   Where labour only is lent then it is easier to infer that the hirer is the employer. Where labour and plant is hired, it is more difficult to rebut the presumption, as the hirer may not have control over the way the plant is used.

On the facts, A had failed to rebut the presumption and remained B's employer for the purposes of vicarious liability.

It is possible that, where an employee is lent out, the permanent employer will remain personally, rather than vicariously liable, where the employee himself is injured (*McDermid* v *Nash* [1987] 2 All ER 878. See 'Employer's liability', pp. 149–54.)

IN THE COURSE OF EMPLOYMENT

The employer will only be liable for torts which the employee commits in the course of his employment. These are probably the most litigated words in the English language and each case will be a question of fact.

The courts have often used a test suggested by Salmond that an act is in the course of employment if it is either:

(a)   a wrongful act authorised by the employer, or
(b)   a wrongful and unauthorised mode of doing some act authorised by the employer.

It is sometimes said that where an employee is outside the course of his employment he is on a frolic of his own.

In some cases it will be clear that the act was outside the course of employment. Where a bus conductor attempted to turn a bus round, he was clearly outside the course of his employment (*Beard* v *London General Omnibus Co* [1900] 2 QB 530). However, the courts may now be prepared to investigate the reasons for driving a vehicle. A fork lift truck driver who had to move a diesel lorry in order to do his job has been held to be within the course of his employment.

The fact that the employee was doing his job negligently, does not take him outside the course of his employment.

Century Insurance Co *v* Northern Ireland Road Transport Board [1942] AC 509

The employee was employed by the defendants as a petrol tanker driver. While he was unloading his tanker he threw away a lighted match, which caused a fire and explosion. The defendants were held vicariously liable for his negligence as he was doing his job at the time of the accident, even if he was doing it in a negligent way.

Express prohibition

It is possible for the employer to be vicariously liable for an act if the prohibition applies to the way in which the job is done, rather than the scope of the job itself. A bus driver is therefore within the scope of his employment when he races other buses when expressly prohibited from doing so (*Limpus* v *London General Omnibus Co* (1862) 1 H & C 526). The driver was still doing what he was paid to do, drive a bus.

A number of cases have involved giving lifts to people.

Conway *v* George Wimpey & Co Ltd [1951] 2 KB 266

The defendants provided transport for their employees on a building site. Drivers were told not to give lifts to employees of other companies. The plaintiff, who was an employee of another company, was given a lift and injured as a result of the negligence of the driver. It was held that the defendants were not vicariously liable, as at the time of the accident the driver was doing an unauthorised act, not simply doing an authorised act in an unauthorised mode.

Twine *v* Bean's Express Ltd (1946) 62 TLR 458

The plaintiff's husband was given a lift in a van driven by the defendant's employee. He was killed as a result of the employee's negligence. The driver had been prohibited from giving lifts to prohibited persons and there was a notice on the side of the vehicle stating who could be carried. The deceased was not an authorised passenger. The defendants were held not to be vicariously liable, as the driver was outside the course of his employment by doing an unauthorised act.

Rose v Plenty [1976] 1 WLR 141

The defendants had prohibited their employees from carrying boys on their milk floats. The thirteen year old plaintiff was injured while being carried on a milk float, due to the negligence of an employee. It was held that the defendants were vicariously liable as the prohibition had not affected the course of the employee's employment, simply the method by which he could do his job.

There is clearly a problem with distinguishing this case from *Twine*. The majority in the Court of Appeal (Denning MR and Scarman LJ) said that in *Twine* the plaintiff was a trespasser and owed no duty of care. This point was no longer valid in the light of case law that held that a limited duty of care was owed to a trespasser. Secondly, in *Twine* the lift was not given for a purpose beneficial to the employer, but in *Rose* the boy was assisting with the delivery of milk.

Despite the efforts of the Court of Appeal it may be that the cases are irreconcilable and *Rose* represents a pragmatic approach to the question of course of employment. Previous case law had demonstrated the latitude given to the court when they asked the questions of what was the employee paid to do and what was he doing at the time of the accident. The modern approach may be to define the scope of employment in wide terms, so as to enable the plaintiff to satisfy judgment.

Detours

A number of cases have involved drivers who make a detour from their authorised route and are involved in an accident. Are they still within the course of their employment? One test is whether they are on a frolic of their own or still on the employer's business.

An employer was held not liable when the driver completed his work and then went to visit a relative. This was a new and independent journey which had nothing to do with his employment (*Storey* v *Ashton* (1869) LR 4 QB 476).

Whether a lunch break is within the course of employment will depend on whether the employee is authorised to take one. The question of fact in each case will be whether the driver was going about the employer's business or not. Therefore a bus driver who detoured while carrying children, in order to please the children, was still within the course of his employment (*Williams* v *Hemphill Ltd* (1966) SLT 259).

Accidents on the way to work have been considered.

Smith v Stages [1989] 2 WLR 529

Stages and another employee were travelling to their homes in the Midlands, after working in South Wales. The car crashed and both men were injured. The employers were paying travelling expenses but did not stipulate the means of travel and the men were paid for the day they travelled. The House of Lords held that the men were in the employer's time and were therefore within the course of their employment. However, most journeys to and from work by employees will be outside the scope of employment, unless a person is on the employer's business.

Criminal acts

A criminal act by an employee is likely to take the form of an assault or dishonesty. In the case of assaults the courts are reluctant to find that the employee was in the course of employment.

Warren v Henley's Ltd [1948] 2 All ER 935

The employee was employed as a pump attendant at a garage by the defendants. He accused a customer of being about to drive away without paying. The customer threatened to report him to the police and the defendants. The employee then gave the customer 'one on the nose to get on with'. This was held to be an act of personal vengeance and outside the course of his employment.

In cases of dishonesty, the fact that the offence was committed for the employee's benefit will not take him outside the course of his employment (*Port Swettenham Authority* v *TW Wu* [1979] AC 580). The question will still be, what was the employee paid to do and what was he doing at the time of the offence.

Lloyd v Grace Smith & Co [1912] AC 716

A solicitor's clerk was held to have acted within the scope of his employment when he fraudulently induced a client to convey properties to him. As the clerk was paid to do conveyancing, he was within the course of employment.

THE EMPLOYER'S INDEMNITY

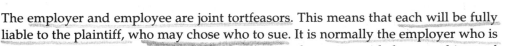

P can choose who to sue.

The employer and employee are joint tortfeasors. This means that each will be fully liable to the plaintiff, who may chose who to sue. It is normally the employer who is sued. As the employee is jointly liable, the employer is entitled to sue him and recover an indemnity.

Lister v Romford Ice & Cold Storage Ltd [1957] AC 555

A lorry driver knocked over his father who was acting as his mate on the lorry. The father recovered damages on the basis of the employer's vicarious liability for the driver's negligence. The damages were paid by the employer's insurers, who then exercised their right of subrogation to bring proceedings against the driver for an indemnity. The House of Lords held that there was an implied term in the employee's contract of employment that he would perform his contractual duties with reasonable care. He had broken this and the insurers were entitled to recover the money which they had paid to the father.

Since this case, the result of which received considerable criticism, the employer's insurance companies have reached a gentlemen's agreement, that they will not pursue their rights under the *Lister* principle unless there is evidence of collusion or misconduct. The decision in *Lister* did seem to undermine the principle of vicarious liability, that the employer is the best person to insure against such losses. Allowing the insurance company to get their money back from the employee looks like having your cake and eating it. The employers pay a premium for the insurer to take a non-existent risk.

It should be noted that the gentlemen's agreement was made before the statutory right to an indemnity under Civil Liability (Contribution) Act 1978, s. 1.

EMPLOYERS AND INDEPENDENT CONTRACTORS

The basic rule is that an employer is not liable for the torts of his independent contractors. There are, however, occasions where the employer will be primarily responsible where damage was caused by his independent contractor.

The employer may be under a non-delegable duty which cannot be discharged by entrusting work to an independent contractor. Examples of this are the employer's personal duty of care to his employees; liability under the rule in *Rylands* v *Fletcher*; work done by an independent contractor on or over the highway.

The employer will be liable where he has authorised the independent contractor to commit a tort.

PRINCIPAL AND AGENT

It is possible for a principal to be vicariously liable for the tort of his agent where the agent commits a tort in the course of his employment.

Ormrod v Crossville Motor Services [1953] 1 WLR 1120

The owner of a car asked a friend to drive the car to Monte Carlo from Birkenhead. The owner planned to compete in a car rally in Monte Carlo and the two were to go on holiday together afterwards. The friend caused damage to the plaintiff's bus in an accident caused by his negligence. It was held that the owner was liable for his friend's negligence, even though the friend was going on the journey partly for his own purposes.

Morgans v Launchbury [1973] AC 127

A husband sometimes used his wife's car. The wife was concerned about the husband's drinking habits and said he had to get a friend to drive him home if he had too much to drink. The husband did this and the friend negligently caused an accident. An action was brought against the wife, claiming she was vicariously liable. The House of Lords held that the husband was using the car for his own purposes and not hers. The driver was therefore not an agent of the wife.

23 | Joint and several liability

INTRODUCTION

If there is more than one breach of duty which causes the plaintiff damage, the liability of the defendants may be independent, several or joint.

Independent liability arises where the plaintiff suffered damage as a result of two completely separate torts. Each tortfeasor is liable for the damage he inflicts. If A's car is damaged on the right hand side by B's negligence and a week later C drives negligently into the left hand side of the car, B and C are independently liable for the damage they inflicted.

If more than one tortfeasor acts independently to cause the same damage to the plaintiff then they are severally liable. An example would be where two careless motorists collide and injure a pedestrian. In cases of several liability each tortfeasor is separately liable in respect of the damage but the plaintiff may only recover damages once.

Joint liability may arise in a number of ways. If two or more tortfeasors commit a joint breach of duty or act in furtherance of a common design then they are joint tortfeasors.

Brooke v Bool [1928] 2 KB 578

The plaintiff leased a shop from the defendant who remained entitled to enter the premises. A lodger in the shop told the defendant he could smell gas and both men investigated. The lodger was told to light a match by the defendant and there was an explosion. The defendant was held jointly liable for the damage caused by the lodger's negligence.

Joint liability also arises where an employer is held to be vicariously liable for the negligence of his employee. The employer and the employee are joint tortfeasors.

Similarly, where the employer is under a non-delegable duty and damage is caused by the tort of his independent contractor and in principal–agent cases.

In cases of joint liability each tortfeasor is liable for the full amount but the plaintiff can only recover once.

Two problems are raised by joint and several liability; successive actions by the plaintiff and contribution between defendants. The position has now been changed by statute but it is still relevant to look at common law.

SUCCESSIVE ACTIONS

If two or more persons were found to be joint tortfeasors at common law then two consequences followed.

A judgment against one tortfeasor barred a subsequent action against the others. This was so even if the judgment was unsatisfied. Judgment also meant that the plaintiff could not continue the action against other tortfeasors. This rule was reversed by the Law Reform (Married Women and Tortfeasors) Act 1935, s. 6 (now Civil Liability (Contribution) Act, s. 3).

Judgment recovered against any person liable in respect of any debt or damage shall not be a bar to an action, or to the continuance of an action, against any other person who is (apart from any such bar) jointly liable with him in respect of the same debt or damage.

If the plaintiff does bring a second action against a joint or several tortfeasor then s. 4 provides that he shall be refused costs in the later action unless the court is satisfied that there was reasonable ground for bringing it.

The statutory provision removed an important distinction between joint and several liability, as the common law rule against successive actions did not apply to several (concurrent) tortfeasors.

Where the plaintiff sues joint or several tortfeasors together, one judgment is given for a single sum.

The second consequence of joint liability at common law was that the release of one joint tortfeasor had the effect of releasing the other tortfeasors. This was based on the reason that in cases of joint liability only one tort was committed. Where liability was several, the release of one tortfeasor did not affect the liability of the others. The severity of the rule in cases of joint liability has been mitigated by courts drawing a distinction between an agreement not to sue, which preserves the cause of action against the rest, and a release, which extinguishes the liability of the rest. In practice the courts are very reluctant to find that there has been a release and even where there has been a release, this does not extinguish the action if there is an express or implied reservation of the action against the others.

CONTRIBUTION BETWEEN TORTFEASORS

At common law the rule was that a joint or several tortfeasor could not recover a contribution or indemnity from other tortfeasors in the absence of an agreement between them to the contrary.

This rule was reversed by statute and this is now the Civil Liability (Contribution) Act 1978, ss. 1 and 2.

Section 1 provides:

> Subject to the following provisions of this section, any person liable in respect of any damage suffered by another person may recover contribution from any other person liable in respect of the same damage (whether jointly liable with him or otherwise).

The person seeking a contribution must be actually or hypothetically liable.

Section 1(6) provides:

> References in this section to a person's liability in respect of any damage are references to any such liability which has been or could be established in an action brought against him in England or Wales by or on behalf of the person who suffered the damage.

Therefore if the plaintiff could not establish liability, e.g. because the action was statute barred, no contribution is recoverable. However, if the person has paid the plaintiff, then s. 1(2) provides that he will be entitled to a contribution even though he has ceased to be liable to the plaintiff, provided he was liable immediately before he made the payment. There is a two year limitation period from the date of judgment or settlement in which a contribution can be sought.

The person from whom the contribution is sought will be liable to make the contribution even though he is no longer liable to the original plaintiff. This is unless the claim for contribution itself is defeated by the two year limitation period.

If the plaintiff's action against the person from whom contribution is sought was blocked by a limitation period, this does not stop another tortfeasor claiming a contribution unless his action is blocked by the two year limitation period (s. 1(3)).

A complication arises in respect of s. 1(5). This states:

> A judgment given in any action . . . by or on behalf of the person who suffered the damage in question against any person from whom contribution is sought . . . shall be conclusive in the proceedings for contribution as to any issue determined by that judgment in favour of the person from whom the contribution is sought.

This section would appear to contradict s. 1(3), as literally interpreted it would mean that a court's judgment on limitation in an action between the plaintiff and the person from whom contribution is sought in the latter's favour, would be conclusive that no contribution could be claimed.

Section 1(4) provides:

> A person who has made or agreed to make any payment in bona fide settlement or compromise of any claim . . . shall be entitled to recover contribution in accordance

with this section without regard to whether or not he himself is or ever was liable in respect of the damage, provided, however, that he would have been liable assuming that the factual basis of the claim against him could be established.

This section recognises the fact that most civil actions are settled and do not go to trial. Provided the settlement is bona fide and not collusive, then the person settling is entitled to a contribution.

Section 2 deals with the amount of contribution a person may be entitled to. This is the amount that the court finds to be just and equitable having regard to that person's responsibility for the damage in question. The court has to take into account all the relevant circumstances, such as the degree of blameworthiness and the parties role in bringing about the damage.

Fitzgerald v Lane [1988] 2 All ER 961

The plaintiff stepped out into traffic on a busy road. He was struck by a vehicle driven by D1. This pushed him into the path of a vehicle being driven by D2. D1 and D2 were held to have been negligent. The House of Lords held that the plaintiff's conduct had to be looked at in the light of the totality of D1 and D2's conduct. The plaintiff was held to be 50% to blame. Then the court had to decide the amount of contribution payable. It was held that D1 and D2 were equally to blame and they had to contribute equally to the remaining 50% of the plaintiff's damages.

The court may also exempt a party from having to pay a contribution, or may order a party to pay a complete indemnity.

The amount which can be recovered by contribution is limited to the amount that the plaintiff could have recovered from that particular defendant.

Example

A collision occurs between three cars driven by D1, D2 and D3. As a result, a pedestrian, P, is injured.

P has a choice as to whether to sue D1, D2 or D3, or he could issue a single writ against all three.

If P chose to sue D1 and was successful, recovering £30,000 in damages, D1 could then bring contribution proceedings against D2 and D3 within two years. The court would then have to determine the relative contributions of the three parties. If D1 was held to be 25% to blame then he could recover £22,500 from D2 and D3. If D2 was found to be 50% to blame, then D1 would recover £15,000 from him and the remainder from D3.

Suppose P sued all three defendants and was awarded £30,000. He would then have a choice as to which defendant(s) to enforce the judgment against. That person would then have to seek a contribution from the others. This leaves the plaintiff with the option of enforcing against a solvent defendant.

24 | Limitation

INTRODUCTION

A defendant ought not to have the threat of litigation hanging over him indefinitely and there are therefore statutory limitation periods within which the plaintiff must either serve his writ or lose his remedy. The present complex law is contained in the Limitation Act 1980 (as amended).

The legal effect of the expiration of a limitation period is to bar the remedy but not the right: e.g. where a debt is owed but the limitation period has expired, the creditor cannot sue for the money but the debt is still owed.

The major difficulty in fixing limitation periods is to draw a fair line between the defendant's interest in having a clearly defined and short limitation period and not barring the plaintiff before he is aware that he has an action. This problem arises particularly in two areas.

Where the claim is for personal injuries but the nature of the plaintiff's illness means he is not aware of it for many years: e.g. X worked in Y's factory from 1976–84. In 1991 he discovers that he is suffering from asbestosis contracted during his employment by Y. Should X be allowed to claim?

If the claim is for a defective building the damage may take many years to manifest itself: e.g. X builds a house in 1975. The house is purchased by Y in 1978. In 1990 large cracks appear in the walls of the house and Y discovers that these are due to faulty foundations. Should Y be able to sue X?

ACCRUAL OF CAUSES OF ACTION

The limitation period starts to run when the cause of action accrues. Where the tort is actionable *per se* (without proof of damage), time starts to run from the date of the defendant's act. Where the tort is actionable only on proof of damage, the cause of action accrues when the damage is sustained. If the tort is of a continuing nature, such as nuisance, then a fresh cause of action arises each time that damage is inflicted.

In the asbestosis and defective building examples given above there may be problems in ascertaining when damage occurred. This problem is widespread and it is a question of fact in each case whether damage has been established: e.g. it has been held that damage occurs when burglars enter premises rather than when a defective safety gate was installed (*Dove* v *Banhams Patent Locks* [1983] 1 WLR 1436). A further problem is that if the damage was unobservable (latent) when it occurred then the claim could be statute barred before the plaintiff is aware of it. This problem is dealt with by the legislation.

In some cases the plaintiff may have a choice of action in either contract or tort. One of the factors which may affect his decision is the relevant limitation period. Limitation periods in contract accrue when a breach of contract occurs.

Midland Bank Trust Co Ltd v Hett, Stubbs and Kemp (a firm) [1979] Ch 384

The plaintiff was given an option to purchase a farm. The defendant solicitor negligently failed to register the option. More than six years later the farm was sold to a third party. The damage for the purposes of a negligence action was held to occur when the farm was sold. The negligence action was therefore not statute barred. The contract action was also held not to be barred as the breach of contract was an omission which continued until the sale of the farm. Had the breach of contract been an act then the limitation period would have run from then.

LIMITATION PERIODS

Normal periods

The basic rule is that a tort action must be brought within six years of the accrual of the cause of action (Limitation Act, 1980 s. 2).

Damages for personal injuries and death

Where the damages claimed by the plaintiff consist of or include a claim for damages for personal injuries, the limitation period is three years (Limitation Act 1980, s. 11(4)).

Cartledge v E Jobling & Sons Ltd [1963] AC 758

The plaintiff contracted pneumoconiosis as a result of the defendant's breach of duty. He did not know he had the disease until well after the three year time period had expired. It was held that his action was statute barred. The damage occurred when the lung tissue was scarred, although a medical examination might not have revealed the damage at that stage.

The obvious injustice of this decision was almost immediately reversed by statute (now Limitation Act 1980, s. 11(4)). This allowed the plaintiff to claim within three years of the date of knowledge.

Knowledge is defined by s. 14 as knowledge of certain facts:

(a)   That the injury in question was significant.
(b)   That the injury was attributable in whole or in part to the act or omission which is alleged to constitute negligence, nuisance or breach of duty.
(c)   The identity of the defendant.
(d)   If it is alleged that the act or omission was that of a person other than the defendant, the identity of that person and the additional facts supporting the bringing of an action against the defendant. (This would cover cases of vicarious liability.)

An injury is significant:

> if the person whose date of knowledge is in question would reasonably have considered it sufficiently serious to justify his instituting proceedings for damages against a defendant who did not dispute liability and was able to satisfy a judgment (s. 14(2)).

The relevant knowledge required is of facts not of law (s. 14(1)). Therefore it is irrelevant whether or not the plaintiff was aware that the defendant's act or omission amounted to a tort. It also means that incorrect legal advice will not stop time running against the plaintiff. If the plaintiff is aware of the facts but is advised that he has no cause of action, time will run against him. (But the court may apply the discretion.)

Knowledge may be either actual or constructive (s. 14(3)). It therefore includes: facts observable or ascertainable by him; and facts ascertainable by him with the help of medical or other appropriate expert advice which is reasonable for him to seek. If the plaintiff has symptoms of e.g. asbestosis and fails to seek medical advice then he will have constructive knowledge. However, if he has sought medical advice but the doctor has failed to diagnose the appropriate facts, then time will not run against him.

The court is given a power to disapply the provisions relating to personal injuries or death (s. 33). In deciding whether to apply this discretion the court must have regard to certain factors:

(a)   The length of, and the reasons for, the delay on the part of the plaintiff.
(b)   The effect of the delay on the cogency of the evidence in the case.
(c)   The conduct of the defendant after the cause of action arose, including his response to the plaintiff's request for information.
(d)   The duration of any disability of the plaintiff arising after the cause of action.
(e)   The extent to which the plaintiff acted promptly and reasonably once he knew of the facts which afforded him a cause of action.

(f)   The steps taken by the plaintiff to obtain medical, legal, or other expert advice and the nature of any such advice received.

This equitable discretion was originally supposed to be limited to exceptional cases. However, it has been given a broad interpretation by the courts (*Thompson* v *Brown* [1981] 1 WLR 744). But the discretion can only be applied where the plaintiff is prejudiced by the operation of the provisions of the Act. It will not apply where prejudice is caused by failure to serve the writ or where the action is discontinued.

DEFECTIVE BUILDINGS AND LATENT DAMAGE

Just as disease in a person may not manifest itself for a lengthy period of time, so a building may outwardly seem healthy but have serious latent defects. The legal problem raised is not to prejudice the plaintiff by fixing a cut off point before he realises he has a cause of action and avoiding making the defendant liable decades after the alleged breach of duty.

The law is now contained in the Latent Damage Act 1986. A three stage analysis is made.

(a)   Initially the limitation period runs for six years from the date of the damage (Limitation Act 1980, s. 14A(4)(a)). This confirms the House of Lords decision in *Pirelli General Cable Works Ltd* v *Oscar Faber & Partners* [1983] 2 AC 1. The difficulty here is that where the original defect about which the complaint is made is e.g. in the foundations, no damage may be observable until the six year period has expired.

(b)   The second period runs for three years from the earliest date on which the plaintiff or his predecessor first knew, or could have known, of the facts required to commence proceedings (Limitation Act 1980 s. 14A(4)(b)). This discoverability test comes from *Sparham-Souter* v *Town and Country Developments* [1976] 1 QB 958. The plaintiff must be aware of all relevant facts before the period begins to run: i.e. he must be aware of the defect or should reasonably be aware of it. The plaintiff is not endowed with the knowledge of an expert and the damage must be sufficiently serious to justify the implementation of proceedings.

(c)   The third provision is a long stop which prevents the discoverability test operating indefinitely. No action may be commenced in cases of latent damage beyond fifteen years of the breach of duty which causes the damage (Limitation Act, s. 14B). The relevant breach of duty will usually be when the building is completed.

For example, A Ltd build a house and construction is completed in July 1988. The house is purchased by B. A Ltd have failed to dig the foundations to the appropriate depth. Damage to the building commenced immediately, so the initial six year period runs from July 1988. B is unaware of the damage as there are no external signs to put him on his guard. In July 1995 a large crack appears in the gable end wall. The three year discoverability period will run from this date. B will have until July 1998 in which to serve his writ. The fifteen year period runs until July 2003, so B is unaffected by this.

NB The above example assumes that B does have an action in tort against A Ltd. (See chapter on Defective Premises.) Defective premises actions may also be brought in contract, when the limitation period is six years from the date of the breach of contract. Or under the Defective Premises Act 1972, where the limitation period is six years from when the building was completed (Defective Premises Act 1972, s. 1(5)).

MISCELLANEOUS LIMITATION PERIODS

Actions under the Consumer Protection Act 1987 must be brought within three years of suffering the relevant damage or within three years of acquiring the necessary knowledge, if this is the later (Consumer Protection Act 1987, s. 5(5) and Schedule 1). The Act also provides a long stop provision of ten years from when the defendant supplied the product to another.

In cases of personal injury followed by death, if the plaintiff dies after the expiration of the limitation period the claim does not survive for the benefit of his estate. The personal representatives may ask the court to exercise the discretion. Where the plaintiff dies before the expiration of the limitation period, a new limitation period begins to run for three years from the date of death or the date of the personal representatives knowledge, whichever is later (Limitation Act 1980, s. 11(5)).

FRAUD OR CONCEALMENT

Where the plaintiff's action is based on the defendant's fraud or where any fact relevant to his right of action is concealed by the defendant, the limitation period does not begin to run until the plaintiff has, or ought with reasonable diligence to have discovered the fraud or concealment (Limitation Act 1980, s. 32(1)).

25 | General defences

INTRODUCTION

Defences in tort actions can be divided into two categories. First, those which are only applicable to particular torts. Examples would include fair comment in a defamation action and distress damage feasant in a trespass to land action. These defences can be found in the chapter on the relevant tort.

The second group of defences are those which have general application in tort cases. The defences of *volenti non fit injuria*, contributory negligence and illegality may arise in a number of torts but have a particular importance in negligence actions. For this reason, they were dealt with in a separate chapter in the negligence section. (See Chapter 9.) The remainder of the general defences will be dealt with here.

MISTAKE

Mistake is not generally a defence to a tort action as a mistake as to law or fact will not usually exclude the defendant from liability. For example, it is not a defence to trespass to land for the defendant to argue that he mistakenly thought that the land was his. Neither is it a defence in a medical negligence action for the defendant doctor to claim that he made a mistake in diagnosing the patient's condition, if that mistake amounted to negligence.

Mistake may be relevant where reasonableness is required. A reasonable mistake of fact may be relevant to a defence. Where a police officer arrests a person and has reasonable grounds for suspecting that an arrestable offence has been committed, the tort of false imprisonment is not committed, even if no such offence has been committed.

In the tort of deceit, if the defendant honestly believed the truth of his statement, there is no liability.

INEVITABLE ACCIDENT

An accident will be inevitable where it was not intended by the defendant and could not be avoided by the use of reasonable care. In a fault based tort this only means that the defendant was not at fault. As the burden of proof is on the plaintiff to establish fault, inevitable accident is not a defence. At the time when the burden of proof in trespass to the person actions was on the defendant he could avoid liability by proving that the event complained of was an inevitable accident. This is no longer the case. (See Chapter 19, p. 212.)

NECESSITY

This defence is usually raised in connection with actions for intentional interference with persons or property. The defence is essentially that the defendant's action was necessary to prevent greater damage to the defendant or a third party.

Where self-defence is used, the defendant has responded to the plaintiff's threatened or actual tortious behaviour. With necessity, the plaintiff may well be an innocent third party.

The courts seem to take the view that where personal injury is threatened, then any necessary damage to property will be justified. If a ship is threatened with sinking in a storm, the decision to throw goods overboard to try and save the ship's crew could be defended by necessity.

In battery cases involving lack of consent on the part of a patient, where the patient is incapable of giving a valid consent, the test is whether the treatment was in the best interests of the patient (*F v West Berkshire Health Authority* [1989] 2 All ER 545). If the patient is capable of giving a valid consent and refuses, then the doctor must abide by that refusal or face a battery action. (See Chapter 14, p. 157.)

Where property damage is threatened, the question is whether the defendant acted in the way that a reasonable man would have done. If he sees a fire on the plaintiff's land which he reasonably thinks is liable to spread to his own land and cause damage, he may enter the plaintiff's land and attempt to extinguish the fire.

Would it make any difference if the fire was started by the defendant's own negligence? In *Rigby* v *Chief Constable of Northamptonshire* [1985] 2 All ER 985, it was stated that where the need to act was brought about by the defendant's negligence, then necessity would not be a good defence. Necessity can therefore never be a defence to negligence.

It should be noted that the courts are very hesitant about allowing a defence of necessity, as it means inflicting loss on the plaintiff. The Court of Appeal, for example, has refused to accept necessity as a defence to squatting (*Southwark London Borough Council* v *Williams* [1971] Ch 734).

26 | Remedies

INTRODUCTION

Remedies in tort are classified as either judicial or extra-judicial. Judicial remedies are the sort that a judge may make such as an award of damages or an injunction. Extra-judicial remedies comprise some form of self-help such as distress damage feasant or abatement of a nuisance.

DAMAGES

Damages in tort may be either compensatory or non-compensatory.

Non-compensatory damages

These may be nominal, contemptuous or exemplary.

Nominal damages

Nominal damages are awarded for a tort actionable *per se*, i.e. where a legal right has been violated but the plaintiff has suffered no actual loss. The damages are awarded for the wrong itself rather than any loss suffered. The amount awarded will be small, normally £2, and the fact that nominal damages have been awarded does not mean that the plaintiff should be regarded as a successful plaintiff for the purposes of costs.

Contemptuous damages

These are usually only awarded in defamation actions. They consist of an award of the least valuable coin of the realm. Contemptuous damages acknowledge that the plaintiff's legal rights have suffered a technical infringement but express derision of his conduct in the matter. A plaintiff who is awarded contemptuous damages is unlikely to recover costs.

Exemplary damages

Exemplary or punitive damages are awarded to punish the defendant for his conduct and are in addition to compensatory damages. The award of exemplary damages in tort is controversial as many people feel that the punitive function of the law should be performed by the criminal rather than the civil law.

The award of exemplary damages in tort actions has been considered by the House of Lords and the principles are laid down in *Rookes* v *Barnard* [1964] AC 1129. The House was generally unhappy with the award of exemplary damages as this tended to confuse the respective roles of civil and criminal law. Exemplary damages were therefore confined to three categories. Statute and precedent prevented their abolition. The three categories were confirmed by the House of Lords in *Cassell & Co Ltd* v *Broome* [1972] AC 1027.

(a)   Express authorisation by statute

The Reserve and Auxiliary Forces Act 1951, s. 13(2) allows an award of exemplary damages. This appears to be the only statutory provision in this category.

(b)   Conduct calculated to make a profit

Such damages are usually awarded in defamation cases and are primarily to reverse unjust enrichment but may also take into account the plaintiff's difficulties in litigating.

Cassell & Co Ltd *v* Broome [1972] AC 1027

The plaintiff was a retired naval officer. The defendants published a book about a wartime convoy with which the plaintiff was involved. The plaintiff sued for libel and was successful. The jury awarded £25,000 exemplary damages which was upheld by the House of Lords because of the profit which the defendant would have made. It was not necessary that the defendant calculated that the profit would exceed the damages. The major factor was that the defendant was prepared to hurt somebody in order to make a profit.

(c)   Oppressive conduct by government servants

This category covers not only government servants in the strict sense but also persons exercising governmental functions, such as police officers. A court may award exemplary damages where there has been oppressive, arbitrary or unconstitutional action by government servants. However, in *Holden* v *Chief Constable Lancashire* [1987] QB 380, it was held that this category covers wrongful arrest regardless of whether there was oppressive behaviour or aggravating circumstances. The court read the requirement of or 'unconstitutional action' literally.

This category has justified the award of substantial amounts of damages against police officers in cases of wrongful arrest and malicious prosecution. In *Taylor* v *Metropolitan Police Commissioner* (1989), £70,000 was awarded in exemplary damages for false imprisonment and malicious prosecution.

In rare cases a local authority may be liable to pay exemplary damages where it has practised sexual and racial discrimination in the recruitment of its employees (*Bradford City Metropolitan Council* v *Arora* [1991] 3 All ER 545).

Despite the reluctance of the courts to extend the range of exemplary or punitive damages, the Lord Chancellor has remitted to the Law Commission the issue of whether punitive damages would be appropriate in the disaster cases.

Aggravated damages

It is convenient at this point to discuss the expression aggravated damages. This is an expression used by judges and some confusion surrounds the question as to whether they are compensatory or non-compensatory. They are awarded where there is outrage to person or property and are best regarded as compensatory. They are to compensate for injury to the plaintiff's pride or feelings. They may be awarded in deceit (*Archer* v *Brown* [1985] QB 401) or cases involving rape or sexual assault (*W* v *Meah* [1986] 1 All ER 935). They are apparently not suitable for medical negligence cases even where horrific and totally unacceptable treatment caused excruciating pain (*Kralj* v *McGrath* [1986] 1 All ER 54).

Compensatory damages for personal injuries

Introduction

The basis of an award of compensatory damages in a tort action is that the plaintiff should be awarded such a sum of money as will, as nearly as possible, put him in the position he would have been in if he had not sustained the injuries. The damages must (in the absence of a statutory exception) be awarded on a once and forever basis in the form of a lump sum.

The expression personal injuries covers physical harm to the person, disease and illness (including psychiatric illness).

Damages for personal injuries are normally treated separately as they raise problems not encountered with other types of loss. Where damage to property is caused then financial compensation is adequate. Where a person is deprived of a leg by tortious conduct, money is the only compensation available but this requires the court to fix the market value of a leg and to engage in the difficult task of assessing damages for intangibles such as pain, shock and suffering. Other serious difficulties are posed by the problems of calculating future pecuniary losses and estimating future medical condition.

Classification of damages

In personal injuries cases damages are divided into pecuniary and non-pecuniary losses. Pecuniary damages are those that can be estimated in monetary terms, such as loss of earnings, medical and other expenses. Non-pecuniary damages cover intangibles such as loss of physical amenity, pain, shock and suffering.

Form and basis of the award

The judge is required to itemise the award, showing how much has been awarded for each head of loss. The reason for this is that different rates of interest are applied to pecuniary and non-pecuniary damages. The advantage of the system in practical terms is that practitioners are aware of the going rate for each type of loss and this encourages out of court settlements.

The basis of the award is full compensation. The plaintiff must be compensated for all pecuniary losses which he has suffered as a result of the tort. The system of full compensation is subject to two particular criticisms. A high cost is involved for small claims. This could be avoided by excluding compensation for the first few days. Secondly, there is no incentive for the victim to recover and return to work.

At this stage it would be helpful to set out an example drawn from a case.

Lim Poh Choo v Camden and Islington Area Health Authority [1979] 2 All ER 910

Dr Lim Poh Choo was admitted to a national health service hospital for a minor operation. In the recovery room following the operation she suffered a cardiac arrest. This was the result of the negligence of a person for whom the health authority was vicariously liable. At the time of the accident the plaintiff was 36 years old and a senior psychiatric registrar. After the accident, which caused her irremediable brain damage, she was barely sentient and totally dependent on others.

Liability was admitted by the defendants, so the one issue at trial was damages. The trial judge had awarded damages as follows:

1.	Pain, suffering, loss of amenities	£20,000	
	Interest from date of writ	£5,930	£25,930
2.	Out of pocket expenses, including £680 for cost of stay in hospital and nursing home	£3,596	
3.	Cost of care to date of judgment: 40 months at £200 per month	£8,000	

4.	Interest on (2) and (3) from date of accident (1 March 1973) to judgment	£2,482	£14,078
5.	Loss of earnings to date of judgment	£14,213	
6.	Interest on (5) from date of accident to judgment	£3,044	£17,257
7.	Cost of future care: Malaysia, 7 years at £2,600 per annum discounted to England, 11 years at £8,000 per annum	£17,500 £88,000	£105,000
8.	Loss of future earnings: 14 years at £6,000 Loss of pension	£84,000 £8,000	£92,000

Total: £254,765

The defendants appealed to the House of Lords on quantum of damages. The House held:

(a)   The overall amount awarded was not excessive.
(b)   The award for pain, suffering and loss of amenities was correct.
(c)   The award for loss of earnings, to date and future, was correct.
(d)   Some alteration was needed to the cost of care to avoid duplication between this, loss of earnings and loss of amenities.

The result was that (excluding interest) the plaintiff was awarded £229,298.64.

The lump sum

It can be seen from the above case that once the plaintiff has succeeded in an action then damages will be awarded in a lump sum.

The lump sum is said to have the advantages of enabling the plaintiff to concentrate on recovery without reducing his entitlement to compensation; enable the insurer to pay up and incur no further inconvenience; and enable the plaintiff to plan his life taking into account any disability suffered.

The disadvantages are that the plaintiff may use the capital unwisely; no account can be taken of any improvement or deterioration in the plaintiff's medical condition; and the lump sum system takes no account of inflation, which may erode what at the time was adequate compensation.

There is now a statutory power to award provisional damages (Supreme Court Act 1981, s. 32A). If there is a chance that at some future time, the injured person may develop some disease or suffer deterioration in his physical or mental condition, he may be awarded damages on the basis that this will not occur, with a proviso that further damages will be awarded at a later date if it does occur. The section must be specifically pleaded by the plaintiff, who may be awarded a higher amount at trial if he does not plead the provision. The right to have the award adjusted may only be exercised once.

Interim damages may be awarded at the interlocutory stage where the defendant admits liability but contests quantum. The defendant must be insured, or be a public body, or have the resources to make an interim payment (Supreme Court Act 1981, s. 32).

Pecuniary losses

(a)   Loss of earnings

Damages for loss of earnings come into two categories. Loss of earnings suffered by the plaintiff before the trial have to be pleaded as special damages. The plaintiff must show what his net loss has been as a result of his injury. At this stage inflation can be taken care of, e.g. if the accident occurred in 1985 and the trial in 1990. If the plaintiff was earning £10,000 per annum in 1985 and but for the accident would have been earning £15,000 in 1990 then an average figure of £12,500 will be taken and multiplied by five.

Future loss of earnings (i.e. from the trial onwards) are claimed as general damages. This causes severe problems for the courts as it involves guessing what would have happened to the plaintiff had the accident not occurred.

The first stage in calculating future loss of earnings is to take the plaintiff's net annual loss, i.e. the difference between what he would have earned and what he is earning. The court will then adjust this figure to take into account factors such as promotion prospects. The second stage is to apply the multiplier to this figure. The multiplier is calculated by working out the number of years that the disability is likely to continue. This figure is then reduced to take into account the contingencies of life, i.e. the plaintiff might not have lived or worked until retirement age and he has received a capital sum which can be invested and make money which would otherwise not be available to him. At this stage a simple example would be useful.

Example

The subject is a twenty-seven year old man who has been rendered totally unfit for work by a negligently caused accident. Before the accident he worked as a roofer and earned £20,000 per annum. The accident took place in 1987 and the trial in 1990. Had the accident not occurred he would have been earning £22,000 in 1990.

(i)   Pre trial loss of earnings, £21,000 less tax and national insurance which would have been paid: £14,000 × 3 = £42,000

(ii)   Future loss of earnings (assuming no promotion prospects): net annual loss of £14,000. Multiplier of 15 = £210,000.

The objective of this exercise is that the plaintiff should receive a sum, which when invested will produce a figure equal to the lost sum.

Where the plaintiff is a child below working age, the court will take into account national average earnings during early working years and apply a low multiplier. The reason for the low multiplier is that the child might never have become a wage earner (*Croke* v *Wiseman* [1981] 3 All ER 852).

The lost years: one problem which may evolve in calculating damages for future loss of earnings are the so called lost years. This occurs where the plaintiff's life expectancy is reduced by the accident. Damages for loss of earnings are based on the plaintiff's life expectancy before the accident (*Pickett* v *British Rail Engineering Ltd* [1980] AC 136) but a deduction is made for the amount that the plaintiff would have spent on his own support during the lost years.

If our subject in the above example had his life expectancy reduced in that he would now die at 40, damages are recoverable by him for the period 40–65 years of age but subject to a deduction for his living expenses.

No damages are recoverable for loss of expectation of life itself but non-pecuniary damages may be awarded for mental suffering caused by the knowledge that life has been cut short.

(b)   Other pecuniary losses

The plaintiff can recover any expenses reasonably incurred as a result of treatment of his injuries. Any medical expenses reasonably incurred may therefore be recovered. The plaintiff has a choice as to whether he is treated privately or not (Law Reform (Personal Injuries) Act 1948, s. 2(4)). But if the plaintiff is treated by the national health service then the living expenses which he saves are set off against his loss of earnings (Administration of Justice Act, s. 5)

If a friend or relative has incurred financial loss in caring for the plaintiff then the plaintiff can recover this amount as damages. This is the plaintiff's loss because of his need for care (*Housecroft* v *Burnett* [1986] 1 All ER 332). In the absence of any contract between the third party and the plaintiff, the obligation on the plaintiff to reimburse the third party is only a moral one.

Non-pecuniary losses

(a)   Loss of amenity

The plaintiff may recover damages for the injury itself and any consequent inability to enjoy life. These damages are calculated on an objective basis and do not take into account the plaintiff's inability to appreciate the disability. Unconscious plaintiffs may therefore recover for loss of amenity (*West* v *Shephard* [1964] AC 326).

Loss of amenity may include loss of capacity to enjoy sport or other pastimes which the plaintiff engaged in before the injury. Impairment of one of the five senses, inability to play with one's children, diminution of marriage prospects, impairment of sexual life and destroyed holidays may also be compensated under this heading.

The courts work from a tariff which is laid down by the Court of Appeal. The tariff figure can be adjusted in the light of the particular circumstances of the plaintiff.

(b)   Pain and suffering

The court will award damages for any pain and suffering which can be attributed to the injury itself and to any consequential surgical operations. The award will cover past and any future pain. Compensation neurosis may also be compensated. This is a medically recognised condition caused by awaiting the outcome of litigation.

An unconscious plaintiff cannot recover damages for pain and suffering. A conscious plaintiff may recover for any mental suffering caused by the knowledge that life has been cut short (Administration of Justice Act 1982, s. 1(b)) or that his ability to enjoy life has been diminished by physical handicap.

Damages for nervous shock are awarded as damages for pecuniary loss and as damages for pain and suffering and loss of amenity.

Damages for bereavement are only awarded in actions under the Fatal Accidents Act 1976 to certain classes of dependants (see below, p. 282.). No damages can be awarded for grief or sorrow (*Hinz* v *Berry* [1970] 2 QB 40).

Deductions

A victim of an accident may be in receipt of money from sources other than tort damages. As the objective of the damages award is to compensate the plaintiff for losses incurred as a result of his injury, it is necessary for the courts to work out to what extent these other sources must be set off against damages. The plaintiff may be entitled to state benefits as a result of his injuries and may also have private insurance or become entitled to payments by his employer.

The philosophy employed by the courts is not to punish a thrifty plaintiff. On this basis personal accident insurance money is generally non-deductible, as are pensions (*Parry* v *Cleaver* [1970] AC 1). If an employee has received sick pay or wages from an employer then this will be deducted unless the sick pay has to repaid out of any damages received.

There has been considerable controversy over whether social security benefits should be deductible from tort damages for personal injuries. It should be remembered that social security payments are the main source of compensation for accident victims. Parliament has now accepted the case against double-compensation. The law is now contained in Social Security Act 1989, s. 22 and Sch 4 as amended by Social Security Act Sch 1 and the Recoupment Regulations 1990, SI 1990, No 322. The law applies to payments made on or after 3 September 1990 in relation to accidents occurring on or after 1 January 1989. Virtually all social security payments can be recouped by the Department of Social Security. The compensator (who will normally be an insurance company) must pay all benefits received by the plaintiff before a compensation payment is made. The system applies to settlements out of court.

The scheme does not apply to small payments of under £2,500. The Law Reform Act 1948, s. 2(1) applies to these. Half of any of the relevant benefits paid for a five year period will be deducted from the damages awarded.

Examples

(a) X is awarded £50,000 damages and has received £12,000 in benefits. X will receive £38,000 in damages.

(b) X is awarded £20,000 in damages reduced by 50% for contributory negligence and has received £10,000 in benefits. X will receive nothing in damages.

(c) X is awarded £2,000 in damages and has received £1,500 in benefits. Assuming the benefits are deductible, X will receive £1,250 in damages.

One difference between (c) and the other two examples, is that in (c) the deduction will be made by the court. In (a) and (b) the deduction and payment to the Department of Social Security will be made by the compensator.

Structured settlements

The haphazard effect of the lump sum award of damages in personal injuries cases has brought about many calls for reform. The plaintiff is generally at a disadvantage because of the difficulty of estimating the amount that will be awarded at trial. This, combined with delay and the stress of the litigation process, leads to plaintiffs accepting low figures in negotiated settlements. As no judicial or legislative reform has been forthcoming, it has been left to the insurance companies to produce structured settlements which provide pensions instead of lump sum damages for future losses.

The structured settlement works by the insurer buying an annuity which covers the liability involved and is held for the injured person. This pension can be varied and the payments structured over a period of time. The system offers two direct benefits to the plaintiff. The income which is generated can be guaranteed against erosion by inflation; and the income is paid free of tax to the plaintiff. The latter factor increases by a quarter the value of the lump sum paid by the insurer.

The first part of a structured settlement is a lump sum to cover financial losses incurred up to the date of settlement. The second part is a pension which will usually last for the remainder of the plaintiff's life. This pension covers future loss of income, non-pecuniary losses, medical expenses and the cost of future care.

The court has no power to order a structured settlement so these are only available where the parties agree. A second limitation is that they are only appropriate in connection with future losses, they are not appropriate to past losses. The damages must be large enough to justify using a structured settlement. At present cases must be worth at least £50,000 to make it worthwhile.

EFFECT OF DEATH ON AN AWARD OF DAMAGES FOR PERSONAL INJURIES

Introduction

If the defendant in a tort action dies then the cause of action will usually survive against his estate. Where the plaintiff dies, his cause of action will generally survive for the benefit of his estate and a new cause of action will be created for his dependants. An important exception to this principle is in actions for defamation where the death of a party terminates the action.

The estate's action (Law Reform (Miscellaneous Provisions) Act 1934)

At common law the action did not survive the death of the plaintiff. The introduction of compulsory third-party insurance for motor cars made it unjust that if the defendant killed his victim instead of maiming him he could escape civil liability. The 1934 Act removed the rule that the action did not survive death.

The Act does not create liability. It preserves the deceased's subsisting action for the benefit of his estate (s. 1(1)). The action is the one that the deceased would have brought had he lived.

This principle does not create difficulties for damages accruing during the deceased's lifetime: e.g. the deceased was injured in a car accident caused by the defendant's negligence and died three months later. The estate will recover damages for pecuniary and non-pecuniary losses based on the normal principles.

Problems do arise with losses accruing after the death. There is a difficulty with overlap with the dependant's action. To avoid this, the Act provides (s. 1(2)) that no damages may be recovered by the estate for loss of earnings for the lost years. It is also provided that no damages may be recovered by the estate for bereavement (s. 1(A)).

The action is not for death caused by the defendant and so the defendant need not be responsible for the death. But where the defendant's wrong has caused the death, then any losses or gains to the estate consequent on the death are ignored in the calculation of damages (s. 1(4)). An example of a loss would be the termination of an annuity. An example of a gain would be an insurance payment. One exception to this rule is that the court may award the estate any funeral expenses incurred.

The dependant's action (Fatal Accidents Act 1976)

Who can claim?

A definition of dependants is given in s. 1(3) of the Act. The normal action will be brought by the surviving spouse and children but parents and other ascendants, siblings, uncles and aunts and their issue are included. One category which deserves special mention is cohabitees. If the claimant had lived with the deceased as husband or wife for a period of at least two years then that person is classed as a dependant.

The action is brought by the personal representatives of the deceased or after six months of the appointment of the personal representatives, by any dependant on behalf of himself or others.

The nature of the action

This is a new right of action given to the dependants and is not a survival of the deceased's right of action. The death must have been caused by the tortious act of the defendant (s. 1(1)) and the dependants have to show that the deceased had a right of action in order to be able to claim. This means that if the deceased had settled the claim or obtained judgment, the dependants have no claim. But the dependants will not be bound by any limitation on the amount the deceased could have claimed.

The action is often said to be for the loss of a breadwinner. Where a spouse is deprived of the other spouse's earnings or a child is deprived of a parent's earnings, there will be a claim.

The amount recoverable

The main head of damages is the pecuniary loss suffered by the dependants from the date of death. The method of assessing damages was stated by Lord Wright in *Davies* v *Powell Duffryn Collieries Ltd* [1942] AC 601.

The starting point is the amount of wages which the deceased was earning, the ascertainment of which to some extent may depend upon the regularity of his employment. Then there is an estimate of how much was required or expected for his own personal and living expenses. The balance will give a datum or base figure which will generally be turned into a lump sum by taking a certain number of years' purchase. That sum, however, has to be taxed down by having due regard to uncertainties.

An award may be made from the date of death up to the date of trial. The earnings the deceased would have made are calculated and the sum he would have spent on his own support is deducted. The second stage is to assess losses into the future. The annual value of dependency is estimated (the multiplicand) and the appropriate multiplier used. The aim is to give a lump sum which, when invested, will produce an income equivalent to the dependant's loss of income over the period of dependancy. This will give a global figure which is available for distribution between the dependants.

Dependency

The dependency must not arise from a business relationship. In *Malyon* v *Plummer* [1964] 1 QB 330, the plaintiff had been paid £600 per annum for services rendered to her husband's company. The value of these services was calculated at £200 per annum. The balance was attributable to her relationship with the deceased. Her loss of dependency was therefore £400 per annum.

Where the court is calculating the damages to be awarded to a cohabitee it must take into account the fact that the dependant had no enforceable right to financial support by the deceased (s. 3(4)).

When assessing a wife's claim in respect of her husband's death the court must take no account of her remarriage or prospects of remarriage (s. 3(3)).

Bereavement

Damages for bereavement may be awarded to certain classes of dependants. The spouse of the deceased or the parents of an unmarried child may claim. The damages are for mental distress at the death and are fixed by statute at £7,500 (s. 1A). There is no attempt to reflect the subjective level of grief.

Deductions

In assessing the damages in respect of a person's death, any benefits which have accrued or may accrue to any person from his estate or otherwise as a result of death are disregarded (s. 4). Therefore any insurance money, pensions or damages for pain and suffering inherited as part of the deceased's estate are disregarded.

Defences

If the deceased could have had a defence raised successfully against him by the defendant, then the dependants may have the same defence raised against them. *Volenti* or *ex turpi causa* will therefore bar the claim. Any contributory negligence on the part of the deceased will be reflected in a deduction of damages.

Example

Fred was injured in an accident at work due to negligence and breach of statutory duty on the part of Gareth, his employer. The accident rendered Fred unfit for work and he died as a result of his injuries, two years after the accident.

Fred is survived by his wife Sally and two children, Alan (aged 9 years) and Becky (aged 7 years). At the time of the accident Fred earned £15,000 per annum (net). His employment prospects were good but he was unlikely to earn a higher salary later in his working life.

Six months after Fred's death Sally started proceedings in tort against Gareth and two years after the writ was issued a judge approved a settlement of the action on the following basis.

The estate

Fred had died intestate and his property therefore devolved to his wife and children.

Pecuniary losses; two years loss of earnings	=	£30,000
other losses	=	£6,000
Non-pecuniary losses; pain, shock and suffering	=	£9,000
loss of amenity	=	£8,000
Damages to the estate	=	£53,000

The dependants

Fred's only dependants were his wife and two children.

Pecuniary losses; from date of death to date of trial (2½ years) from the trial (settlement)	=	£37,500
Multiplicand of 15,000; multiplier of 15	=	£225,000
Damages for bereavement to Sally	=	£7,500
Damages to the dependants	=	£270,000

INJUNCTIONS

An injunction is a court order requiring that the defendant do some act or refrain from doing some act.

The injunction may be mandatory, ordering the defendant to do something, or prohibitory, ordering him not to do something.

A mandatory injunction requires the defendant to undo something which he has done in breach of a tortious obligation. There must be a strong probability of grave damage to the plaintiff and damages must be inadequate. They are not granted as a matter of course and the court will take into account any hardship which would be caused to the defendant and the defendant's behaviour.

Prohibitory injunctions are granted to prevent continuing tortious misconduct. They are normally used in trespass to land and nuisance actions to protect the plaintiff's proprietary interest. They are also granted in other torts which can be repeated, such as trespass to the person and defamation. The principle behind the prohibitory injunction is that the defendant should not be allowed to buy the right to inflict damage. They are granted more readily than mandatory injunctions and hardship to the defendant is not a ground for the court refusing the injunction. (See also 'Remedies for nuisance', pp. 182–3.)

The injunction may be final or interlocutory. A final injunction is awarded at the end of the trial to the successful party. An interlocutory injunction is awarded pending trial of the action. This is done to prevent harm to the plaintiff where damages would not be an adequate remedy if he succeeded in his action.

Specific restitution

This remedy is available in actions for conversion. If the defendant is found liable, the court has a discretion to order the return of the plaintiff's goods. This remedy is unlikely to be exercised where the goods are of no special value.

SELF-HELP

There are areas of tort where the plaintiff may avail himself of self-help, although it is fair to say that the law does not generally favour this. Details of self-help can be found in the individual torts.

In actions for trespass to land the plaintiff may exercise a right of re-entry on to the land. Where chattels have come onto his land he may exercise a right of distress damage feasant.

In actions for nuisance it may be possible for the plaintiff to take steps to abate the nuisance.

QUESTION

Alan and Bob went on a pub crawl together. Alan offered Bob a lift home in his car, which Bob accepted although he knew Alan was drunk. On the way home, they stopped at an off-licence and threw a brick through a window. Disturbed by a policeman, Alan drove off at high speed and, due to Alan's negligent driving, collided with a car driven by Charles.

Bob, who was not wearing a seat belt, was badly injured and Charles suffered serious injuries to his legs. Charles refused a blood transfusion at the hospital as it was contrary to his religious beliefs. As a result, he had to have one leg amputated. Depressed by this, Charles committed suicide three months later.

Advise Bob, and Charles's wife, Diana, as to their prospects of succeeding in a tort action against Alan.

Suggested approach

Bob's action. In normal circumstances Bob would have a relatively straightforward action against Alan in negligence. On the facts of this case Bob may have a problem in establishing that he was owed a duty of care by Alan because of the maxim *ex turpi causa*. A duty of care may not be owed to a person who suffers damage while participating in a criminal activity (*Pitt v Hunt*). The facts are similar to the case of *Ashton v Turner* where it was held at first instance that one of the grounds for denying the plaintiff an action was *ex turpi causa*.

If a duty of care was owed to Bob in respect of Alan's driving, there is an established breach of duty and reasonably foreseeable damage caused as a result. Are there any defences which Alan could raise?

Volenti non fit injuria is a possible defence to negligence. Bob was aware that Alan had been drinking and might not be capable of driving safely. Was he *volenti* by getting into the car with Alan? There is no express agreement between the parties that Bob will assume the risk of harm. Would the court imply such an agreement? From the cases it would appear not. (See *Nettleship* v *Weston; Owens* v *Brimmell.*) The plaintiff may be aware of the risk but does not consent to the act of negligence which causes his injury. In *Pitt* v *Hunt* it was held by the Court of Appeal that Road Traffic Act 1988, s. 149, meant that *volenti* was not available where a passenger in a car sues the driver in circumstances where insurance is compulsory.

Has Bob been contributorily negligent? In order to establish this as a defence the defendant must prove that the plaintiff failed to take reasonable care for his own safety and that this failure was a cause of his injuries. It appears that Bob may have been contributorily negligent in getting into the car with a driver whom he knew was incapable and by failing to wear a seat belt. In either case the court will have a power to reduce Bob's damages by the proportion for which he was responsible under the Law Reform (Contributory Negligence) Act 1945.

Diana's action. Diana may be able to bring an action as Charles's estate and/or as his dependant. Charles was owed a duty of care by Alan as one road user to another and Alan was in breach of that duty by driving negligently. The problem in the action by the dependent is establishing the chain of causation between the original action and the death.

Alan would have been liable for the original damage to Charles's legs as this was caused by his breach of duty and was not too remote. Would he have been liable for the amputation? Assume that the amputation would not have been necessary but for the refusal of the blood transfusion. Was the amputation too remote? The test for remoteness in a negligence action is whether the kind of damage suffered by the plaintiff was reasonably foreseeable (*Wagon Mound (No 1)*). If the extent of the damage was due to a physical characteristic of the plaintiff then the defendant is liable even if he could not have foreseen the extent of the damage. This is known as the egg-shell skull rule (*Smith* v *Leach Brain*). It is not known whether this principle extends to non-physical characteristics in civil law. If it does, then Alan would be liable for the amputation.

Would Alan be liable for Charles's suicide? The courts seem to have abandoned public policy as a method of denying relief to the estate of a suicide (*Kirkham* v *Chief Constable of Greater Manchester Police*). The question would be whether the suicide was caused by the breach of duty using the but for test. This would appear to be satisfied on the facts. Would the suicide be too remote? It has been held using the direct consequence test that a suicide is not too remote (*Pigney* v *Pointers Transport*). Would suicide be reasonably foreseeable? Again the egg-shell skull rule could be used.

Diana's action as the estate is essentially the action which Charles would have had, had he lived. Alan will be liable for all pecuniary and non-pecuniary losses between the breach of duty and the death (Law Reform (Miscellaneous Provisions) Act 1934). This would depend on the court's finding as to causation and remoteness as discussed above. Any loss of earnings, expenses and damages for pain, shock and suffering may be recovered. No damages are recoverable for the period after the death.

Diana's action as a dependant is under the Fatal Accidents Act 1976 and is essentially for loss of a breadwinner. She would have to establish that the death was caused by the breach of duty. Diana as spouse is a dependant and has two heads of damage to claim for. She would be entitled to £7,500 for bereavement. She could also claim for loss of dependency. This would be the amount in monetary terms which she could have expected to receive from Charles had he lived. This is done by taking Charles's net income and deducting the amount he would have spent on his own support had he lived. The appropriate multiplier is then applied and the resulting figure is the amount available for distribution to the dependants.

Further reading

Atiyah, PS *Accidents, Compensation and the Law* (4th edn by P Cane, 1987) Chs 7 and 18
Burrows, AS *Remedies for Torts and Breach of Contract* (1987)
Harris, D *Remedies in Contract and Tort* (1988)
Harris, D (et al) *Compensation and Support for Illness and Personal Injury* (1984)

Index